FRONTO

II

LCL 113

FRONTO

CORRESPONDENCE

II

WITH AN ENGLISH TRANSLATION BY

C. R. HAINES

HARVARD UNIVERSITY PRESS

CAMBRIDGE, MASSACHUSETTS

LONDON, ENGLAND

First published 1920
Revised and reprinted 1929

ISBN 978-0-674-99125-5

Printed on acid-free paper and bound by
The Maple-Vail Book Manufacturing Group

CONTENTS

THE CORRESPONDENCE OF
M. CORNELIUS FRONTO

M. CORNELII FRONTONIS

ET M. AURELII, L. VERI, ALIORUMQUE EPISTULAE

De Feriis Alsiensibus,[1] (Naber, p. 223).

Ambr. 218 | MAGISTRO meo.

Ferias apud Alsium quam feriatas egerimus non scribam tibi, ne et ipse angaris et me obiurges, mi magister. Lorium autem regressus domnulam meam <leviter> febricitantem repperi. Medicus dicit, si cito nobis me . . . . tu quoque . . . .[1] <si tu> valeas, <ego> laetior sim. Nam oculis spero te iam utentem sanis visere . . . . Vale, mi magister.

De Fer. Als. 2 (Naber, p. 223).

DOMINO meo Antonino Augusto.

Ferias Alsienses . . . . in novellae quid cantetur vineae atque . . . .[2] quid multarum rusticarum. Catonem quoque in oratione adversus Lepidum verbum cantari solitum commemorasse, quom ait *statuas positas Ochae atque Dionysodoro effeminatis, qui*

[1] About eight lines are lost.
[2] In these lacunae twelve lines are lost.

[1] On the Etrurian coast, twenty-four miles from Rome.

THE CORRESPONDENCE OF
M. CORNELIUS FRONTO

Marcus Antoninus to Fronto

162 A.D.

To my master.

In what holiday-wise we have kept our holiday at Alsium[1] I will not put on paper, that you may not be yourself troubled and scold me, my master. On my return to Lorium[2] I found my little lady[3] slightly feverish. The doctor says, if we soon . . . . If you were well, I should be happier. For I hope to see you already enjoying the use of sound eyes . . . . Farewell, my master.

Fronto to Marcus Antoninus

162 A.D.

To my Lord Antoninus Augustus.

Your Alsian holiday . . . . of many rustic things. That Cato also in his speech *Against Lepidus* mentioned a word in everyone's mouth when he spoke of *statues*[4] *set up to such unmanly creatures as*

[2] Half-way to Alsium from Rome.
[3] Probably his daughter Cornificia.
[4] According to Plutarch, Cato preferred that statues of himself should be conspicuous by their absence.

magiras facerent. Id in . . . . velint post redire . . . . facit. Opportune . . . . cantandi ludendique initium capiunt. Et . . . .[1] paravit.

De Fer. Als. 3 (Naber, p. 224).

Ambr. 217 | Domino meo Antonino Augusto.

1. Quid? ego ignoro ea te mente Alsium isse ut animo morem gereres ibique ludo et ioco et otio libero quatriduum universum operam dares? Nec dubito quin te ad ferias in secessu maritimo fruendas ita compararis: in sole meridiano ut somno oboedires cubans, deinde Nigrum vocares, libros intro ferre iuberes, mox ut te studium legendi incessisset, aut te Plauto expolires aut Accio expleres aut Lucretio delenires aut Ennio incenderes, in horam istic[2] Musarum propriam, quintam; redires inde libris . . . . eres diss . . . . mitteres; Ciceronis si sermones ad te detulisset, audires; inde <de>vius quantum potis ad[3] litus pergeres et raucas paludes ambires; <tum> vel, si videretur, aliquam navem conscenderes, ut[4] aethere tranquillo in altum <provectus> portisculorum et remigum visu audituque te oblectares; actutum inde balneas peteres, corpus
Ambr. 234 ad sudorem uberem commoveres, | convivium deinde

[1] From *opportune* to *paravit* the Codex has eleven lines not deciphered.

[2] Niebuhr *istam*; Rob. Ellis *istius*, *i.e.* of Ennius.

[3] For Mai's *poteras*.

[4] Buttmann for Cod. *vel*.

Ocha and Dionysodorus who practised cooking . . . .
. . . . a beginning of singing and playing . . . .

FRONTO TO MARCUS

162 A.D.

To my Lord Antoninus Augustus.

1. What? Am I not aware that you went to Alsium with the intention of indulging yourself and there giving yourself up to recreation and mirth and complete leisure for four whole days? And I have no doubt that you have set about enjoying the holiday at your seaside resort in this fashion: after taking your usual siesta at noonday, you would call Niger[1] and bid him bring in your books; soon when you felt the inclination to read, you would polish your style with Plautus or saturate yourself with Accius or soothe yourself with Lucretius or fire yourself with Ennius, to the hour in that case appropriate to the Muses, the fifth[2] . . . .
. . . .; if he had brought you treatises of Cicero, you would listen to them; then you would go as far as possible off the beaten track to the shore and skirt the croaking marshes; then even, if the fancy took you, get on board some vessel, that, putting out to sea in calm weather, you might delight yourself with the sight and sound of the rowers and their time-giver's[3] baton; anon you would be off from there to the baths, make yourself sweat profusely,

[1] Not mentioned again. He would most likely be the secretary or librarian of Marcus, possibly his anagnostes or reader.

[2] This seems a punning reference to Quintus, the praenomen of Ennius.

[3] The master of the rowers (something like our bo'sun) gave them the time by the beats of a hammer or baton.

regium agitares conchis omnium generum, Plautino *piscatu hamatili,* ut ille ait, *et saxatili,*[1] altilibus veterum saginarum, matteis pomis bellariis crustulis vinis felicibus calicibus perlucidis sine delatoria nota.

2. Quid hoc verbi sit, quaeras fortasse: accipe igitur. Ut homo ego multum facundus et Senecae Annaei sectator Faustiana vina de Sullae Fausti cognomento *felicia* appello; calicem vero *sine delatoria nota* quom dico, sine puncto dico. Neque enim me decet, qui sim tam homo doctus, volgi verbis Falernum vinum aut calicem acentetum appellare. Nam qua te dicam gratia Alsium, maritimum et voluptarium locum, et ut ait Plautus, *loc<ul>um lubricum*[2] delegisse, nisi ut bene haberes genio, utique verbo vetere faceres animo *volup.*[3] Qua, malum! *volup*? Immo, si dimidiatis verbis verum dicendum est, uti tu animo faceres *vigil*—vigilias dico—aut ut faceres *labo* aut ut faceres *mole*—labores et molestias dico—. Tu umquam volup? Volpem facilius quis tibi quam voluptatem conciliaverit. Dic, oro te, Marce, idcircone Alsium petisti, ut in prospectu maris esurires? Quid? tu Lorii te fame et siti et negotiis agendis
Ambr. 223 adfligere nequibas? In apopsi | . . . . . iucundiores tibi esse videntur . . . . memini me ad . . . . pueros in balneis esse . . . . rescribas . . . . liber . . . . mare ipsum aiunt, ubi alcedonia sint, fieri feriatum. An alcedo cum pullis suis tranquillo otio

[1] Plaut. *Rud.* II. i. 10. [2] Plaut. *Mil. Glor.* III. ii. 38.

[3] Plaut. *Asin.* V. iii 1. *cp. cael.* = *caelum*, *gau* = *gaudium* (Ennius), and *nol* = *nolu'ris* (Lucilius). *cf.* Pal. *Anthology*, VI. 85, and Elizabethan usage, *e.g. sor* = sorrow.

then discuss a royal banquet with shellfish of all kinds, a Plautine *catch hook-taken, rock-haunting,* as he says, capons long fed fat, delicacies, fruit, sweets, confectionery, felicitous wines, translucent cups with no informer's brand.

2. Perhaps you will ask what *do* you mean? Listen then! I as a man greatly eloquent and a disciple of Annaeus Seneca call Faustian[1] wines *felicitous* wines from Faustus Sulla's title; moreover when I speak of a cup without an informer's brand, I mean a cup without a spot. For it does not become a man so learned as I am to speak in everyday terms of Falernian wine or a flawless cup. For to what end can I say that you chose Alsium, a seaside and pleasure resort and, as Plautus has it, a *slippery spot,* if not to indulge yourself and, in ancient parlance, take your *pleasu?* How—the mischief! —pleasu? Nay, if the truth must be told in docked words, that you might to your heart's content indulge in *watchin'*—I mean watching—, in *labors*—I mean labours—, in *vexats*—I mean vexations. You ever indulge in pleasu? It were easier to reconcile you to a polecat than to pleasure. Tell me, Marcus, I beseech you, have you repaired to Alsium only to fast with the sea in sight? What, could you not wear yourself out at Lorium with hunger and thirst and doing business? With a fine view . . . . seem to you more delightful? I remember (telling) you . . . .
The very sea, they say, keeps holiday, when the halcyon broods.[2] Is a halcyon with her chicks

[1] The *ager Faustianus* was part of the Falernian district. Felix was a title of Faustus Sulla. Fronto is sarcastic in his allusion to Seneca, whom he disliked.

[2] See Plutarch *On Water Animals*, xxxv.

dignior est quam tu cum tuis liberis? . . . . <v>etere<s> <tyr>annos.[1]

3. At enim res plane iam postulat—num studium? num laborem? num <vigilias?> num munera?[2] Quis arcus perpetuo intenditur? Quae fides perpetuo substrictae sunt?[3] Oculi conivendo[4] <tantum> durant, qui uno obnixi obtutu interissent.
Ambr. 226 Hortus qui crebro pangitur, ope <si> stercoris | indiget, herbas et holuscula nihili procreat; frumento vero et solidis frugibus requietus ager deligitur; ubertas soli otio paratur.

4. Quid maiores vestri qui rempublicam et imperium Romanum magnis auctibus auxerunt. Proavus vester summus bellator tamen histrionibus interdum se delectavit, et praeterea potavit satis strenue. Tamen eius opera populus Romanus in triumphis mulsum saepe bibit. Avum item vestrum,[5] doctum principem et navum et orbis terrarum non regendi tantum sed etiam perambulandi diligentem, modulorum tamen et tibicinum studio devinctum fuisse scimus, et praeterea prandiorum opimorum esorem optimum fuisse. Iam vero pater vester, divinus ille vir, providentia pudicitia frugalitate innocentia pietate sanctimonia omnes omnium principum virtutes supergressus, tamen et palaestram[6] ingressus est et hamum[7] instruxit et scurras risit.

[1] These two words do not appear in Mai. Naber seems to have got them from du Rieu.

[2] Cod. illegible except for letter *u*.

[3] Mai has *suo strictae sono*. [4] Cornelissen for Cod. *coniugio*.

[5] Charisius (i. 127), who quotes this passage, adds *duum* (= *duorum*).

worthier of quiet ease than you with your children?

. . . .

3. But you say that circumstances now plainly demand—not study surely? not toil? not wakefulness? not duties? What bow is for ever strung[1]? what chords for ever stretched? By winking alone can eyes keep their sight, which could not but fail if fixed in one unwavering stare. A garden repeatedly planted, if it lack the aid of manure, bears only weeds and stunted vegetables of no value; for corn, however, and staple crops land that has lain fallow is chosen; rest restores fruitfulness to the soil.

4. What of your ancestors who enlarged the state and empire of Rome with huge additions? Your great-grandfather, consummate warrior as he was, yet at times took pleasure in actors[2] and, moreover, drank pretty stoutly. Yet thanks to him the Roman people often drank mead at his triumphs. We know, too, that your grandfather, a learned ruler and a strenuous, loving not only to govern the world, but to go up and down in it, was yet devoted to music and flute-players, and was withal a right good eater of right rich banquets. Again, your father, that godlike man, who in his foresight, continence, frugality, blamelessness, dutifulness, and personal righteousness excelled the virtues of all rulers, yet visited the palaestra, and baited a hook and laughed at buffoons.

[1] Hor. *Od.* II. x. 20.
[2] So *Princ. Hist. ad fin.*

---

[6] Galen, vi. 406 (Kühn) says the same of Marcus.
[7] The margin of Cod. has *theatrum* twice, and implies that it was another reading. Capit. *Vit. Pii* xi. 2 says Pius was fond of fishing.

5. Nihil de Gaio Caesare dico acerrimo Cleopatrae hoste <post moecho>,[1] nihil de Augusto Liviae viro. Romulum ipsum urbis huius conditorem, quom hostium ducem manu comminus conserta obtruncavit Ambr. 225 quomque spolia opima | Feretrio vexit, huncne tenui victu usum putas? Profecto neque esuriens quisquam neque abstemius animum induxisset virgines adultas de spectaculis rapere. Quid? Numa senex sanctissimus nonne inter liba et decimas profanandas et suovetaurilia mactanda aetatem egit, epularum[2] dictator, cenarum libator, feriarum promulgator? Saturatum et feriatum dico. E<x o>mn<ibus tu>[3] esuriales ferias celebras? Nec Chrysippum tuum praeteribo, quem cotidie ferunt madescere solitum. Et pleraque . . . . Socratem <plane ipsum ex> Socraticorum *Symposiis* et *Dialogis* et *Epistulis* existimes hominem multum scitum et facetum fuisse—Socratem intelleges Aspasiae discipulum, Alcibiadi magistrum.

6. Iam si bellum indixti ludo otio satietati voluptati, at tu dormi saltem, quantum libero homini satis est. Intensius ad supremam . . . . ad luminis . . . .?[4] An tandem si ignem de caelo nemo sur-

[1] From the margin of Cod.

[2] Niebuhr *epulonum* for Cod. *epulorum*. Cicero (*De Orat.* iii. 19) says that the Epulones were instituted by the Pontifices.

[3] So Brakman. It would also be possible to read *dico eum. Num tu* . . . Before *Socratem* three lines are missing.

[4] Query *horam diei quom tu labores suscepisti, ad luminis adventum protrahes*? Cf. Suet. *Vitell.* 17.

5. I say nothing of Gaius Caesar, Cleopatra's keenest foe and afterwards paramour, nothing of Augustus, the husband of Livia. As regards Romulus himself the founder of this city, when he slew the leader of the enemy in a hand-to-hand combat and brought the *Spolia Opima*[1] to Jupiter Feretrius, do you think he was content with half rations? Verily no hungry or ascetic man could have conceived the idea of carrying off grown-up maidens from a public festival.[2] What? did not the aged Numa, most holy of men, pass his life putting sacred offerings and tithes to secular uses, and sacrificing bulls, sheep, and swine, he the dictator of festivals, the inaugurator of banquets, the promulgator of holidays? I call him a gourmand and a holiday-maker. And do you of all men keep your holidays fasting? Nor will I pass over your own Chrysippus,[3] who used to get mellow, so they say, every day in the year. And very many . . . . Plainly Socrates himself, as you may gather from the *Symposia*, the *Dialogues*, and the *Letters of the Socratics*, was a man of much shrewdness and wit—the Socrates, mark you, who was Aspasia's pupil and Alcibiades's teacher.

6. Now if you have declared war on play, relaxation, good living, and pleasure, yet do sleep as a freeman should. (When you have worked) hard till the last (hour of the day, will you continue your labours) till the dawn? Prithee, if no one had

[1] The choice spoils taken by a general from the general of the enemy slain in single combat.

[2] The rape of the Sabine women.

[3] So Diog. Laert. *Chrys.* 4. Horace (*Odes*, III. xxi. 11) says the same of Fronto's hero Cato.

ripuisset, sol non esset tibi satis ad iudicandum? Nae <tu> cum animo tuo reputes[1] cotidiano te mendacio adstringi, quom te diem cognitioni dare
Ambr. 220 ais et nocte cognoscis, | tum sive condemnes sive absolvas mendax futurus. Si quempiam condemnas, *parum cavisse uidetur*[2] ais: istuc quidem, si lucernae removeantur, nihil videri poterit.

7. At tu obsecro vel ioco vel serio te exorari a me patere, ne te somno defraudes utique terminos diei et noctis serves. Agere de finibus <nondum divi>[3]duis claros et nobiles Vesperum et Luciferum puta: utrique demonstrationem sui quisque limitis ostendunt. Horum cognitioni interesse postulat Somnus, nam se quoque[4] adfinem esse negotio et adtingi iniuria ait. Vellem autem tantum mihi vigoris aut studii adesse, quantum adfuit quom illa olim nugalia conscripsi, *Laudem Fumi et Pulveris*.[5] Nae ego somni laudem ex summis opibus conscripsissem.[6] Nunc quoque, si tibi fabulam brevem libenti est audire, audi.

8. Iovem Patrem ferunt, quom res humanas a primordio conderet, aevom vi<tae>[7] medium uno ictu percussum in duas partes undique pares diffidisse: partem alteram luce, alteram tenebris amicisse, diem noctemque appellasse, noctique otium diei negotium tradidisse. Tum Somnus necdum natus erat et omnes pervigiles aetatem agebant;

[1] From the margin of Cod. for text *reputas*.
[2] A legal expression.
[3] Brakman.
[4] Orelli for Cod. *quisque*.
[5] See i. p. 38 (*Laudes*).
[6] He seems to have done so before: see i. p. 96.
[7] Heindorf.

stolen fire from heaven, would not the sun suffice you for your judicial duties? Do realise in your conscience that you are tied to a daily falsehood, for, when you say that you "appoint the day" for trial of cases and yet try by night,[1] then you are bound to be untruthful, whether you condemn or acquit. If you condemn anyone, you say, *there appears to have been gross negligence;* where indeed but for the lights nothing could appear at all.

7. But do, I beseech you, in jest or earnest let yourself be persuaded by me not to rob yourself of sleep, and to keep the boundaries of day and night distinct. Imagine that two noble and illustrious litigants, Evening and Morning, are having a law-suit about boundaries not yet marked out. Each party puts in a description of his own frontier. Sleep claims to intervene in their trial, for he too is connected with the business, and declares that he suffers prejudice. Would that I had as much vigour and enthusiasm as I enjoyed when long ago I composed those trifles in praise of *Smoke* and of *Dust.* Verily I would have written a eulogy of Sleep to the top of my skill! Now, too, if you care to hear a short apologue on Sleep, listen.

8. They tell us that Father Jove, when at the beginning of things he was founding the human race, with one stroke clave asunder the continuity of man's life into two parts in every respect equal; the one he clothed with light, the other with darkness; called this day and that night, and assigned to night rest and to day work. As yet Sleep had not been born, and all men passed their whole lives awake.

[1] Dio, lxxi. 6, § 1 (of Marcus), νυκτὸς ἔστιν ὅτε δικάζων.

Ambr. 219 sed quies nocturna vigilantibus pro somno adhuc[1] | erat promulgata. Paulatim deinde, ut sunt ingenia hominum inquieta et agitandi et turbandi cupida, noctes diesque negotiis exercebant, horam otio nullam impertibant. Tum Iovem ferunt, ubi iam iurgia et vadimonia nocturna sisti et noctes quoque comperendinari videret,[2] cum corde suo agitasse de suis germanis fratribus unum praeficere, qui nocti atque otio hominum curaret: Neptunum multas et graves curas maritimas causatum, ne fluctus terras totas cum montibus obruerent neve motu[3] venti cuncta funditus percellerent, silvas et sata radicitus haurirent; Ditem quoque Patrem causatum multa opera multaque cura templa infera[4] aegre coerceri, amnibus et paludibus et stagnis Stygiis Acheruntem aegre commoeniri, canem denique custodem apposuisse umbris territandis quae aufugere ad superos cuperent, eique cani trinas latrandi fauces ac trinos hiatus trinasque dentium formidines addidisse.

9. Tum Iovem deos alios percontatum animadvertisse, gratiam vigiliae aliquantum pollere; Iunonem plerosque partus nocturnos ciere; Minervam artium
Ambr. 214 atque artificum magistram | multum vigilari velle; Martem nocturnas eruptiones et insidias muta re iuvare; Venerem vero et Liberum multo maxime

[1] This word is doubtful.
[2] Heindorf for Cod. *videat.*

But in lieu of sleep the hush of night had been hitherto established for wakeful men. Then, little by little, men's disposition being restless and prone to action and excitement, they began to employ nights as well as days in business, giving not an hour to rest. Then they say that Jove, seeing that now quarrels and recognizances were fixed for the night, and suits were even put off from one night to another, took counsel with his own heart to set up one of his own brethren to preside over night and the repose of mankind. But Neptune pleaded his many heavy cares upon the seas, that the waves should not overflow whole lands, mountains and all, or cyclones in their fury level everything with the ground and suck up the woods and the crops by their roots. Father Dis too made his plea that hardly with immense pains and immense anxiety were the nether precincts kept under control, hardly was Hades impaled in on every side with rivers and marishes and the Stygian fens; that he had even set up a watch-dog to terrify any Shades that had a mind to escape to the upper air, and had given him to boot a triple throat for barking, three gaping jaws, and threefold terror of teeth.

9. Then Jove after question had with other Gods perceived that a liking for wakefulness was considerably in the ascendant; that Juno called most children to birth at night; that Minerva, mistress of arts and artificers, was for much wakefulness; that Mars by the silence of the surroundings aided nightly sallies and ambuscades; that Venus, however, and Liber were by

[3] Hauler (*Vers. d. Phil.* 41, p. 79) reads *coorti.*
[4] Lucr. vi. 141.

pernoctantibus favere. Capit tum consilium Iuppiter Somni procreandi eumque in deum numerum adsciscit, nocti et otio praeficit eique claves oculorum tradit. Herbarum quoque sucos, quibus corda hominum Somnus sopiret, suis Iuppiter manibus temperavit: securitatis et voluptatis herbae de caeli nemore advectae, de Acheruntis autem pratis leti herba petita. Eius leti guttam unam aspersit sed[1] minimam, quanta dissimulantis lacrima esse solet.

Hoc, inquit, *suco soporem hominibus per oculorum repagula inriga: cuncti quibus inrigaris ilico post procumbent et artubus mortuis immobiles iacebunt. Tum tu ne timeto, nam vivent et paulo post, ubi evigilaverint, exsurgent.*

10. Post id Iuppiter alas non ut Mercurio talares sed ut Amori humeris exaptas Somno adnexuit. *Non enim te soleis,* ait, *et*[2] *talari ornatu ad pupulas hominum et palpebras incurrere oportet* <*aut*>[3] *curruli strepitu et cum fremitu equestri, sed placide et clementer*
Ambr. 218 *pinnis teneris in modum hirun|dinum advolare nec ut columbae alis plaudere.*

11. Ad hoc, quo iucundior hominibus Somnus esset, donat ei multa somnia amoena ut, quo studio quisque devinctus esset, aut[4] histrionem in somniis fautor spectaret, aut tibicinem audiret, aut aurigae agitanti[5] monstraret, milites somnio vincerent, imperatores somnio triumpharent, peregri-

[1] For Cod. *aspersisse.* Brakman would supply *ferunt.*
[2] Bährens for Cod. *aut.* [3] Heindorf.
[4] For Cod. *ut,* and so in the two following cases.
[5] For Cod. *agitandi.* Pearce (cp. Suet. *Vitell.* 17) suggests *ministraret.*

far the most in favour of the night-wakers. Jupiter then made up his mind to beget Sleep, and enrolled him among the Gods, set him in charge of night and repose, and gave into his keeping the keys of men's eyes. He also mixed with his own hands the juice of herbs, wherewith Sleep might soothe to rest the hearts of men. The herbs of security and delight he culled from the groves of Heaven, but the herb of death was sought in the meadows of Acheron. Of that death he mingled but one drop and that the tiniest, as is the tear of one who would hide his tears.

With this juice, said he, *instil slumber into men through the gateways of their eyes: all, into whom thou dost thus instil it, will thereafter at once fall down and lie prone with limbs motionless as though dead. But fear thou not, for they will be alive and anon, when they awake, will rise again.*

10. That done, Jupiter furnished Sleep with wings, not as Mercury's attached to the ankles, but like Love's fitted to the shoulders. *For thou must not,* said he, *dash into the eyelids and pupils of men with sandals and winged ankles, with the whirling of chariots and the thunder of steeds, but fly to them quietly and softly with gentle wings like a swallow and not with clapping of pinions like pigeons.*

11. Furthermore, that Sleep might be the more welcome to men, he endowed him with many a lovely dream that, according to each sleeper's favourite hobby, he might—in his dreams—either watch an actor and clap him or listen to a flute-player or shout advice to a charioteer in his course; that soldiers might conquer and generals triumph[1]—in

[1] *cp.* Lucan, *Phars.* vii. 7 ff.

nantes somnio redirent. Ea somnia plerumque ad verum convertunt.

12. Igitur, Marce, si quo tibi somnio hinc opus est, censeo libens dormias tantisper dum quod cupis quaque exoptas vigilanti tibi optingat.

De Fer. Als. 4 (Naber, p. 230).

MAGISTRO meo salutem.

Modo recepi epistulam tuam, qua confestim fruar. Nunc enim imminebant officia δυσπαραίτητα. Interim quod cupis, mi magister, breviter ut occupatus parvolam nuntio nostram melius valere et intra cubiculum discurrere.

Dictatis his legi litteras Alsienses meo tempore, mi magister, quom alii cenarent, ego cubarem tenui cibo contentus hora noctis secunda—multum, inquis, cohortatione mea <commotus>! Multum, mi magister, nam verbis tuis adquievi saepiusque legam ut
Ambr. 149: Quat. xl. ends saepius adquiescam. Ceterum verecundia | officii, quam sit res imperiosa, quis te magis norit? Sed oro te, illud quid est, quod in fine epistulae manum condoluisse[1] dicis? Illatenus dolueris, mi magister, si me compotem voti di boni faciunt. Vale mi magister optime, φιλόστοργε[2] ἄνθρωπε.

[1] Naber for Cod. *consoluisse.*
[2] See i. p. 280. Lit. "man of warm affections."

their dreams; and wanderers come home—in their dreams. Such dreams generally turn out true.

12. So, Marcus, if you need a dream hereafter, I advise you to sleep with a will, until such time as what you desire and as you wish it may fall to your lot in your waking hours.

Marcus Antoninus to Fronto

162 A.D.

To my master, greeting.

I have just received your letter, which I will enjoy presently. For at the moment I have duties hanging over me that can hardly be begged off. Meanwhile I will tell you, my master, shortly, as I am busy, what you want to hear, that our little daughter[1] is better and can run about the bedroom.

After dictating the above I read the Alsian letters, my master, at my leisure, while the others were dining and I was lying down at eight o'clock, satisfied with a light repast. *Much good has my advice done you,* you will say! Much, my master, for I have rested[2] upon your advice, and I shall read it the oftener that I may the oftener rest upon it. But who knows better than yourself how exacting a thing is obedience to duty? But what I beseech you is that which you say at the close of your letter, that your hand pained you. If the Gods are kind, my master, and grant my prayers, you will not have suffered pain since. Farewell, my best of masters, man of the warm heart.

[1] Probably Cornificia.
[2] A play on the word.

(Naber, p. 217.)

De Bello Parthico

<Ad Antoninum Imperatorem.>

Ambr. 236, following 244

1\. . . . . <qui deus tan>[1]|tam genuit gentem Romanam, aequo animo patitur fatisci nos interdum et pelli et vulnerari. An cunctetur de militibus nostris Mars Pater illa dicere?—

Ego quom genui, tum morituros scivi et ei rei sustuli;
Praeterea, quom in terrae orbem misi ob defendendum imperium,
Scibam me in mortifera bella non in epulas mittere.[2]

Haec verba Telamo Troiano bello de suis liberis semel elocutus est; Mars de Romanis saepe multisque in bellis hoc carmine usus est: Gallico bello apud Alliam, Samniti apud Caudium, Punico ad Cannas, Hispanico apud Numantiam, Iugurthino apud Cirtam, Parthico ad Carrhas. Sed semper et ubique aerumnas adoreis terroresque nostros triumphis commutavit.

2\. Sed ne nimis vetera alte petam, vestrae familiae exemplis utar. Traiani proavi vestri ductu auspicioque nonne in Dacia captus vir consularis?

[1] Heindorf.

[2] From Ennius's tragedy *Telamon*, quoted also by Cic. *Tusc.* iii. 13. Fronto adapts the words of Ennius, which are *ad Troiam quom misi ob defendendam Graeciam.* He also has *mortiferum bellum.*

M. CORNELIUS FRONTO

On the Parthian War[1]

162 A.D.

To the Emperor Antoninus.

1. . . . . The God who begat the great Roman race has no compunction in suffering us to faint at times and be defeated and wounded. Or would Father Mars hesitate to say of our soldiers the words?—

Full well I knew when I begot you, you would die: I reared you for that end;
Aye, when I sent you forth the wide world through the empire to defend,
Full well I knew to deadly wars and not to feasts my children I should send.

These words were uttered by Telamon to his sons once in the Trojan war. But Mars has spoken of the Romans in the same strain many a time and in many a war: in the Gaulish war at Allia,[2] in the Samnite at Caudium,[3] in the Punic at Cannae,[4] in the Spanish at Numantia,[5] in the Jugurthine at Cirta,[6] in the Parthian at Carrhae.[7] But always and everywhere he turned our sorrows into successes and our terrors into triumphs.

2. But not to hark back too far into ancient times, I will take instances from your own family. Was not a consular taken prisoner in Dacia under the leadership and auspices of your great grandfather

[1] The Parthian war broke out soon after the death of Pius. Fronto is consoling Marcus for a disaster in Armenia, when Severianus the legatus and his legion were destroyed at Elegeia in 162 by the Parthians. See also *Princ. Hist. ad fin.*
[2] July 16, 390 B.C.
[3] 321 B.C.
[4] Aug. 2, 216 B.C.
[5] 138 B.C.
[6] Apparently the defeat of Albinus in 109 B.C. is meant.
[7] 52 B.C.

Nonne a Parthis consularis aeque vir in Mesopotamia trucidatus? Quid? avo vestro Hadriano imperium optinente quantum militum ab Iudaeis, quantum ab Britannis caesum. Patre etiam vestro imperante, qui omnium principum <felicissimus erat>[1] . . . .
Ambr. 235, followed by 281 and 232 . . | . . Si Marso quis patre natus viperas lacertas et natrices timeret, nonne degenerasse videretur[2]? . . . . pauculis diebus in fasciis tenentur, illi in pannis degunt omnem aetatem.[3]

3. Itaque bonus ille imperator . . . . venire captivos jubebat . . . . sint ingratiis. Quid ego, quippe cui . . . . Piscibus in caudis est <virtus>,[4] avibus in pennis, anguibus serpendi vi . . . . quod
Ambr. 228 quis . . . . | et gloriam Romani nominis restituendam et insidias fraudesque hostium <puniendas>, quae comparata . . . . vendere nugaci . . . . consulta sunt tam<en> . . . . iure meritoque . . . .
Ambr. 227 neque . . . . | vocent paratos progredi remanere, porro retro, illic <istic>.[5] Haudquaquam utile est homini nato res prosperas perpetuo evenire: fortunae variae magis tutae.

4. Et <magnis firmatus> opibus et omnium quaecumque intenderat sine offensione potitus, <Polycrates>[6] nihil in aetate agunda duri aut acerbi

[1] Niebuhr, but perhaps *pacatissimus*. A lacuna follows of not less, as it seems, than a page.
[2] From the margin of Codex.
[3] From margin of p. 232 of Codex.
[4] Or possibly *robur*.
[5] Mai.
[6] Heindorf, who also suggested *redegisset* below. The other long insertions are my own, merely to make a readable translation possible. They mostly differ from Naber's. Such indications as there are in the Codex have been followed.

Trajan?[1] Was not a consular likewise slain by the Parthians in Mesopotamia?[2] Again under the rule of your grandfather Hadrian what a number of soldiers were killed by the Jews,[3] what a number by the Britons![4] Even in the principate of your Father, who was the most fortunate of princes . . . . Should we not think the son of a Marsian[5] father degenerate, if he were afraid of vipers, lizards, and water-snakes? . . . .[6] are kept a few days in swaddling bands, the others pass their whole lives in rags.

3. And so that excellent emperor[7] . . . . bade his captives be sold . . . . The strength of fishes lies in their tails, of birds in their wings, of snakes in their power of crawling . . . . both the restoration of the prestige of the Roman name, and the punishment of the enemy's traps and treachery, ... call upon those to halt who are ready to advance, forward, backward, here, there. It is by no means advantageous to a man that is born of woman that prosperity should always attend him: changing fortunes are more secure.

4. Take Polycrates[8]: strong in his vast wealth, and successful without a stumble in all that he undertook, he is said in the course of his life to have experienced no hard fortune or disappointment,

[1] Longinus; see Dio, lxviii. 12.
[2] Maximus; see *ibid.* lxviii. 30, and below, *Princ. Hist. ad fin.*
[3] See Dio, lxix. 14.
[4] Not recorded elsewhere; but see Spart. *Vit. Hadr.* 5.
[5] The Marsians were supposed to have power over snakes: see Pliny, *N.H.* vii. 2; xxv. 5.
[6] In this gap (Ambr. 231) there was a reference to the Parthians, as we see from a marginal note.
[7] Trajan (?).
[8] Tyrant of Samos, who died 522 B.C.

expertus esse dicitur, quin sub manus quom cuncta <redegisset> prorsus <haberetur omnium regum> beatissimus. <Cui, ut fertur,> rex Amasis Aegyptius sapiens fortuna de eximia[1] consultus, scriptis familiaribus litteris suasit semet[2] ipsum voluntario aliquo damno sciens multaret eoque dolore <deis invidis se conciliaret> . . . . <ille autem aureo> habebat <in> anulo manupretio summo[3] facie eximia lapidem smaragdum, <quam prae ceteris suis bonis rebus . . . . aestimabat>. Eum Polycrates anulum nave longa in altum provectus sponte in mare abiecit, unde numquam postilla emergeret.

5. Tum quod sciens sponteque <fecit>[4] abiectum lapidem dolebat. <Sed mox grandem> piscator <piscem retibus> saepe <iactis tandem> nactus, indignum duxit ad venales deferre, sed dignitati parens regi obtulit. Rex gratum acceptumque
Ambr. 222 habuit | s<ibique> apponi iussit: quo iusso piscique opera <data> se<rvi> contrectantes <eum> anulum in alvo repertum ad regem gaudentes detulerunt. Tum Polycrates litteras ordine de casu et postliminio anuli perscriptas ad regem Amasim mittit. Amasis magnum et maturum malum Polycrati coniectans amicitiam hospitiumque renuntiat, ut alieno potius, suo quam hospiti aut amico fortunam commutatam ipse minus aegre ferret.

[1] Cod. *fortunatissimis*. Heindorf reads *fortunae peritissimus*.
[2] Mai. Brakman says the Codex has *semper* (?).
[3] In the Codex follows *smaragdum*. [4] Brakman.

such as to prevent him, when he had brought everything under his power, being counted the most fortunate of all kings. To him, as the story goes, Amasis the wise King of Egypt, being consulted about his unique good fortune, wrote a friendly letter, advising him of his own accord to inflict some loss knowingly upon himself, and by that penance disarm the envy of the Gods. . . . . Now he had an emerald of extraordinary lustre set in a gold ring of the finest workmanship, which he valued above all his other possessions. Polycrates putting out to sea in a ship of war, cast this ring of his own accord into the water, making sure that he should never afterwards see it again.

5. Deliberate and premeditated as his act had been, he subsequently regretted the jewel he had cast away. But shortly after a fisherman, who with repeated casting of his nets had at length caught a huge fish, thought it too fine to take to the dealers, and in virtue of its excellence presented it to the king. The king was much pleased with the gift, and ordered it to be served at his own table. When the slaves in pursuance of this order were busy with the fish preparing it for the table, they found the ring in its stomach and brought it joyfully to the king. Then Polycrates sent King Amasis a letter with full particulars of the sacrifice and recovery of the ring. Whereon Amasis, forecasting for Polycrates a disaster signal and speedy, renounced all friendship and ties of hospitality with him, that when his fortune changed he might regard it with less concern as affecting a stranger rather than his own guest or friend.

6. Sed somnium filiae Polycrati iam ante insigne optigerat. Patrem suum videre sibi visa erat aperto atque edito loco sublimem ungui et lavi Iovis et Solis manibus. Harioli autem laetam et pinguem fortunam portendi eo[1] somnio interpretati. Sed omne contra evenit. Nam deceptus ab Oroete Perse Polycrates captusque in crucem sublatus est. Ita ei crucianti somnium expeditum. Manibus <enim Iovis quom plueret lavabatur, unguebatur Solis, dum ipse e corpore humorem emitteret>.[2] Huiuscemodi[3] exorsus <felices ha>bent <exitum> interdum <infaustum>. Non est exultandum nimia Ambr. 221 et diutina prosperitate, | nec si quid malae pugnae acciderit defetiscendum. Sed victoriam brevi spera, namque semper in rebus gestis Romanis crebrae fortunarum commutationes extiterunt.

7. Quis ita ignarus est bellicarum memoriarum, qui ignoret populum Romanum non minus cadendo quam caedendo imperium peperisse? legiones nostras saepe <fusas fuga>[4]tasque armis barbarorum esse? Quamvis in<festi et>[5] truces tauri subigi iungendo domarique potuerunt: aeque ac[6] nostri exercitus olim[7] sub iugum missi sunt. Sed eosdem illos, qui sub iugum egerant, paulo post ante triumphum nostri egere et captivos sub corona vendidere.

[1] For Cod. *portendier*. [2] Chiefly from Mai.
[3] Mai *huius* [*fabulae*]; Mähly *huiusque modi*.
[4] Alan. [5] Brakman. [6] For *potuere*, *praequam*.
[7] For Cod. *sili*; Naber *illi*.

6. But the daughter of Polycrates had previously had a remarkable dream. She had seemed to see her father, raised aloft on an open and conspicuous spot, being laved and anointed by the hands of Jupiter and the Sun. The diviners read the dream as foretelling a rich and happy fortune.[1] But it turned out wholly otherwise. For Polycrates, beguiled by Oroetes the Persian, was seized and crucified. And so the dream was fulfilled in his crucifixion. For he was laved by Jove's hands when it rained, and anointed by the hands of the Sun, when the dew of agony came out upon his skin. Such prosperous beginnings as his have not seldom a disastrous ending. There should be no exultation over excessive and prolonged prosperity, no fainting away when a reverse has been sustained. You may soon hope for a victory, for Rome in her history has ever experienced frequent alternations of fortune.

7. Who is so unversed in military annals as not to know that the Roman people have earned their empire by falling no less than by felling? that our legions have often been broken and routed by the arms of barbarians? It has been found possible to subject to the yoke and to tame bulls, however savage and dangerous; and in the same way our armies have in former times been made to pass under the yoke. But those very foes, who forced us under the yoke, have our generals but a little later forced to march at the head of their triumphs and have sold them as slaves by auction.

[1] Periander, the tyrant of Corinth, had a similar dream, and Artemidorus (a writer of the time of Marcus), *On Dreams*, 4, said it signified great honours and riches.

8. Post Cannensem cladem Poenus imperator anulorum aureorum, quos caesis equitibus Romanis Poeni detraxerant, tres modios cumulatos misit Carthaginem. Sed non multo post Carthago capta est: illis, qui anulos detraxerant, catenae inditae sunt. In ea pugna Scipio quantum hominum Poenorum Afrorumque cepit aut occidit aut in deditionem accepit! Si eorum linguas resecari imperasset, navem onustam linguis Romam inegisset.

Ambr. 216 9. Quod te vix quic|quam nisi *raptim* et *furtim* legere posse prae curis praesentibus scripsisti, fac memineris et cum animo tuo cogites C. Caesarem atrocissimo bello Gallico cum alia multa militaria tum etiam duos *De Analogia* libros scrupulosissimos scripsisse, inter tela volantia de nominibus declinandis, de verborum aspirationibus et rationibus inter classica et tubas. Cur igitur tu, Marce, non minore ingenio praeditus quam C. Caesar, nec minus ordine insignis nec paucioribus exemplis aut documentis familiaribus instructus, non vincas negotia et invenias tibimet tempora, non modo ad orationes et poemata et historias et praecepta sapientium legenda sed etiam syllogismos, si perpeti potes, resolvendos?

---

[1] He quotes Marcus's own phrase (see above, *Ad Anton.* ii. 1) in the letter from Minturnae (probably), where Marcus was trying to get a little respite from the anxieties caused by the Parthian invasion of Roman provinces and the disaster at Elegeia.

8. After the disaster at Cannae the Carthaginian general sent to Carthage three bushels of golden rings heaped up, which Carthaginians had drawn from the fingers of Roman knights slain in the battle. But not many years later Carthage was taken, and chains were put on those who had drawn off the rings. In that battle what a multitude of Carthaginians and Africans did Scipio capture or slay or reduce to submission! Had he given orders for their tongues to be cut out, he could have sent into Rome a ship freighted with the tongues of his enemies.

9. With respect to what you say that you can scarcely read anything except *by snatches* and *by stealth*[1] in your present anxieties, recall to your mind and ponder the fact that Gaius Caesar, while engaged in a most formidable war in Gaul wrote besides many other military works two books of the most meticulous character *On Analogy*,[2] discussing amid flying darts the declension of nouns, and the aspiration of words and their classification mid the blare of bugles and trumpets. Why then, O Marcus, should not you, who are endowed with no less abilities than Gaius Caesar, and are as noble in station and fortified by no fewer examples and patterns at home, master your duties and find time for yourself not only for reading speeches and poems and histories and the doctrines of philosophers, but also for unravelling syllogisms, if you can endure so far.

[2] Cicero quotes this work (*Brutus*, 72) as meaning *De ratione Latine loquendi*. Caesar wrote it while crossing the Alps on his way from his winter quarters at Luca, in north Italy, to the seat of war in Gaul.

10. **Nunc, ut orationem istam M. Tulli, quam tibi legendam misi, paucis commendem.** Mihi profecto ita videtur, neminem umquam neque Romana neque Graecorum lingua facundius in contione populi laudatum quam Gnaeus Pompeius in ista oratione laudatus est: ut mihi ille videatur non ita suis virtutibus ut Ciceronis laudibus *Magnus* nominatus.[1] Tum praeterea multa istic reperies praesentibus consiliis tuis capita apte considerata, de ducibus Ambr. 215 exercituum de|ligendis, de commodis sociorum, tutela provinciarum, di<sciplina mili>tum[2]; quibus artibus praeditos esse oporteat imperatores bella et cetera ge<rentes>[3] . . . . tractatus . . . . quos . . . . intentionem . . . . consuevi. Ne . . . . velim . . . . quia ego intento maiore vel aliquando repraesentatas has res arbitror profuturas. Velis dumtaxat. Et si quis . . . . quod . . . .[4] Neque mihi succenseas, quod non mea manu tibi rescripserim, praesertim quom a te tua manu scriptas litteras acceperim. Digitis admodum invalidis nunc utor et detractantibus; tum haec epistula multorum verborum indigebat,[5] mea autem dextera manus hac tempestate paucarum litterarum.

Ad Antoninum Imp. i. 1 (Naber, p. 94).

Vat. 83 *ad init* | Magistro meo.

Bonum annum, bonam salutem, bonam fortunam peto a deis die mihi sollemni natali tuo, com-

[1] *Ac . non . . patus* is apparently the reading of the Codex, according to du Rieu. The margin of Cod. has *cognominatus.*

[2] Buttmann for Cod. *de . . . . tum.* Brakman prefers *defendendis, tum* for *disciplina militum.*

[3] Brakman.

[4] Twenty-six lines are lost.

10. Now to say a few words in praise of that speech[1] of M. Tullius which I sent you to read. It seems to me the very truth that no one was ever praised either in Greek or Latin before an assembly of the people more eloquently than Gnaeus Pompeius in that speech, so much so that to me he seems to have earned his title of *Great* not so much by reason of his own merits as of Cicero's praises. Then besides you will find in it many chapters full of reflections well suited to your present measures, touching the choice of generals, the interests of allies, the safeguarding of provinces, the discipline of soldiers, the necessary qualifications of commanders for duties in the field and elsewhere . . . .

. . . .

because I think that these considerations, even occasionally brought forward with greater earnestness, would be profitable. At all events you would wish it; and if anyone . . . . Do not be offended with me for not having answered your letter in my own hand, and that though the letter I had from you was in yours. My fingers just now are very weak and refractory; then this epistle required many words, but my right hand is at this moment one of few letters.

Marcus Antoninus the Emperor to Fronto

162 A.D.

To my master.

A good year, good health, good fortune do I ask of the Gods on this your birthday, a red-letter

[1] Surely the *Pro Lege Manilia*; but Mai refers it to a speech on the Mithridatic War.

[5] Buttm. for Cod. *ingerebat.* Perhaps *multam vim . . . ingerebat* would stand.

potemque me voti fore confido, nam quem sponte dei iuvisse volunt et dignum ope sua iudicant, eum commendo benignitati eorum. Tu quom alia laetabilia, mi magister, in tuo animo festo hoc die agitabis, numerato apud te qui te valde diligant: in iis primis hunc tuum discipulum ponito, inibi Dominum meum fratrem, πάθει φιλοῦντάς σε ἀνθρώπους. Vale, et perennem multis annis bonam valetudinem, mi magister, optine laetissimus incolumitate filiae nepotum generi.

Nostra Faustina reficit sanitatem. Pullus noster Antoninus aliquo lenius tussit. Quantum quisque in nidulo nostro iam sapit, tantum pro te precatur.
Vat. 98 Iterum atque iterum ac | porro in longam senectam bene vale, iucundissime magister. Peto a te—sed impetratum sit—ne te ob diem natalem Cornificiae Lorium vexes. Dis volentibus Romae paucis diebus nos videbis. Sed post diem natalem tuum, si me amas, nox quae sequitur iam placide quiescas sine ullius instantis officii cogitatione. Hoc Antonino tuo da sollicite et vere petenti.

Ad Antoninum Imp. i. 2 (Naber, p. 94).

ANTONINO AUGUSTO Fronto.

1. Seni huic et, ut tu appellas, magistro tuo bona salus bonus annus bona fortuna res omnis

[1] Hor. *Od.* IV. xi. 17.
[2] Victorinus, who married Gratia about 160.

day[1] for me, and I am assured that they will grant my prayer, for I commend to their bounty him whom the Gods themselves delight to aid and deem worthy of their help. You, my master, when other joyous thoughts pass through your mind on this your festal day, count over to yourself those who dearly love you: among the chief of these set this your pupil, set the Lord my brother there, both of us men that love you passionately. Farewell, my master, and may you for many years to come enjoy unbroken good health with your daughter, grandchildren and son-in-law[2] spared to make your happiness complete.

Our Faustina is recovering her health. Our little chick Antoninus[3] coughs rather less. The occupants of our little nest, each as far as he is old enough to do so, offer prayers for you. Next year and the year after and right on into a long old age, most delightful of masters, may you have the best of good health. I ask of you—and do not refuse me—not to take the trying journey to Lorium for Cornificia's[4] birthday. God willing, you shall see us at Rome a few days hence. But if you love me, pass the coming night in peace and quiet without attending to any business however pressing. Grant this to your Antoninus, who asks it with sincerity and concern.

162 A.D.

FRONTO to Antoninus Augustus.

1. For this old man and, as you style him, your master, good health, a good year, good fortune,

[3] Antoninus (Geminus) and Lucius Aurelius Commodus, afterwards emperor, were born on Aug. 31, 161. The former died four years later. [4] The daughter of Marcus.

bona, quae tu scribis eo[1] te mihi ab deis die tibi sollemnissimo natali meo precatum, omnia mihi ista in te tuoque fratre sita sunt, Antonine meo cordi dulcissime: quos ego postquam cognovi meque vobis transdidi, nihil umquam prae vobis dulcius habui neque habere possum; tametsi alios annos totidem de integro, quantum[2] vixi, vivam. Hoc igitur unum coniunctis precibus ab deis precemur, uti vos incolumes et florentes et reipublicae familiaeque vestrae prospere potentes aetatem longam degatis. Nec quicquam est praeterea, quod ego tanto opere vel ab
Vat. 97 deis vel a forte fortuna vel a nobis ipsis impetratum | cupiam, quam ut vestro conspectu et adfatu vestrisque tam iucundis litteris frui quam mihi diutissime liceat; eique ego rei, si fieri posset, repuerascere opto.

2. Nam quod ad ceteras res alioqui adtinet, sat vitae est. Video te, Antonine, Principem tam egregium quam speravi; tam iustum tam innocentem quam spopondi; tam gratum populo Romano et acceptum quam optavi; tam mei amantem quam ego volui; tam disertum quam ipse voluisti. Nam ubi primum coepisti rursum velle, nil offuit interdum noluisse. Fieri etiam vos cotidie facundiores video

[1] Cod. *ea*. [2] Query *quot iam*.

---

[1] So Melito in his *Apology* (Eus. *H.E.* iv. 26, § 7) calls him εὐκταῖος.

everything good, which you write you have prayed of the Gods for me on this my birthday, above all others a red-letter day for you—all these good things are in your keeping and your brother's, O Antoninus, sweetest joy of my heart: whom, since I have known you and given myself up to you, I have ever held sweeter than all things, and will so hold you, although I live again other years as many as I have lived. This one thing, therefore, let all of us with joint prayers ask of the Gods, that you may both pass long lives in health and vigour, exercising your power to the advantage of the state and of your own households. Nor is there aught else I could wish so much to obtain either from the Gods or from Fairy Fortune or from yourselves, as that it may be my lot as long as possible to enjoy your presence, your converse, and your delightful letters; and to that end I am ready, if it were possible, to be a boy again.

2. Otherwise, as far as everything else is concerned, I have had my fill of life. I see you, Antoninus, as excellent an Emperor as I hoped; as just, as blameless as I guaranteed; as dear and as welcome[1] to the Roman People as I desired; fond of me to the height of my wishes, and eloquent to the height of your own. For now that you once begin to feel the wish again, to have lost the wish for a time proves to have been no set-back.[2] Indeed I see both of you becoming more eloquent

[2] About the year 146 Marcus devoted himself more exclusively to philosophy and neglected rhetoric (see *Ad Mar.* iv. 13, i. p. 216). Later he eschewed it entirely; see *Thoughts*, i. 7; i. 17, § 4. But there was rhetoric in his writings, and Dio, lxxi. 35, § 1, says he was "practised in rhetoric."

et exulto quasi adhuc magister. Nam quom omnes
virtutes vestras diligam et amplectar, fateor tamen
praecipuum me et proprium gaudium ex eloquentia
vestra capere. Itidem ut parentes, quom in voltu
liberum oris sui lineamenta dinoscunt, ita ego quom
in orationibus vestris vestigia nostrae sectae animadverto—γέγηθε δὲ φρένα Λητώ: meis enim verbis
exprimere vim gaudii mei nequeo. Nec te recor-
datio ista urgeat nec omnino angat, quod tibi conscius es non perpetuam operam eloquentiae dedisse.
Vat. 92 Nam ita | res habet: qui magno ingenio praeditus
recta via ad eloquentiam ab principio inductus atque
institutus fuerit, tametsi interdum concessarit aut
restiterit, ubi primum progredi denuo et pergere
visum erit, coeptum illud iter confecerit setius fortasse aliquo, minus tamen nihilo. Crede autem hoc
mihi, omnium, quos ego cognoverim, uberiore quam
tu sis ingenio adfectum comperisse me neminem:
quod quidem ego magna cum lite Victorini nostri et
magna eius cum bile adiurare solebam, quom eum
adspirare ad pulchritudinem ingenii tui posse ne-
garem. Tum ille meus Rusticus Romanus, qui
vitam suam pro unguiculo tuo libenter dediderit
atque devoverit, de ingenio tamen invitus et tristis
aegre concedebat.

---

1 Hom. *Od.* vi. 106 = Verg. *Aen.* i. 502.

2 About this time Consul II. and *praef. urbi*. For Marcus's

every day, and I am elated as if I were still your master. For while I love and cherish all your merits, yet I confess that I derive my chief and peculiar pleasure from your eloquence. Just as it is with parents, when in their children's faces they discern their own lineaments, so it is with me when in the speeches of either of you I detect marks of my school—*and glad in her heart was Latona:* [1] for I cannot express in my own words the intensity of my joy. And do not feel compunction at the recollection, or be vexed in the least with the consciousness, of not having devoted yourself continuously to eloquence. For the fact is that, if a man endowed with great natural capacity has been from the first brought into and trained in the right way of eloquence, although he have given it the go-by for a time or rested on his oars, as soon as ever he resolves to make a fresh start and set forward, he will get to the end of his journey somewhat less quickly of course, but less successfully not a whit. But believe me when I say that, of all the men whom I have ever known, I have never met with any one gifted with richer ability than yourself: I used, indeed, to affirm this with an oath to the immense disagreement of our dear Victorinus and his immense disgust, when I said that he could not aspire to the charm of your natural gift. Then that friend of mine, the Roman Rusticus,[2] who would gladly surrender and sacrifice his life for your little finger, yet on the question of your natural ability gave way against his will and with a frown.

relations with him see *Thoughts*, i. 17, §§ 4, 6. Soon after this letter was written he condemned Justin Martyr and his companions to death as Christians.

3. Unum tibi periculum fuit, Antonine, idem quod omnibus qui sublimi ingenio extiterunt, ne in verborum copia et pulchritudine clauderes; quanto enim ampliores sententiae creantur, tanto difficilius verbis vestiuntur; nec mediocriter laborandum est ne procerae illae sententiae male sint amictae neve indecorius cinctae neve sint seminudae.

Vat. 91 | Meministi eius orationis tuae, quam vixdum pueritiam egressus in senatu habuisti? in qua quom imagine *utriculi* ad exemplum accomodandum usus esses, anxie verebare ne parum pro loci et ordinis dignitate τὴν εἰκόνα usurpasses, meque primam illam longiusculam ad te epistulam scripsisse qua id, quod res est, augurabar, magni ingenii signum esse ad eiusmodi sententiarum pericula audaciter adgredi, sed quod eo opus esset, tuo te studio et nonnulla nostra opera adsecuturum, ut digna tantis sententiis verborum lumina parares; quod nunc vides provenisse et, quamquam non semper ex summis opibus ad eloquentiam velificaris, tamen sipharis et remis te tenuisse iter, atque ut primum vela pandere necessitas impulit, omnes eloquentiae studiosos ut lembos et celoces facile praetervehi.

4. Haec ut scriberem productus sum proxima epistula tua, qua scripsisti "exolescere paulatim quaecumque didicisses"; mihi quidem nunc cum

---

[1] Perhaps when he entered the Senate as *quaestor*, but very possibly his Caesar-speech. See i. p. 19.

3. You had, Antoninus, but one danger to fear, and no one of outstanding ability can escape it—that you should limp in respect of copiousness and choiceness of words. For the greater the thoughts, the more difficult it is to clothe them in words, and no small labour is needed to prevent those stately thoughts being ill-clothed or unbecomingly draped or half-naked.

Do you remember that speech of yours,[1] which you delivered in the Senate when scarcely more than a boy, in which you made use of that simile of a *leathern bottle* by way of illustration, and were much concerned lest you had employed an image little suited to the dignity of the place and of a senator? and that first rather long letter[2] I wrote to you, in which I drew the inference—and it is a true inference—that it is a mark of great abilities to encounter boldly the difficulties in thoughts of that kind, but that by your own application and some help from me you would attain what was needed therein, the command of luminous expression[3] to match such great thoughts. This you see has now come to pass, and although you have not always set every sail in pursuit of eloquence, yet you have held on your course with topsails and with oars, and as soon as ever necessity has forced you to spread all your canvas, you are easily distancing all devotees of eloquence like so many pinnaces and yachts.

4. I have been prompted to write this by your last letter,[4] in which you said that you were gradually forgetting all that you had learnt, but to me it seems

[2] The letter printed first in this edition: *cp.* the reference to *audacia*. [3] *cp. De Eloqu.* iii. below.

[4] This letter is not in the collection, but *cp.* i. p. 39.

maxime florere quae didicisti atque adolescere videntur. An parum animadvertis, quanto studio quantoque favore et voluptate dicentem te audiat senatus
Vat. 82 |populusque Romanus? Et spondeo, quanto saepius audierit, tanto flagrantius amabit, ita multa et grata sunt ingenii et oris et vocis et facundiae tuae delenimenta. Nimirum quisquam superiorum imperatorum—imperatoribus enim te comparare malo, ne viventibus comparem[1]—quisquam illorum his figurationibus uteretur, quae Graeci σχήματα vocant? Ne longius repetam, vel proximo senatu quom Cyzicenorum gravem causam commemorares, ita orationem tuam figurasti—quam figuram Graeci παράλειψιν appellant—ut praetereundo tamen diceres et dicendo tamen praeterires. In qua[2] multa simul laudanda sunt: primum hoc, te doctissime perspexisse sociorum graves aerumnas non perpetua neque recta aut prolixa oratione exaggerandas, indicandas tamen impensius, ut digni senatus misericordia et auxilio viderentur; deinde ita breviter rem omnem atque ita valide elocutus es, ut paucissimis verbis omnia quae res posceret, continerentur, ut non ocius aut vehementius terra urbem illam quam

[1] Mai for Cod. *compararem*. [2] For Cod. *quo*.

---

[1] These are the technical figures of rhetoric, whether of language, such as alliteration, antithesis, etc., or of thought, such as παράλειψις (= a passing by) here.

that now more than ever is blossoming all that you have learnt and growing to maturity. Or do you fail to notice the eagerness, partiality, and pleasure with which the Senate and the Roman People listen to your speeches? And I go bail for it, the oftener they listen the more passionately will they love, so many and so ingratiating are the charms of your genius, your countenance, your voice, and your eloquence. In fact, is there one among former Emperors—I prefer to compare you with Emperors that I may not compare you with contemporaries—is there one who used these rhetorical figures which the Greeks call *σχήματα*?[1] Not to go further back, even at the last sitting of the Senate, when you spoke of the serious case of the Cyzicenes, you embellished your speech with a figure, which the Greeks call *παράλειψις*, in such a way that while waiving a point you yet mentioned it, and while mentioning it you yet waived it. In this speech many things at once call for praise: the first, that you most judiciously grasped the fact that the heavy trials of the allies should not be made too prominent by a continuous or direct or lengthy speech upon them, but should at the same time be pointed out with earnestness, so as to seem worthy of the compassion and help of the Senate; then you set forth the whole case so briefly, and yet so forcibly, that all that the subject demanded was summed up in the fewest words; so that not more suddenly or more violently was the city stirred by the earthquake[2] than the minds of

[2] The earthquake at Cyzicus is apparently alluded to again in the *De Eloquentia* 1 *ad fin.* It has a bearing on the date of the disputed *Letter to the Commune of Asia* relative to the Christians (Euseb. *H.E.* iv. 13: Justin, *Apol.* i. *ad fin.*).

animos audientium tua oratio moverit. Ecquid ad-
Vat. 81 gnoscis formam sententiae tullianae— | *ut non ocius aut vehementius terra urbem illam quam animos audientium tua oratio moverit?* Ut quisque amore quempiam deperit, eius etiam naevolos saviatur.

5. Sed mihi crede amplissimum te iam tenere in eloquentia locum, brevique summum eius cacumen aditurum, locuturumque inde nobiscum de loco superiore, nec tantulo superiore, quanto rostra foro et comitio excelsiora sunt, sed quanto altiores antennae sunt prora vel potius carina. Praecipue autem gaudeo te verba non obvia adripere, sed optima quaerere. Hoc enim distat summus orator a mediocribus, quod ceteri facile contenti sunt verbis bonis, summus orator non est bonis contentus, si sint meliora.

6. Sed haec certo loco ac tempore pluribus vel scribemus ad te vel coram colloquemur. Ut voluisti, Domine, et ut valetudo mea postulabat, domi mansi, tibique sum precatus ut multos dies natales liberorum tuorum prospere celebres. Pullo nostro tussiculam sedaverit et dies clementior et nutrix eius, si cibis aptioribus vescatur, omnia enim remedia atque omnes medelae fovendi[1] infantium
Vat. 10 faucibus | in lacte sunt sitae.

7. In oratione tua Cyzicena quom deos precaveris, *et si fas est, obsecro* addidisti: quod ego me non

[1] m[1] of the Codex has *offendi*. Novák would read *offensis*.

---

[1] Adjoining the Forum. It was where the Romans voted by Curiae. [2] He is referring to Cornificia's birthday.
[3] *i.e.* Antoninus Geminus, see last letter.

your hearers by your speech. Do you recognize the Ciceronian turn of the sentence?—*so that not more suddenly or more violently was the city stirred by the earthquake than the minds of your hearers by your speech.* When a man is deeply in love he kisses even the moles on his beloved's cheek.

5. But believe me you now hold a most distinguished place in eloquence, and will ere long reach its very summit, and speak thence with us from higher ground, and not so much higher only as the Rostrum is than the Forum and the Comitium,[1] but as much as the yards overtop the prow or rather the keel. But above all am I glad that you do not snatch up the first words that occur to you, but seek out the best. For this is the distinction between a first-rate orator and ordinary ones, that the others are readily content with good words, while the first-rate orator is not content with words merely good if better are to be obtained.

6. But I will either write to you or discuss these matters orally with you more fully at some fixed time and place. As you wished, my Lord, and as my health demanded, I have stayed at home and prayed for you that you might keep many happy returns of your children's birthdays.[2] The greater mildness of the weather and his nurse, if he takes more suitable food, will have quieted our little chick's[3] cough, for all remedies and all curatives for throat affections in children are centred in milk.[4]

7. In your Cyzicus-speech, when invoking the Gods, you added *and if it be allowed, I adjure them,* a use of the word[5] which I do not remember to have

[4] See Aul. Gell. xii. 1.

[5] Plautus uses it (*Rud.* III. iii. 32) of supplication to Venus, and Festus defines it as *opem a sacris petere.*

memini legisse. Obsecrari enim et resecrari populus aut iudices solebant. Sed me forsitan memoria fugerit: tu diligentius animadvertito.

8. Me quoque tussicula vexat et manus dexterae dolor, mediocris quidem sed qui a rescribenda longiore epistula impedierit: dictavi igitur.

9. Quoniam mentio παραλείψεως habita est, non omittam quin te impertiam quod de figura ista studiosius animadverterim, neque Graecorum oratorum neque Romanorum, quos ego legerim, elegantius hac figura usum quemquam quam M. Porcium in ea oratione, quae *de Sumptu suo* inscribitur, in qua sic ait:

Iussi caudicem proferri, ubi mea oratio scripta erat de ea re, quod sponsionem feceram cum M. Cornelio. Tabulae prolatae: maiorum benefacta perlecta: deinde quae ego pro republica fecissem leguntur. Ubi id utrumque perlectum est, deinde scriptum erat in oratione: "Numquam ego pecuniam neque meam neque sociorum per ambitionem dilargitus sum." "Attat, noli noli scri-
Vat. 107 *bere,"* [1] *inquam "istud"; nolunt | audire. Deinde recitavit: "Numquam* [2] *ego praefectos per sociorum vestrorum oppida imposivi, qui eorum bona* <*coniuges*>[3] *liberos diriperent." "Istud quoque dele; nolunt audire: recita porro." "Numquam ego praedam neque quod de hostibus captum esset neque manubias inter pauculos amicos meos divisi, ut illis eriperem qui cepissent." "Istuc quoque dele: nihil eo* [4] *minus volunt dici; non opus est recitato." "Numquam ego evectionem datavi, quo amici mei per symbolos pecunias magnas caperent."*

[1] Query *recitare.*
[2] For Cod. *num quos.*
[3] Eckstein.
[4] Alan for Cod. *nihilo.*

read, for it was the people or a jury that used to be adjured or conjured; but perhaps my memory plays me false: do you think over it more carefully yourself.

8. I, too, am troubled with a cough, and pain in my right hand, not very severe it is true, but enough to prevent my *writing* so long a letter: therefore I have dictated it.

9. Since mention has been made of *paraleipsis,* I must not fail to acquaint you with what I have noticed with regard to this figure in a somewhat careful search. None of the Greek or Roman orators that I have read has used this figure more happily than M. Porcius in that speech which is entitled *On his Expenses,*[1] in which he says as follows:

I ordered the volume to be produced containing my speech on the subject of my having made an agreement with M. Cornelius. The tablets were produced: the services of my ancestors were read out: then was recited what I had done for the state. The reading out of both these being finished, the speech went on as follows: "I have never either scattered my own money or that of the allies broadcast to gain popularity." "Oh, don't, don't, I say, record that: they have no wish to hear it." Then he read on: "Never have I set up officials in the towns of your allies to rob them of their goods, their wives, and the children." "Erase that too; they will not listen: go on reading." "I have never divided booty or spoil taken from the enemy or prize money among my select friends so as to rob those who had won it." "Erase as far as that too: they would rather hear anything than that; there is no need to read it." "I have never granted a pass to travel post, to enable my friends to gain large

[1] Nothing more is known of this speech.

"Perge istuc quoque uti cum maxime delere." "Numquam ego argentum pro vino congiario inter apparitores atque amicos meos disdidi neque eos malo publico divites feci." "Enimvero usque istuc ad lignum dele." Vides in quo loco respublica siet, ubi[1] *quod reipublicae bene fecissem, unde gratiam capiebam, nunc idem illud memorare non audeo ne invidiae siet. Ita inductnm est male facere impoene, bene facere non impoene licere.*

10. Haec forma παραλείψεως nova, nec ab ullo alio, quod ego sciam, usurpata est. Iubet enim legi tabulas, et quod lectum sit iubet praeteriri. A te quoque novum factum, quod principium orationis tuae figura ista exorsus es; sicut multa alia nova et
Vat. 90 exi|mia facturum te in orationibus tuis certum habeo, ita egregio ingenio natus es.

Ad Verum (?) *Imp.* i. 1 (Naber, p. 113).

Vat. 2 (somewhere) | <Domino meo>[2].

1. . . . .

Sit quod iubes rectum fortasse sed serum: neque enim omnia, quae ratio postulat, etiam aetas tolerat . . . . An tu cycnum coges in ultima cantione cor-
Vat. 1 nicum voculas aemulari?[3] . . | . . <in>genio discrepanti iuberesne me niti contra naturam adverso quod aiunt flumine? Quid, si quis postularet, ut

[1] Haupt for Cod. *uti*.

[2] For all the first part of this letter see Hauler, *Mitteil. d. könig; deutsch. archäol. Institut*, xix. pp. 317–321, and *Archiv. f. lat. Lexicographie*, xv. 106.

[3] These two sentences are from the margin of Codex.

sums by these warrants." "Be quick, erase as far as that too most particularly." [1] *"I have never shared the money for wine-largess between my retinue and friends, nor enriched them to the detriment of the state." "Marry, erase as far as that down to the wood." Pray mark the pass to which the state has come, when I dare not now mention the very services I have done it, whereby I hoped to gain gratitude, lest it should bring odium upon me. So much has it become the fashion that a man may do ill with impunity, but not with impunity do well.*

10. This form of *paraleipsis* is original and, as far as I know, not employed by anyone else. For Cato bids the tablets be read, and what is read he bids be waived aside. You also have shewn originality by beginning your speech with this figure, just as you will, I am sure, do many other original and brilliant things in your speeches, so great is your natural ability.

Fronto to Marcus Antoninus (?) [2]

? 162 A.D.

To my Lord.

1. . . . . What you enjoin may perhaps be right, but it is too late: nor indeed does age also permit all that reason demands . . . . Would you make a swan in its dying song rival the cawing of crows? . . . . though it is out of keeping with my genius, would you advise me to strive against nature and swim, as they say, against the stream? What, if one called on

[1] Or, "as quickly as possible."

[2] The heading and title to this letter are lost, and its attribution is not certain. It reads like a letter to Marcus. Naber, following Mai, assigns it to Verus.

Phidias ludicra aut Canachus deum simulacra fingeret? aut ut Calamis lepturga[1] aut Polycletus chirurga?[2] Quid, si Parrhasium versicolora pingere iuberet aut Apellen unicolora, aut Nealcen magnifica aut Protogenen minuta, aut Niciam obscura aut Dionysium inlustria, aut lascivia Euphranorem aut Pausiam t<ristiti>a sa<tura>?[3]

2. In poetis autem quis ignorat ut gracilis sit Lucilius, Albucius[4] aridus, sublimis Lucretius, mediocris Pacuvius, inaequalis Accius, Ennius multiformis? Historiam quoque scripsere Sallustius structe Pictor incondite, Claudius lepide Antias invenuste, Sisenna longinque, verbis Cato multiiugis Caelius singulis. Contionatur autem Cato infeste, Gracchus turbulente, Tullius copiose. Iam in iudiciis saevit idem Cato, triumphat Cicero, tumultuatur Gracchus, Calvus rixatur.

3. Sed haec exempla fortasse contemnas. Quid? philosophi ipsi nonne diverso genere orationis usi sunt? Zeno ad docendum plenissimus, Socrates ad
Vat. 4 coarguendum captiosissimus, Diogenes ad | exprobrandum promptissimus, Heraclitus obscurus involvere omnia, Pythagoras mirificus clandestinis signis sancire omnia, Clitomachus anceps in dubium vocare omnia. Quidnam igitur agerent isti ipsi sapientis-

[1] Or m[2] *lepturgata* for m[1] *Turena*.

[2] m[2] *Etrusca. cp. duriora et Tuscanicis proxima* of the works of Callon, Quint. xii. 10. 7.

[3] Or *sa<llita>* Hauler.

[4] Minton Warren *Abuccius* from Varro, *R.R.* iii. 6. 6.

Phidias to produce sportive works or Canachus images of Gods, or Calamis delicate statuary or Polycletus rough handiwork? What if one bade Parrhasius paint rainbow hues or Apelles monochromes, or Nealces grand canvasses or Protogenes miniature[1] ones, or Nicias sombre pictures or Dionysius brilliant ones, or Euphranor subjects all licence or Pausias all austerity?

2. Among poets, who does not know how Lucilius is graceful,[2] Albucius dry, Lucretius sublime, Pacuvius mediocre, Accius unequal, Ennius many-sided? History, too, has been written by Sallust symmetrically by Pictor without method, by Claudius pleasantly by Antias without charm, by Sisenna[3] at length, by Cato with many words abreast by Caelius with words in single harness.[4] In harangue, again, Cato is savage, Gracchus violent, Tully copious, while at the bar Cato rages, Cicero triumphs, Gracchus riots, Calvus quarrels.

3. But perhaps you would make light of these instances. What? have not philosophers themselves used different styles in their speaking? No one could be fuller in exposition than Zeno, more captious in argument than Socrates, more ready than Diogenes at denunciation; Heraclitus was obscure enough to mystify everything, Pythagoras wonderfully prone to give everything religious sanction with secret symbols, Clitomachus agnostic enough to call everything in question. What, pray, would your wisest of

[1] Hauler says this refers to detailed work and not to size.

[2] Aul. Gell. vii. 14, defines *gracilis* of style as combining *venustas* and *subtilitas* (= Greek *ἰσχνός*), and says Varro attributed *gracilitas* to Lucilius.

[3] As the names go in pairs, the contrast to Sisenna must have dropped out, and *longinque* may belong to his *vis-à-vis*.

[4] For Cato's trick of using *atque* . . . *atque* see i. p. 152.

simi viri, si de suo quisque more atque instituto deducerentur? Socrates ne coargueret, Zeno ne disceptaret, Diogenes ne increparet, ne quid Pythagoras sanciret, ne quid Heraclitus absconderet, ne quid Clitomachus ambigeret?

4. Sed ne in prima ista parte diutius quam epistulae modus postulat commoremur, tempus est de verbis primum quid censeas considerare. Dic sodes hoc mihi, utrumne, tametsi sine ullo labore ac studio meo verba mihi elegantiora ultro occurrerent, spernenda censes ac repudianda? An cum labore quidem et studio investigare verba elegantia prohibes, eadem vero, si ultro si iniussu atque invocatu meo venerint, ut Menelaum ad epulas, tu idem[1] recipi iubes? Nam istud quidem vetare durum prorsus atque inhumanum est: consimile ut si ab hospite, qui te Falerno accipiat, quod rure eius natum domi superfiat,
Vat. 8 Cretense postules vel Sa|guntinum, quod—malum!—foris quaerendum sibi atque mercandum sit. Quid . . . . Epictetus incuriosus . . . . Socrates . . . . Xenophon . . . . Antisthenes . . . . Aeschines . . . . Plato[2] . . . . Haud igitur indicarent ea si . . . .[3] Quid nostra memoria Euphrates, Dio, Timocrates, Athenodotus? Quid horum magister Musonius? Nonne summa facundia praediti neque

[1] Rob. Ellis for Cod. *quidem*.
[2] Eleven lines are missing. The names are from the margin. [3] Nine lines are lost.

---

[1] Hom. *Il.* ii. 408.
[2] A Stoic philosopher friend of Pliny the younger. He committed suicide under Hadrian.

men themselves do, if called away from their own individual habits and principles—Socrates from arguing, Zeno from disputing, Diogenes from finding fault, Pythagoras from sanctioning anything, Heraclitus from wrapping anything in mystery, Clitomachus from calling anything in question?

4. But that we may not dwell on this first part longer than is compatible with the compass of a letter, it is time to consider first what is your view about words. Tell me then, pray, whether in your opinion the choicest words must be disdained and rejected, even if they come to me of their own accord, without any toil and pursuit of mine? or, while forbidding the searching out of choice words with toil and eagerness, do you at the same time bid me receive them like Menelaus at the banquet,[1] if only they come of their own accord, unbidden by me and uninvited? For to forbid that indeed is downright harsh and barbarous. It is as though from a host who welcomes you with Falernian wine, which being produced on his own estate is abundant at home, you should call for Cretan or Saguntine, to be got—bad cess to it!—from elsewhere and paid for. What . . . . Epictetus unconcerned . . . . Socrates . . . . Xenophon . . . . Antisthenes . . . . Aeschines . . . . Plato . . . . Would they then not indicate this, if . . . . What in our own recollection of Euphrates,[2] Dio,[3] Timocrates, Atherodotus?[4] What of their master Musonius?[5] Were they not gifted with a supreme command of words, and

[3] Of Prusa, called "Golden-mouthed," orator and philosopher. He died about 117.

[4] Fronto's master.

[5] A Stoic philosopher under Nero and Vespasian.

minus sapientiae quam eloquentiae gloria inclyti extiterunt?

5. An tu <censes Epictetum non> consulto verbis usum fuisse? . . . .[1] ne pallium quidem sordibus obsitum candido et pure lauto praetulisset. Nisi forte Epictetum[2] arbitrare claudum quoque consulto factum et servum consulto natum. Quid igitur est? Tam facile ille . . . . numquam voluntarias verborum sordes induisset. Forte et servus, consulto natus est sapiens. Sed ita eloquentia caruit pedum incolumitate[3] . . . .

(Naber, p. 139.)

De Eloquentia 1

<Antonino Augusto Fronto>.

Ambr. 404, following 427? 1. . . . .[4] | verborum loca gradus pondera aetates dignitatesque dinoscere ne in oratione praepostera ut in temulento ac perturbato convivio conlocentur; quae ratio sit verba geminandi et interdum trigeminandi, nonnumquam quadriplicia, saepe quinquies aut eo amplius superlata ponendi; ne frustra neve temere verborum strues acerventur, sed ut certo ac sollerti termino uniantur.[5]

2. Post ista omnia investigata examinata distincta finita cognita, verborum omnium, ut ita dixerim, de[6]

[1] Four lines are illegible.

[2] From the margin for Cod. *eum tu*.

[3] This sentence is from the margin of the Codex. Possibly the previous clause, *forte*, etc., is not complete.

[4] A column seems to be lost between the end of the last letter and the beginning of this. As Naber points out, the order of the various fragments in this mutilated tractate cannot be certainly determined.

famed as much for their eloquence as for their wisdom?[1]

5. Or do you think that Epictetus did not use words of set purpose? . . . . would have preferred even a mantle foul with dirt to one that was white and spotlessly clean. Unless you think perchance that Epictetus became lame too of set purpose and of set purpose was born a slave. What then is it? So easily he . . . . never would have donned voluntary rags of words. Even a slave by accident he was of set purpose born a wise man. But so eloquence was divorced from soundness of feet[2] . . . .

On Eloquence 1

? 162 A.D.

Fronto to Antoninus Augustus.

1. . . . . to distinguish between the place, rank, weight, age, and dignity of words, that they may not be put together absurdly in a speech, as it might be in a drunken and confused carouse; on what principles words are to be doubled and sometimes trebled, on occasion drawn up four deep, often carried to a fifth place[3] or even extended further than that; that words be not heaped to no purpose or at random but be combined within fixed and intelligent limits.

2. When all these have been examined, tested, distinguished, defined, and understood, then from

[1] All this was surely addressed to Marcus and not Verus.
[2] Epictetus, it is said, was made lame by the cruelty of his master, Epaphroditus.
[3] See for an illustration the first two lines of § 2, and *cp.* last letter, § 2, *verba multiiuga*.

[5] Schäfer prefers *finiantur.*
[6] From the margin.

populo, sicut in bello ubi opus sit legionem conscribere, non tantum voluntarios legimus sed etiam latentes militari aetate conquirimus, ita ubi verborum praesidiis opus sit, non voluntariis tantum, quae ultro obvenerint, utemur sed latentia eliciemus atque ad imperandum indagabimus.

3. Hic illud etiam, ut arbitror, scite a nobis commentandum,[1] quibus rationibus verba quaerantur, ut non hiantes oscitantesque expectemus, quando verbum ultro in linguam quasi palladium de caelo defluat;[2] sed ut regiones verborum et saltus noverimus ut, ubi quaesitis opus siet,[3] per viam potius ad investigandum quam invio progrediamur.

4. Certa igitur loca sunt a vobis <exploranda>[4]
Ambr. 403 . . . . . . | . . In primis oratori cavendum ne quod novum verbum ut aes adulterinum percutiat, ut unum et id<em> verbum vetustate noscatur et novitate delectet[5] . . . . castella verborum . . . . conciliabula verborum[6] . . . .
Ambr. 402 . . . . | . . . . Officiorum genera duo, rationes

[1] Heindorf for Cod. *conventum*; Schäfer would read *commentum*. [2] From the margin of Cod. for *diffluat* in the text.
[3] For Cod. *sit ut*: the phrase is from Plautus.
[4] Heindorf. [5] From the margin of Codex.
[6] These two phrases are separate marginal glosses on the left margin of p. 403.

---

[1] The *palladium* was a supposed image of Pallas that fell from the sky at Troy and was carried off by the Greeks.
[2] In this mutilated passage Fronto is speaking of *sapientia* and *eloquentia* in connexion with a classification of human functions The *officia* or essential functions of man are, he says, of two *genera*, and can be classified under three heads (*rationes* or *species*). The distinction of the two *genera* is not

the whole word-population, so to speak, just as in war, when a legion has to be enrolled, we not only collect the volunteers but also search out the skulkers of military age, so when there is need of word-reinforcements, we must not only make use of the voluntary recruits that offer themselves, but fetch out the skulkers and hunt them up for service.

3. At this point too, as I think, we must seek skilfully to find out the methods by which words are sought for, that we may not wait gaping open-mouthed till such time as a word shall fall of itself upon our tongues like a god-send [1] from heaven; but that we should know their haunts and their coverts, so that, when we have need of choice words, we may follow them up along a beaten track rather than have no path to help us forward.

4. You must therefore scout over definite ground . . . . First of all a speaker must be on his guard against coining a new word[3] like debased bronze, so that each several word may be both known by its age and delight by its freshness . . . . fortresses of words . . . . assembly-places of words . . . . Of obligations [2] the

given in what we have. The three classes are (1) that of existence, that a man must exist and perform certain *munera*, *e.g.* eat, in order to live; (2) of quality, he must be such and such and have such and such habits and idiosyncrasies; (3) of objective or result, the two previous *officia* enabling him to discharge the third. This third class is concerned wholly with *negotia*, work done, and is self-contained. Under this comes *sapientia*. Since a man must live before he can be wise, a *munus*, like eating, is an *officium* of the wise man, though it has no direct connexion with his *negotium*, which is wisdom. Eating belongs to *species prima*, which is common to all men, but wisdom to *species tertia*. The pursuit of eloquence comes under *species secunda*, which varies with every man.

[3] See I. 219; II. 115.

tripertitae. Prima species substantiae, ut sit; altera
qualitatis, ut talis sit; tertia rei, ut rem ipsam,[1]
cuius causa superiora officia suscepit, expleat
Ambr. 401 . . . . <dis>|cendae exercendaeque sapientiae:
tertiam autem hanc speciem rei dico ac negotiis
solam terminatam, se quasi contentam. Hac officiorum partitione, si tamen aut ille verum aiebat,
aut ego olim audita memoria retineo, ut prima
homini ad sapientiam tendenti sint molimenta quae
ad vitam salutemque pertinent conservandam. Igitur et prandere et lavari et ungui et cetera eiusmodi
munera sunt sapientis officia, quamquam neque in
balneis quisquam sapientia <se laverit>, neque ut
circu<li . . . . quom> ad mensam cenarit pran-
dio<que comeso>[2] vomerit, sapientiam ructarit;
<nec vitam quidem potes habere ni>si ederis, <nec
sapientiam> nisi vixeris. Quid igitur istic admon-
endus es? Ne tu <negotium> hoc <sapientiae in>[3]
prandio et mensa situm existimes. Non est sapientiae negotium vesci: sed sine vita, quae cibo constat,
nulla sapientia, studia nulla esse possunt. Nunc
. . . . vides igitur <prima haec> officia <omnium
Ambr. 396 esse hominum>[4] . . | . . . . . . at non aeque
sequentia officia, quae sunt qualitati cuiusque ac-

[1] For Cod. *re ipsa*, Niebuhr.
[2] *Comeso* is from the margin of Codex.
[3] Heindorf.
[4] The additions are by Heindorf. There are seven lines of the Codex from *nunc* to *hominum*.

kinds are two, the categories three-fold. The first class, of existence, that a man be; the second, of quality, that he be such and such; the third, of objective, that he satisfy the very object by reason of which he undertook the foregoing obligations . . . . of learning and practising wisdom: by this third class, however, I mean that of objective and that which has its end in the work to be done and is, as it were, content with itself. By this division of obligations, if indeed either he[1] said what was true, or I carry correctly in my memory things heard long ago, for a man who aspires to wisdom those would count as the first things to be taken in hand which have to do with the preservation of life and health. So dining and bathing and anointing with oil and all functions of such a kind are obligations of the wise man. And yet neither at the baths can anyone lave himself with wisdom, nor when he has dined at table with a select company, and after the meal had occasion to vomit, will he bring up wisdom; but you can neither have life unless you eat, nor wisdom unless you live. What then is the warning here? that you should not think this business of wisdom to lie in dining and the pleasures of the table. The business of wisdom is not to eat, but apart from life, which is derived from food, there can be no wisdom and no pursuits. Now . . . . you see then that these primary obligations apply to all men . . . . but the second class of obligations which are suited to the character of each person, cannot be in the

[1] Probably one of Fronto's teachers, *i.e.* Dionysius or Athenodotus, who must have been mentioned in a lost part of the letter.

commodata,[1] possunt omnium esse communia.[2] Aliud prandium gubernatori commune[3] et aliud pugili de integris tergoribus; aliud prandendi tempus, alia lavatio, alius somnus, alia pervigilatio.

5. Considera igitur an in hac secunda ratione officiorum contineatur eloquentiae studium. Nam Caesarum est in senatu quae e re sunt suadere, populum de plerisque negotiis in concione appellare, ius iniustum corrigere, per orbem terrae litteras missitare, reges exterarum gentium compellare, sociorum culpas edictis coercere, benefacta laudare, seditiosos compescere, feroces territare. Omnia ista profecto verbis sunt ac litteris agenda. Non excoles igitur id quod tibi totiens tantisque in rebus videas magno usui futurum? An nihil referre arbitraris qualibus verbis agas, quae non nisi verbis agi possunt? Erras, si putas pari auctoritate in senatu fore Thersitae verbis expromptam sententiam et Menelai aut Ulixi orationem, quorum Homerus et voltus in agendo et habitus et status et voces canoras ac modulationum eloquentiae genera diversa non <dedignatus est
Ambr. 396 describere> . . . . . . | . .

6. Quisquam vereri potest quem inridet? quisquam dicto oboediret cuius verba contempserit. Quom in officina Apellis Alexander Magnus de picturae arte dissereret, *Tace quae nescis,* inquit, *ne*

[1] The margin of Cod. has *secunda species qualitatis haec est.*
[2] The margin adds *sed diversa sunt et quae communia omnibus,* which Heindorf thinks should be *neque commoda omnibus.* [3] Heindorf *commodum.*

same way common to all. One kind of dinner is usual for the man at the wheel, and another off the whole chine of an ox for the prize-fighter; their times of dining are different, their washing is different, their sleeping, their keeping awake different.

5. Consider then whether in this second category of obligations be contained the pursuit of eloquence. For it falls to a Caesar to carry by persuasion necessary measures in the Senate, to address the people in a harangue on many important matters, to correct the inequities of the law, to despatch rescripts throughout the world, to take foreign kings to task, to repress by edicts disorders among the allies, to praise their services, to crush the rebellious and to cow the proud. All these must assuredly be done by speech and writing. Will you not then cultivate an art, which you see must be of great use to you so often and in matters of such moment? Or do you imagine that it makes no difference with what words you bring about what can only be brought about by words? You are mistaken if you think that an opinion blurted out in the Senate in the language of Thersites would carry equal weight with a speech of Menelaus or Ulysses, whose looks in the act of speaking and their mien and attitude and melodious voices and the difference of cadence in their oratory Homer did not in fact disdain to describe[1] . . . .

6. Can anyone fear him whom he laughs at, or could anyone obey his order, whose words he despised? When Alexander the Great was discussing the art of painting in the studio of Apelles, *Hold your tongue,* said the painter, *about what you*

[1] Hom. *Il.* iii. 212.

te pueri illi, qui purpurissum subterunt, contemnant[1] . . . . Nemo tanta auctoritate est, qui non, ubi peritia deficitur, ab eo qui peritior est, despiciatur . . . . medebor . . . . temnor . . . . mersit[2] . . . .

7. Tibi tanta eloquentia parta est, quae ad laudem
Ambr. 394 etiam supersit . . . . comi | sese . . . . nil, ac capillus etsi non cotidie acu ornandus, tamen pectine
Ambr. 393 cotidie expediendus est . . . . | fuisse Croesum et Solonem, Periandrum et Polycraten, Alcibiaden denique et Socraten.

8. Quis dubitat sapientem ab insipiente vel praecipue consilio et delectu rerum et opinione discerni? ut, si sit optio atque electio divitiarum atque egestatis, quamquam utraque et malitia et virtute careant, tamen electionem laude et culpa non carere. Proprium namque sapientis officium est recte eligere, neque perperam vel postponere vel anteferre.

9. Si me interroges concupiscamne bonam valetudinem, abnuam equidem, si sim philosophus: nihil est enim fas concupiscere sapienti aut adpetere, quod fors fuat an frustra concupiscat; nec quidquam, quod in manu fortunae situm videat concupiscet. Tamen, si necessario sit alterutra[3] res eligenda, Achilli potius pernicitatem eligam quam debilitatem Philoctetae. Simile igitur in eloquentia servandum: non opere nimio concupiscas igitur, nec opere nimio

[1] This whole passage has been restored from the Codex by Hauler, *Wien. Stud.* 35, pp. 398 f. For the earlier part Mai read *inridentius quam dictorum eius causa haud*, the last three words being doubtful.

[2] These isolated words are from the margin of Cod. (Naber.) [3] Brakman for Cod. *altera*.

don't understand, that those boys yonder who are mixing the purple paint may not despise you[1] . . . . There is no one, however authoritative, who when his skill is at fault is not looked down upon by him who has greater skill . . . .

7. You have achieved such great eloquence as is even more than enough for fame . . . . and hair, though it need not be daily set off with a pin, yet must daily be smoothed out with a comb[2] . . . . Croesus and Solon, Periander and Polycrates, Alcibiades in fine and Socrates.

8. Who doubts that a wise man is distinguished from an unwise man preëminently by his sagacity and choice of things and judgment, so that if there be an option and alternative between riches and poverty, though they are both of them devoid of vice and virtue, yet the choice between them is not devoid of praise or blame. For it is the special obligation of the wise man to choose rightly, and not wrongly put this first or that second.

9. If you ask me whether I covet good health, I should, if I were a philosopher, say no; for a wise man must not covet or desire anything which it may be he would covet in vain; nor will he covet anything which he sees to lie in the power of Fortune.[3] Yet were the choice of one or the other forced upon me, I would rather choose the fleetness of Achilles than the lameness of Philoctetes. A similar course must be kept in eloquence. You should, therefore, not covet it too much or too much disdain it: yet if

[1] Pliny gives the story, *N.H.* xxxv. 36, § 12.

[2] This seems to imply that Marcus's eloquence, great as it is, still requires brushing and trimming up.

[3] *cp.* Marcus, *Thoughts*, vi. 41, etc.

aversere: tamen,[1] si eligendnm sit, longe longeque eloquentiam infantiae praeferas.

10. Audivi te nonnumquam ita dicentem: *at enim quom aliquid pulchrius elocutus sum, placeo mihi ideoque*
Ambr. 400 *eloquentiam fugio.* Quin tu potius illud | corrigis ac mederis, ne placeas tibi, non ut id, propter quod places, repudies? Nam ut nunc facis, alibi tu medicamenta obligas. Quid tandem? Si tibi placebis quod iuste iudicaris, iustitiam repudiabis? Si placebis tibi pio aliquo cultu parentis, pietatem aspernabere? Places tibi quom facundus: igitur verbera te: quid facundiam verberas?

11. Tametsi Plato ita diceret itaque te compellaret: *O iuvenis, periculum est tibi praepropera placendi fuga: novissimum namque homini sapientiam colenti amiculum est gloriae cupido, id novissime exuitur:* ipsi ipsi, inquam, Platoni in novissimum usque vitae finem gloria amiculum erit.

Illud autem audisse me memini, pleraque sapientes viros, id est in[2] scitis mentis atque consultis, habere debere, quorum interdum usu abstineant; itemque interdum nonnulla in usu habere debere, quae dogmatis improbent; neque ubique rationem sapientiae rectam et usum vitae necessarium congruere.

12. Fac te, Caesar, ad sapientiam Cleanthis aut Zenonis posse pertingere, ingratiis tamen tibi pur-

[1] Heindorf for Cod. *tum.*
[2] For Cod. *id inest.* Kluss. reads *id institutis mentis.*

a choice must be made you would far and far prefer eloquence to dumbness.

10. I have heard you say sometimes, *But indeed, when I have said something rather brilliant, I feel gratified, and that is why I shun eloquence.* Why not rather correct and cure yourself of your self-gratification, instead of repudiating that which gratifies you. For acting as you now do, you are tying a poultice in the wrong place. What then? If you gratify yourself by giving just judgment, will you disown justice? If you gratify yourself by shewing some filial respect to your father, will you despise filial duty? You gratify yourself, when eloquent: chastize yourself then, but why chastize eloquence?

11. And yet Plato would tell you this and take you thus to task: *Perilous, young man, is that hasty avoidance of self-gratification, for the last cloak that wraps the follower after wisdom is the love of fame, that is the last to be discarded:*[1] to Plato, to Plato himself, I say, will fame be a cloak to his very last day.

This also I remember to have heard, that wise men must needs have many things—I mean in their mental rules and postulates—to which in practice they occasionally give the go-by; and occasionally also must needs allow in practice some things which they cry out upon in their tenets; and that the right rules of wisdom and the necessary practices of life do not everywhere coincide.

12. Suppose that you, O Caesar, succeed in attaining to the wisdom of Cleanthes or Zeno, yet

[1] "The last infirmity of noble mind": see Plato (*ap. Athen.* xi. 507 D), ἔσχατον τὸν τῆς δόξης χίτωνα· ἐν τῷ θανάτῳ αὐτῷ ἀποδυόμεθα. *cp.* also Tac. *Agr.* 9.; *Hist.* iv. 6; Plut. *An Seni, etc.*, 783 D; Lucian, *Peregr.* 38.

pureum pallium erit sumendum, non pallium[1] philo-
Ambr. 399 sophorum soloci lana. Purpureo . . . . . . | . .
Cleanthes aqua de puteo extrahenda victum quaerebat; tibi saepenumero curandum in theatro crocum
Ambr. 398 longe atque alte exprimatur[2] . . . . | . .
Diogenes cynicus non modo nullam pecuniam quaesivit sed etiam propriam neglexit . . . . udaque ea . . . . mensa et . . . . familia tu . . . . famae . . . . Socrate . . . . sapientior . . . . alienum . . . . vocalem . . . . carmina quorundam . . . .

Ambr. 397 13. . . . . <dei> | immortales sirint comitium et rostra et tribunalia Catonis et Gracchi et Ciceronis orationibus celebrata hoc potissimum saeculo conticiscere? orbem terrae quem vocalem acceperis, mutum a te fieri? Si linguam quis uni homini exsecet, immanis habeatur; eloquentiam humano generi exsecare mediocre facinus putas? Num[3] hunc adnumeras Tereo aut Lycurgo? qui Lycurgus quid tandem[4] mali facinoris admisit, quom vites amputavit? Multis profecto gentibus ac nationibus profuisset vinum undique gentium exterminatum. Tamen Lycurgus poenas caesarum vitium luit. Quare metuendam censeo divinitus poenam eloquentiae exterminatae. Nam vinea in unius tutela dei sita: eloquentiam vero multi in caelo diligunt: Minerva orationis magistra, Mercurius nuntiis praeditus,

[1] The margin of Cod. gives, as epithet of *pallium*, *consucidum* = wool newly shorn.

[2] From the margin of Cod. So also the next sentence and the succeeding fragments.

[3] For Cod. *non*. [4] The margin has *tamen*.

against your will[1] you must put on the purple cloak, not the philosopher's mantle of coarse wool. Purple . . . . Cleanthes gained his livelihood by drawing water from a well; you have often to see that saffron-water is sprinkled broadcast and high in the theatre[2] . . . . Diogenes the Cynic not only earned no money but took no care of what he had[3] . . . .

. . . .

. . . .

13. What, will the Immortal Gods allow the Comitium and Rostra and tribunals, that echoed to the speeches of Cato and Gracchus and Cicero, to be hushed in this age of all others? the wide world, which was vocal when you received it, to become dumb by your doing? If one cut out the tongue of a single man, he would be deemed a monster; to cut eloquence out from the human race—do you think that a trivial crime? Do you rank the doer of this with Tereus and Lycurgus? and this Lycurgus, what evil deed pray did he commit when he lopped the vines? It had surely been to the benefit of many a race and nation had the vine been extirpated from the face of the earth. Yet Lycurgus paid dear for his felled vines. Wherefore I hold that the extirpation of eloquence must fear vengeance from Heaven. For the vine is placed under the patronage of one God, while eloquence is the delight of many a denizen of Heaven—Minerva the mistress of speech, Mercury

[1] See Capit. *Vit. Mar.* v. 3, and Marcus, *Thoughts*, v. 16; vi. 12.

[2] For this custom see Pliny, *N.H.* xxi. 6.

[3] This may have been followed by some such sentence as "but you will have to provide for the finances of the state and see that they are husbanded."

Apollo paeanum auctor, Liber dithyramborum cognitor, Fauni vaticinantium incitatores, magistra Homeri Calliope, magister Ennii Homerus et Somnus.

14. Tum si studium philosophiae in rebus esset solis occupatum, minus mirarer, quod tanto opere verba contemneres. Discere te autem *ceratinas* et
Ambr. 392 *soritas* et *pseudomenus*, verba contorta | et fidicularia, neglegere vero cultum orationis et gravitatem et maiestatem et gratiam et nitorem, hoc indicat loqui te quam eloqui malle, murmurare potius et friguttire quam clangere. Diodori tu et Alexini verba verbis Platonis et Xenophontis et Antisthenis anteponis? ut si quis histrioni studiosus Tasurci gestu potius quam Roscii uteretur; ut si in natando, si aeque liceret, ranam potius quam delphinos aemulari mallet, coturnicum potius pinnis breviculis quam aquilarum maiestate volitare?

15. Ubi illud acumen tuum? Ubi subtilitas? Evigila et attende, quid cupiat ipse Chrysippus. Num contentus est docere, rem ostendere, definire, explanare? Non est contentus: verum auget in

---

[1] See i. p. 94, and *cp.* Hor. *Ep.* II. i. 52, *somnia Pythagorea.*

[2] It is by no means clear that Marcus despised words, but he did despise dialectics; see *Thoughts,* i. 7; vii 67; viii. 1.

[3] "Have you lost your horns?" If "yes," then you had horns; if "no," then you still have them.

[4] "How many grains make a heap?" Do two, or three, or what exact number? As *heap* is an indefinite term, the

the controller of messages, Apollo the author of paeans, Liber the defender of dithyrambs, the Fauns inspirers of prophecies, Calliope the instructress of Homer, Homer the instructor of Ennius, and Sleep.[1]

14. Again, if the study of philosophy were concerned with practice alone, I should wonder less at your despising words[2] so much. That you should, however, learn *horn-dilemmas*,[3] *heap-fallacies*,[4] *liar-syllogisms*,[5] verbal quibbles and entanglements,[6] while neglecting the cultivation of oratory, its dignity and majesty and charm and splendour—this shews that you prefer mere speaking to real speaking, a whisper and a mumble to a trumpet-note. Do you rank the words of Diodorus and Alexinus[7] higher than the words of Plato and Xenophon and Antisthenes? as though anyone with a passion for the stage should copy the acting of Tasurcus rather than Roscius; as though in swimming, were both possible, one would choose to take pattern by a frog rather than by a dolphin, and flit rather on the puny wings of quails than soar with the majesty of an eagle.

15. Where is that shrewdness of yours? where your discernment? Wake up and hear what Chrysippus himself prefers. Is he content to teach, to disclose the subject, to define, to explain? He is not content: but he amplifies as much as he can,

answer cannot be given in any definite number of grains. See Hor. *Ep.* II. i. 47, *Elusus ratione ruentis acervi.*

[5] "If a man says he is lying, is he lying or speaking the truth?"

For these fallacies see Diog. Laert. *Euclides*, iv., and Zeller, *Socrates*, ch. xii.

[6] Lit. twisted, or intricate, and entangling.

[7] A captious disputant who made use of the horn-dilemma. Cicero mentions him with Diodorus, and speaks of his *contorta sophismata*. See next page.

quantum potest, exaggerat, praemunit, iterat, differt, recurrit, interrogat, describit, dividit, personas fingit, orationem suam alii accommodat: ταῦτα δέ ἐστιν αὔξειν, διασκευάζειν, ἐξεργάζεσθαι, πάλιν λέγειν, ἐπαναφέρειν, παράπτειν,[1] προσωποποιεῖν.

16. Videsne ab eo paene omnia oratorum arma tractari? Igitur si ipse Chrysippus his utendum ostendit,[2] quid ego amplius postulo, nisi ut ne verbis dialecticorum sed potius Platonis <eloquentia
Ambr. 391 utaris>? . . | . . gladio dimicandum esse contra
. . . . sed interest robiginoso an splendido <gladio>[3]
. . . . Epictetum . . . . sedentem . . . . <in
sel>la placebat . . . . si ausus esset, epitaphium
. . . . aut . . . . illum lau<de sum>ma pertu-
lisset[4] . . . . ira . . . . sub umbra . . . . <ni>hil
umquam <opi>nionis . . . . tot et . . . . Si
us<quam> . . . . Anaxagorae non Alexini syco-
Ambr. 390 phantae auditor . . . . conamen . . . . . . | . .

17. Tragicus Aesopus fertur non prius ullam suo induisse capiti personam, antequam diu ex adverso contemplaret, ut pro personae voltu gestum sibi capessere ac vocem[5] <adsimulare posset> . . . . stillicidiis . . . . An maiorem <rem> tragoediam putas Amphiaraum scribere quam de terrarum hiatu dicere[6]? . . . . tu de fulmine disputas . . . .[7]

[1] Mai for Cod. παραιπτειν. Buttm. prefers παραινεῖν. Some Greek words may have fallen out.
[2] For Cod. *ostendiset.*
[3] From the margin of Cod.
[4] *Ibid.* [5] *Ibid.* [6] *Ibid.*
[7] Six lines lost.

he exaggerates, he forestalls objections, he repeats, he postpones, he harks back, he asks questions, describes, divides, introduces fictitious characters, puts his own words in another's mouth: those are the meanings of αὔξειν, διασκευάζειν, ἐξεργάζεσθαι, πάλιν λέγειν, ἐπαναφέρειν, παράπτειν, προσωποποιεῖν.[1]

16. Do you see that he handles almost all the weapons of the orator? Therefore if Chrysippus himself has shewn that these should be used, what more do I ask, unless it be that you should not employ the verbiage of the dialecticians but rather the eloquence of Plato? . . . . A sword must be used in fight against (opponents), but it matters much whether the blade be rusty or burnished . . . . Epictetus . . . . if he had dared, an epitaph[2] . . . . carried through with the greatest credit . . . . If anywhere . . . . a disciple of Anaxagoras[3] not of the sycophant Alexinus . . . .

17. The tragedian Aesopus is said never to have put on a tragic mask without setting it in front of him and studying it a long time that he might conform his gestures and adapt his voice to the face of the mask . . . . or do you think it a greater task to write the tragedy *Amphiaraus*[4] than to speak on the subject of an earthquake? . . . . you argue about a thunderbolt . . . .

[1] These words mean to amplify, divide, treat fully, recapitulate, hark back, make the application, introduce characters.

[2] The epitaph of Epictetus was: I Epictetus was by name | Who now lie here, | As Irus poor, a slave, and lame | And to the Immortals dear.

[3] *i.e.* Pericles. See Cic. *De Orat.* iii. 34; *Orat.* iv. 15.

[4] He was swallowed up by an earthquake, while trying to escape from the disastrous expedition against Thebes. There seems to be a reference to the Cyzicus earthquake in 162.

18. Dabit philosophia quod dicas, dabit eloquentia qu<omodo dicas> . . . . <nam si quis>[1] dialecticorum verbis scribat, suspirantem, tussientem immo Iovem scripserit, non tonantem. Para potius oratio-
Ambr. 389: the last of Quat. xxvii. nem dignam sensibus, quos e philosophia hauries, et | quanto honestius sentias, tanto augustius dicas. Quin erige te et extolle, et tortores istos, qui te ut abietem aut alnum proceram incurvant et ad chamaetorta[2] detrahunt, valido cacumine tuo excute, et tenta an usquam ab <optima via> discesseris. Sed comitem philosophiae <eloquentiam adscisce et istos>[3] sermones gibberosos retortos <abice quos> . . . .[4] si tenueris, contemnas; quom contempseris, nescias. Dic, obsecro, mihi de dialecticis istis ecquid tenes? Ecquid tenere te gaudes? Nolo mihi dicas: apud te ipse reputa. Ego illud praedico, quom plurimos amicos in hac disciplina tenueris . . . .[5]

(Naber, p. 148.)

De Eloquentia 2

<Antonino Augusto Fronto>.

Ambr. 380: Quat. xxx. begins . . . . | . . . .
nullius ante, nisi unius Gaii Sallusti, *trita solo*, sensum dictu periculosum et paene opstetricium pulcherrimo

[1] Heindorf. [2] Niebuhr prefers *chamaestrota*.
[3] Heindorf: also *abice quos*.
[4] Thirteen lines are lost.
[5] There is a gap, says Naber, of 32 pp. between *tenueris* and *nullius*.

18. Philosophy will tell you what to say, Eloquence how to say it[1] . . . . For, using the language of dialecticians, a writer would speak of a Jove sighing, nay rather wheezing, not thundering. Provide yourself rather with speech worthy of the thoughts you draw from philosophy, and the more noble your thoughts, the more impressive will your utterance be. Nay, lift yourself up and stand upright, and shake off with your strong top those tree-twisters who are bending you down, like a fir or stately alder, and lowering you to the level of stunted bushes, and make trial whether you have anywhere swerved from the right way. But summon Eloquence, the handmaid of philosophy, and cast away those crooked, twisted modes of speech . . . . which if you took them in, you would despise, and ignore when you have despised them. Tell me, I pray you, do you take anything in from your dialectics? are you proud of taking in anything? You need not confess to me, but think it over with yourself. I prophesy this, though you have kept many of your friends loyal to this teaching . . . .

On Eloquence 2

Fronto to Antoninus Augustus. ? 162 A.D.

. . . .

in a field *previously trod by the foot of no one*[2] save Gaius Sallustius alone, you brought to light in a most choice dress and a most becoming setting a

[1] The position of this sentence is not certain. Brakman says it comes two sentences lower down.
[2] Lucr. i. 925.

cultu et honestissimo ornatu protulisti. Εὔφρανας, ὑπερεύφρανας, σώζεο μοι. Quod librari manu epistula scripta est, a labore gravi digitis consului qui sunt iam in suspicione.

(Naber, p. 149.)

De Eloquentia 3

Antonino Augusto Fronto.

1. Quid . . . . scrutetur qua . . . . propera . . . . neque balbam virginem, quae vestalis sit, capi fas est, neque sirbenam[1] . . . . [verba de balbutientibus ponenda varie][2] . . . . minus . . . . balbutientium vox his ferme verbis significatur: vox *impedita*, vox *vincta*, vox *difficilis*, vox *trunca*, vox *imperfecta*, vox *absona*. His contraria quaerenti tibi subvenisse certum habeo, vox *expedita*,[3] vox *absoluta*, vox *facilis*, vox *integra*, vox *lenis*.[4] Tua vox . . . .

Ambr. 380 ends (Brakman; Naber says 379) vere . . . . his omnibus . . . . quibus vocabulis appellentur sirbeni percensio sit | . . . .

Ambr. 374 2. | Vocis modulatae amatores primas audisse feruntur aves vernas luco opaco. Post pastores recens repertis fistulis se atque pecus oblectabant. Visae fistulae longe avibus modulatiores[5] . . . .

Ambr. 373 murmurantium | voculis in loco[6] eloquentiae oblec-

[1] From the margin of the Codex.

[2] *Ibid.*: possibly only a gloss.

[3] m[1] *eximia*.

[4] For the restoration of this passage see Hauler, *Wien. Stud.* xxii. The contrary to *imperfecta* seems to have dropped out.

[5] The above are from the margin. The rest of Ambr. 374 is illegible.

[6] Margin *luco*.

meaning hard to express and needing almost a midwife's aid. You have given me joy, you have overjoyed me, may you be preserved to me. In having this letter written by my secretary I have saved my fingers from a heavy task,[1] as they are not at present to be trusted.

On Eloquence 3

? 162 A.D.

Fronto to Antoninus Augustus.

1. . . . . Neither a virgin that lisps may be chosen as a Vestal nor one that speaks indistinctly[2]. . . . Words descriptive of stammerers to be variously employed . . . . the utterance of stammerers is generally described as follows: an impeded utterance, a tied utterance, a laboured, a defective, an imperfect, a discordant utterance. The contraries of these have, I doubt not, already rewarded your search: a free utterance, a distinct, an easy, a perfect, a smooth utterance. Your utterance . . . . A survey of all the terms applied to indistinct speakers . . . .

2. The lovers of melodious utterance are said to have listened first to the birds in a shady covert. Next shepherds delighted themselves and their flocks with the newly-invented pipes. Pipes seemed far more melodious than birds . . . . they take delight by way[3] of eloquence in the soft notes of

[1] A great part of this letter has obviously been lost.

[2] See Aulus Gellius, i. 12. This paragraph seems rather out of place. It has much affinity with the similar passage in *De Orationibus, ad. med* below.

[3] Reading *luco*, we must translate "of whisperers, or warblers, in the grove of eloquence."

tantur. Ennium deinde et Accium et Lucretium ampliore iam mugitu personantes tamen tolerant. At ubi Catonis et Sallustii et Tullii tuba exaudita est, trepidant et pavent et fugam frustra meditantur. Nam illic quoque in philosophiae disciplinis, ubi tutum sibi perfugium putant, Platonis phonemata erunt audienda.

3. Haec in eos fabula competit, qui nulla indole praediti eloquentiam desperantes fugitant. Tibi, Caesar, ut cui maxime, sublime et excelsum et amplificum ingenium ab deis datum est. Nam primi tui sensus et incunabula studiorum tuorum mihi cognita sunt. Elucebat iam tunc nobilitas mentis et dignitas sententiarum, quibus sola tum deerant verborum lumina: ea quoque variis exercitationibus instruebamus.

4. Ibi tu mihi videre mor<e iuven>ali et laboris taedio defessus, eloquentiae studium reliquisse, ad philosophiam devertisse, ubi nullum prohoemium cum cura excolendum, nulla narratio breviter et dilucide et callide collocanda, nullae quaestiones partiendae, nulla argumenta quaerenda, nihil ex-
Ambr. 378 aggerandum . . . . . . | . . [mutilum perficere, hiulcum fartis iugare] . . . . consiliario huic magis aetati opus est quam auxiliario <amico>[1] . . . . mutilum perficere, hiulcum explere, asperum levigare[2] . . . .

[1] From the margin of Cod.; *cp.* Plaut. *Truc.* II. i. 8.
[2] *Wien. Stud.* 23, p. 338, Hauler.

mutterers. Anon they nevertheless put up with Ennius and Accius and Lucretius, resonant now with a fuller bass. But when the trumpet of Cato and Sallust and Tullius is heard upon the air, they are excited and affrighted and bethink them of flight, vainly, for even there in the teachings of Philosophy, where they think they have a safe refuge, the resonant periods of Plato will have to be heard.

3. This little story [1] applies to those who having no aptitude for it, shun eloquence in despair. But to you, O Caesar, if ever to man, has been given by the Gods a sublime and lofty and splendid genius; for your earliest thoughts and the infancy of your studies came under my ken. From the very first there was no hiding your nobility of mind and the dignity of your thoughts: they wanted then but one thing, the illumination of words: that too, we were providing by a varied course of study.

4. At this point, in the manner of the young and from a dislike of drudgery, you seem to have deserted the pursuit of eloquence, and to have turned aside after philosophy,[2] in which there is no exordium to be carefully elaborated, no marshalling of facts concisely and clearly and skilfully, no dividing of a subject into heads, no arguments to be hunted for, no amplification . . . . to complete what is imperfect, to fill up gaps with padding . . . . this age requires a friend for counsel rather than for help . . . . to complete what is imperfect, to fill up a hiatus, to make rough places smooth . . . .

[1] The evolution of eloquence just given.

[2] See i. p. 217, *Ad M. Caes.* iv. 13, and *cp. Thoughts*, i. 7 and 17, § 4.

Ambr. 377 5. | Nonne omnes oratorum copias sectabare,[1] refutandi sollertiam, augendi facultatem, eludendi venustatem, permovendi delectandique, deterrendi incitandique, hortandi[2] conciliandi, inflammandi[3] laxandi audientium animos aut alliciendi, rectam quandam in dicendo potentiam ac potestatem?

Tum si quando tibi negotiis districto perpetuis orationis conscribundae tempus deesset, nonne te tumultuariis quibusdam et lucrativis studiorum solaciis fulciebas, synonymis colligendis, verbis interdum singularibus requirendis? ut veterum commata, ut[4] cola, synonymorum ratione converteres, ut de volgaribus elegantia, de contaminatis nova redderes, imaginem aliquam accommodares, figuram iniceres, prisco verbo adornares, colorem vetusculum appingeres. Haec si propterea contemnis, quia didicisti, philosophiam quoque discendo contemnes.

6. Sed non ea sunt ista quae possis contemnere: possis sane non amare. Ut olim Crassus tristis risum oderat, ut nostra hic memoria Crassus lucem fugitabat; ut nostra ibidem memoria vir consularis campos formidabat, Pomptinum Campum multaque
Ambr. 386 loca clausa lecticula praetervehebatur[5] . . . . . . | . . an tibi saepe . . . . supersit . . . . tamen si dixisses nonnumquam . . . . satis consuluisses . . . . modum.[6] Virum etiam saepe vir sapientissi-

[1] Niebuhr for Cod. *sectavere*. [2] Beltrami for Cod. *ornandi*.
[3] Niebuhr for Cod. *infamandi*.
[4] Margin *et cola synonimorum*.
[5] The last five words from the margin of the Codex.
[6] The lost passage was on Friendship, as we learn from a marginal note.

5. Were you not eager for all the resources of orators, their adroitness in refuting, their talent for amplifying, their charm in evasion, and I know not what kind of downright power and potency, that lies in speaking, of moving and delighting, of deterring and provoking, of exhorting, of conciliating, of inflaming, of calming the minds of hearers or alluring them?

Then if on occasion hindered by perpetual business you had no time to compose a speech, did you not fortify yourself with certain hurried yet valuable recreations in the way of study, by collecting synonyms, at times by searching out remarkable words? so as to turn the periods of old writers and their clauses by the system of synonyms[1]; to render refined what was vulgar, and fresh what was soiled, fit in some image, throw in a figure, embellish with a good old word, add a patina of age. If you despise all this only because you have learnt it, you will also despise philosophy in the learning.

6. But these are not things which you could despise: dislike them of course you might. As in old days a morose Crassus[2] hated laughter, as in our time here a Crassus[3] hid from the daylight, and again in our time a man of consular rank had a horror of plains, and traversed the Pomptine plain and many other places with his litter closed

. . . .

. . . . But often even the wisest of men does not know how to speak in a

[1] *i.e.* apparently paraphrasing old writers by using synonymous but more striking expressions.

[2] The grandfather of Crassus the triumvir, called ἀγέλαστος.

[3] Probably Crassus Frugi, Spart. *Vit. Hadr.* 5.

mus . . . . <eloqui> nescit novo plane modo. Sed ita res tulerunt . . . . de puteo quoque. Puteus
Ambr. 385 istic minus sorderet . . . . <senten>|tias inopinatas, aliis <quidem novas et prius in>tactas. Tanto maius periculum sententiis inest, nisi figurationibus moderatis temperantur. Graecis verbis fortasse apertius significabo: τὰ καινὰ καὶ παράδοξα τῶν ἐνθυμημάτων εἰ . . . . <εἶ>πεν αὐτὰ πλα . . . . <εἶ>πεν ἢ πιθανὰ . . . . Hoc ego animo . . . . nullis rationibus . . . . liber quem misti[1] rarus. Scias igitur in hoc uno eximiam eloquentiam tuam claudere.

7. Moneo igitur Marcum meum etiam atque etiam, et ut meminerit obsecro, quotienscumque ἀδοξότερον ἐνθύμημα conceperis, volvas illud tecum[2] et diversis et variis figurationibus verses temptesque et verbis splendidis excolas. Nam quae nova et inopinata audientibus sunt, periculum est nisi ornentur et figurentur ne videantur absurda.

8. Cetera omnia tibi in eloquentia expolita et explanata[3] sunt. Scis verba quaerere, scis reperta recte collocare, scis colorem sincerum vetustatis appingere, sententiis autem gravissimis et honestissimis abun-
Ambr. 376 das . . . .[4]<pri>|ma conditio est; ubi semel patefactae sunt, facile cognitae negleguntur. Contemni denique et nullo honore esse rhetora videas; observari autem et omnibus officiis coli dialecticos, quod

[1] Hauler's reading. Mai and Brakman saw *mire* in the margin. [2] Heindorf for Cod. *temet*.

[3] This is Mai's reading. Niebuhr prefers *expedita*.

[4] Neither Mai nor Naber tell us the extent of the lacuna here, but Mai follows it with the passage which Naber puts first in his *De Eloquentia* 1.

style obviously new. But circumstances have so . . . . a well there would sound less vulgar . . . . thoughts unexpected, to others indeed new and previously unused. So much greater peril is there in thoughts if they are not qualified with figures of speech sparingly used. I can perhaps express my meaning more clearly in Greek words: τὰ καινὰ καὶ παράδοξα τῶν ἐνθυμημάτων[1] . . . .
. . . .
. . . . the book which you sent a scarce one. Know then that in this one point your eloquence limps, splendid as it is.

7. I warn you, therefore, again and again, my Marcus, and beseech you to remember, as often as you conceive in your mind a startling thought, think over it with yourself and turn and try it with various figures of speech and dress it out in splendid words. For there is a danger that what is new to the hearers and unexpected may seem ridiculous unless it be embellished and made figurative.

8. All else in eloquence are for you smoothed and made clear. You know how to search out words, you know how to arrange them correctly when found, you know how to invest them with the genuine patina of antiquity, and you have an abundance of the weightiest and noblest thoughts . . . . is the first essential; as soon as they have been exposed they are easily known and disregarded. In a word, you could see that the rhetorician is despised and of no account, while the dialecticians are courted and treated with

[1] "New and startling thoughts." Fronto urges Marcus to aim at striking and unconventional ideas, but to be careful that they should be toned down by their setting, so as not to strike the hearers as bizarre.

in eorum rationibus semper obscuri aliquid et tortuosi <sit>, eoque fit ut magistro discipulus haereat semper et inserviat, vinctus perpetuis quibusdam vinculis adtineatur.

Dicet aliquis *tu igitur praeter ceteros nimirum verbis pulchris et insignibus uteris?*[1] Ego immo volgaribus et obsoletis. Quid igitur est? Nisi istud saltem scirem, deterioribus uterer.

(Naber, p. 153.)

De Eloquentia 4

Antonino Augusto Fronto.

1. Pleraque in oratione recenti tua, quod ad sententias adtinet, animadverto egregia esse; pauca admodum uno tenus verbo corrigenda; nonnihil interdum elocutione novella parum signatum. Quae melius visum est particulatim scribere, ita enim facilius perpendes singula et satis temporis ad inspiciendum habebis, ut qui plurimis negotiis aut agendis occupatus sis aut actis defessus.

2. Igitur in prohoemio quae egregie a te dicta putem, quaeque arbitrer corrigenda, scripsi tibi.
Ambr. 375 Scripturum deinceps pro amore in | te meo confide cetera. Prima ergo pars tota mirifica est, multis et gravibus sententiis referta, in quibus eximiae sunt . . . . Si recte . . . . quo genere Cato . . . . Si

[1] Niebuhr for Cod. *utens.*

every respect, because in their ratiocinations there is always something obscure and intricate, and hence it results that the disciple always hangs upon his master and is his slave, held fast bound with a kind of everlasting fetter.

Someone will say *You then, of course, beyond all others use choice and striking words.* Nay, I use common and old ones. What then? If I knew not that much, I should use words still worse.

On Eloquence 4

? 162 A.D.

Fronto to Antoninus Augustus.

1. Most things in your late speech, as far as the thoughts go, I consider were excellent, very few required alteration to the extent of a single word; some parts here and there were not sufficiently marked with novelty of expression.[1] I have thought it better to write to you on these points in detail, for so you will the more easily consider them separately and have time to look into them, being as you are busied with the actual discharge and wearied with the past performance of very many duties.

2. Well then I have written to tell you what I consider excellently said by you in your exordium, and what in my opinion needs alteration. Do not doubt that what I shall further write will be written in the spirit of my love for you. All the first part then is wonderfully fine, packed with many weighty thoughts, in which these stand out . . . . in which kind Cato . . . . if sparingly and with dignity

[1] Professor Mackail takes this to mean the "new Latin" style introduced by Fronto.

parce et cum dignitate . . . . multo deinde gravior et severior subiuncta <est sententia> . . . . si
Ambr. 384 nihil . . . . nobis opinionis . . . . | tralatum, tum . . . . <si> res ita impulerint . . . . vincas. Inesse . . . . alterum proprium *comes*, alterum tralatum *opifex*. Neque ulla verbis istis inter se communio est neque propinquitas. Offendit igitur aures ingruens diversitas naturae . . . .[1] sapere . . . . Sallustius . . . . *quique manu ventre pene bona patria laceraverat*. Vides quantum similitudine verborum formae assecutus sit, ut verbum postremum, quamquam parum pudicum, non indecorum esse videatur; ideo scilicet quod <duo> verba similia praecedant. Quodsi ita haec verba contra dixisset: *quique pene bona patria laceraverat*, indita[2] obscenitas verbis appareret . . . . manu ventre. Ad . . . . aures;
Ambr. 388, following 383, which is totally illegible tertioque . . . . | διασκευῇ et παρεκβάσει carendum.

3. Enimvero ad philosophum librum legas; magistro interpretante tacitus attendas; intellexisse adnuas; aliis legentibus ipse plerumque dormites; audias τί τὸ πρῶτον; τί τὸ δεύτερον; diu multumque numerari: εἰ ἡμέρα ἐστιν, φῶς ἐστίν, fenestris patentibus laborari. Securus inde abeas, cui nihil per noctem meditandum aut conscribendum, nihil magistro recitandum, nihil de memoria pronuntiandum, nulla verborum indagatio, nullius synonymi ornatus, nihil de Graeca in nostram linguam pariter vertendum. In eos quoque meus magister Dionysius

[1] The margin of Cod. has *in alio: petere*.
[2] Query *inscita . . . verbi*. Several have proposed *insita*.

. . . . then follows a much weightier and austerer thought . . . . if circumstances so compel . . . . the one word specific—*companion,* the other figurative—*artizan.* Nor is there any connexion or relationship between these words. The ear therefore is offended by the inherent contrast obtruded upon it . . . . Sallust says . . . . "and one who had also wasted his patrimony *manu ventre pene.*"[1] You see how much the writer has effected by the likeness in the form of the words, so that the last word though far from modest does not strike one as indecent: for the reason doubtless that two similar words precede it. But if on the other hand he had spoken the words thus: *quique pene bona patria laceraverat,* the obscenity attached to the words would be obvious . . . . must lack disposition and digression.

3. To be sure you would read a book to your philosopher;[2] listen in silence while your master explained it; shew by nods that you understood him; while others were reading, you would yourself mostly sleep; would hear reiterated at length and often *What is the first premiss? What is the second?* with windows wide open hear the point laboured, *If it is day, it is light.* Then you would take your departure without a care, as one who had nothing to think over or write up the whole night long, nothing to recite to a master, nothing to say by heart, no hunting up of words, no garniture of a single synonym, no parallel turning of Greek into our own tongue. Against them[3] too did my master Dionysius the

[1] *Catil.* 14.

[2] Fronto is making fun of the dialectic method of teaching contrasted with the rhetorical.

[3] The dialecticians.

Tenuïor et compositam fabulam protulit de disceptatione vitis et arboris ilicis.

4. Vitis se ante ilicem ferebat, quod suavissimum fructum hominum conviviis et Osiris[1] altaribus crearet, idem dulce esu, idem haustu iucundum. Tum se maiore cura quam Cleopatram reginam ornari, comptius quam Laidem formosam. Pampinos suos ita pulchros esse ut necterentur ex eis Libero thyrsi, corona Sileno, Nymphis Bacchisque redimicula; ilicem esse horridam infructuosam inamabilem; creare boni aut amoeni numquam quic-
Ambr. 387 quam | praeter glandem . . . . et in lacerata. Item vos . . . .[2] Nunc ego consulto in fabulis finem facio, ut, si qua acrius dicta sunt, permixta fabulis molliantur.[3]

Ad Verum Imp. ii. 6 (Naber, p. 133).

<Domino meo Vero Augusto>

Ambr. 434, following 435 . . . . | animi mei perturbatione non possem. Sed acceptis litteris tuis, ea re iam primum bona spes mihi ostentata est, quod tua manu scripseras; deinde quod post apstinentiam tridui et sanguinem satis strenue et prompte demissum, liberatum esse te periculo impendentis valetudinis nuntiabas. Respiravi igitur et revalui et apud omnes foculos aras

[1] See Hauler (*Vers. d. Phil.* 41, p. 79) for this passage.
[2] About a column and a half are lost in the lacunae.
[3] This sentence is from the margin.

---

[1] He was called λεπτός (see Athen. xi. 7), and also ἀσκάλαφος, from a line in Homer (*Il.* ii. 512) which he often quoted.

Slender[1] indite a quite artistic apologue on a dispute between the *Vine and the Holm-oak tree.*

4. The vine vaunted herself above the holm-oak because she bore the most delicious of all fruits for the banquets of men and the altars of Osiris, alike sweet to eat and delightful to quaff. Then, again, she was arrayed with more care than queenly Cleopatra, with more taste than lovely Lais. So fair were her branches that from them were wound the thyrsus-wands for Liber, a garland for Silenus, and chaplets for the Nymphs and Maenads. But the holm-oak was rough, barren, unattractive, and never produced anything of any goodness or beauty except acorns . . . . Now I purposely end with fictions that, if I have said anything too severe, it may be softened down by being mingled with fictions.

Fronto to Lucius Verus

162 A.D.

To my Lord Verus Augustus.

. . . . I was so distressed in mind that I could not . . . . But on the receipt of your letter, the very fact that you had written with your own hand raised my hopes at the outset; then came your good news that after three days' fasting and a prompt and rather drastic letting of blood you had been freed from the risk of a threatened illness.[2] So I breathed again and recovered and made my prayers at every

[2] Capit. (*Vit. Veri*, 6) tells us that Verus, while on his way to Asia for the Parthian war, was taken ill at Canusium. It appears that he narrowly escaped having a stroke, such as caused his death in January, 169, at the age of thirty-nine.

lucos sacros arbores sacratas—nam rure agebam—supplicavi. Et nunc expecto[1] cognoscere ex tuis litteris, quantum medii[2] isti dies promoverint ad vires reficiendas. Enimvero nunc maiore multo cura diligentiaque opus est, ut paulatim temet compleas, nec properes ad detrimenta virium resarcienda. Nam id quidem omnium opinione compertum et traditum est, sanguinem ubi abundet incursim detrahendum, postea pedetemptim esse reparandum.

Fac, oro te et obsecro, Domine, quod tuo egregio ingenio decet, temperes et reparcas et modificeris desideriis omnibus, quae nunc acriora solito et procaciora existere necesse est post apstinentiam, qua
Ambr. 433 necessario in tem|pore usus es.

Fratrem Dominum saluta, quem salvom habebis, si tu salvos eris. Vale, Domine dulcissime.

Ad Amicos, i. 11 (Naber, p. 181).

Ambr. 319 *ad med.* col. 1 | Fronto Velio Rufo Seni salutem.

Figurae orationis sunt quae maxime orationem ornant. Duplex autem genus est figurarum. Aut enim verborum figurae sunt aut sententiarum. In figuris verborum est tropos, metaphora. Hac figura usus sum quom *stagnum*[3] dixi de corpore in quo

[1] Haupt *expeto.*
[2] Haupt for Cod. *mediei.* Naber reads *medici* (? misprint).
[3] Klussmann for Cod. *figuram.*

---

[1] If Capit. (*Vit. Ver.* 6, § 7) is to be trusted, there was much need of this exhortation.

hearth, altar, sacred grove and consecrated tree—for I was staying in the country. And now I am waiting to hear from your next letter how much the intervening days have done towards restoring your strength. For, indeed, much greater care and attention are required now, that you may fill your veins gradually and not be in too great a haste to repair your lost strength. For it is a belief verified and traditional that blood when in excess must be promptly drawn off, but must subsequently be regained by slow degrees.

I pray and beseech you, my Lord, take heed, as befits your eminent character, to be sparing and temperate and restrained [1] in all your desires which now, after the abstinence which you have practised on a necessary occasion, must necessarily make themselves felt more keenly and more importunately than usual.

Greet my Lord your brother,[2] whose health you will ensure if you are well. Farewell, most sweet Lord.

? 162 A.D.

Fronto to Velius Rufus Senex,[3] greeting.

The figures in a speech are what most set off a speech. There are two kinds of figures, for there are verbal figures or figures of thought. Among the former are trope and metaphor.[4] I employed this figure [5] when I applied the word *slough* to a body in

[2] Marcus hurried to Canusium to see him; see Capit. *ibid.*
[3] Nothing more is certainly known of him.
[4] Cicero (*Brut.* 17), following Greek precedent, separated *tropes* from *figures*. We use trope for the metaphorical use of a word.
[5] Perhaps in the speech *Pro Bithynis* mentioned below.

neque <sucus>[1] sincerus neque aqua pura neque ullus humor liquidus, sed ita ut in palude corrupta omnia. Quod autem plerosque fugit,[2] te hominem vehementem et cum doctrina tum multo magis natura validum esse [scirem artes][3] eius modicae . . . .[4] as aliter . . . .[5]

Ad Amicos, i. 15 (Naber, p. 184).

FRONTO Praecilio Pompeiano salutem.

Verum ex me, mi Pompeiane, uti res est,
Ambr. 312, following 313 audies; velimque te mihi verum | dicenti fidem habere. Orationem istam *Pro Bithynis* ante annum fere in manus sumpseram et corrigere institueram. Tibi etiam Romae tunc agenti nonnihil de ista oratione promiseram. Et quidem, si recte memini, quom sermo inter nos de partitionibus orationum ortus esset, dixeram et prae me tuleram, satis me diligenter in ista oratione coniecturam, quae in crimine mandatae caedis verteretur, divisisse argumentis ac refutasse. Interea nervorum dolor solito vehementior me invasit, et diutius ac molestius solito remoratus est. Nec possum ego membris cruciantibus operam ullam litteris scribendis legendisque impendere; nec umquam istuc a me postulare ausus sum. Philosophis etiam mirificis hominibus dicentibus, sapientem virum etiam in Phalaridis tauro inclu-

[1] Brakman. [2] Mai gives this, but with doubt.
[3] Mai gives these two words doubtfully. Brakman says *validum* is followed by *esse*. [4] Four letters lost.
[5] A lacuna of four pages follows to *meremur* in *Ad Amicos*, i. 12, below.

which there is no sap pure, no water uncontaminated, no fluid clear, but, as in a morass, everything rotting. What, however, escapes most people, I should know, that you, a strenuous man and a strong by training, and much more by nature . . . .

? 162 A.D.

FRONTO to Praecilius Pompeianus,[1] greeting.

You shall hear from me, my Pompeianus, the true state of the case; and I would ask you to accept it from me as the truth. It is nearly a year ago that I took that speech *For the Bithynians*[2] in hand and set about revising it. I also made certain promises to you about the speech when you were in Rome at that time. And, indeed, if I remember rightly, when we were discussing the rhetorical heads of a speech, I claimed, and with some pride, that I had in that speech very thoroughly analyzed in argument and confuted the assumption which turned on the charge of murder by mandate. Meanwhile, a more than usually severe attack of neuritis came on, which proved to be more persistent and troublesome than usual. And I cannot pay any attention to writing or reading letters when my limbs are racked with pain; nor have I ever ventured to make such a demand upon my strength. When philosophers, those wondrous creatures, tell us that the wise man, even if shut up in the Bull of Phalaris,[3] would still

[1] Nothing is known for certain about him. He was possibly a fellow-countryman of Fronto's from Cirta.

[2] Nothing more is known of this speech beyond what Fronto tells us.

[3] A commonplace of the orators. See Cic. *Tusc.* ii. 7; Seneca, *Ep.* 66, etc.

sum beatum nihilominus fore, facilius crediderim beatum eum fore quam posse tantisper amburenti in aheno prohoemium meditari aut epigrammata[1] scribere.

Reconciliata deinde mihi longo post tempore commoda valetudine alias egi res potius: adversus istam orationem alienato animo fui, nec pudebit me fateri
Ambr. 311 odium ac simultatem . . . . . . | . . Rediit igitur post repudium renuntiatum oratio domum meam et mecum denuo mansitavit[2] . . . . ab anu anucella[3] . . . .

Ad Amicos, i. 16 (Naber, p. 185).

<Fronto> Praecilio Pompeiano <salutem>.

Ambr. 294 Lege, carissime mihi[4] <Pompeiane> . . . . . . | . . Venetus[5] venalis est. Scis hoc perpetuum Veneti fatum esse, ut numquam venierit, veneat
Ambr. 293 semper[6] . . . . | das curare. Rescribit mihi litteras se nullas accepisse. Tu certum . . . . loquar . . . . quidquid . . . . consenuisse . . . . sim . . . . carissima[7] . . . .

Ad Amicos, i. 17 (Naber, p. 185).

<Fronto> Claudio Iuliano <salutem>.

Habuisti igitur domi,[8] <mi Naucelli>. . . . . Ita instituimus amicitiam, ut haec volgata officia negle-

[1] Niebuhr would read *epicheiremata* (arguments).
[2] From the margin of Cod. [3] *Ibid.*
[4] From the Index (Naber, p. 172). [5] Mai has *Venetis.*
[6] From the margin of Cod. So also the fragments that follow.
[7] These five words may belong to the next letter. There are also two words, *Has saltem*, given by Mai, which Niebuhr places between *semper* and *das curare.* [8] From the Index.

be happy, I could find it more easy to believe that he would be happy than that he would be able, while baking in the brass, to muse the while on an exordium or write pointed phrases.

Then when after a long interval I had recovered my health, I turned to other matters in preference. I took a dislike to that speech, and will not be ashamed to confess hatred and aversion . . . . So the speech has come back home to me after I had publicly disowned it, and taken up its abode with me again . . . .

? 162 A.D.

Fronto to Praecilius Pompeianus,[1] greeting.

My very dear friend Pompeianus, read . . . . Venetus[2] is for sale. You know that it is the perpetual fate of Venetus to be always going, never gone . . . . He writes in answer that he has never received my letter . . . .

? 162 A.D.

Fronto to Claudius Julianus, greeting.

You have had then at home, my Naucellius,[3] . . . . Our friendship has been on such a footing that we could dispense with these conventional

[1] There was another letter to him in this collection (Naber, p. 172), but only the opening words remain (from the Index, as read by Hauler, *Wien. Stud.* 33, pt. 1, p. 175): *Labris eius labra fovi*, I kissed him lip to lip.

[2] *Venetus* may be a proper name, or = *Venetianus* (*i.e.* a partizan of the "Blues" in the Circus), or mean a Venetian.

[3] One of the names of Julianus, who was consul under Pius and provincial legate under Marcus.

geremus vero amore contenti . . . . Cum amico omnia amara et dulcia communicata velim . . . . salus lumina . . . . eo pervenit ut esset mihi non tantum carissimus is sed paene solus . . .

Ad Amicos, i. 18 (Naber, p. 185).

<Fronto> Claudio Iuliano <salutem>.

Ambr. 280 Nescio quo pacto fit[1] . . . . | omnes provinciales loqui; multa etiam laboriosius facere quam ipsa res postulat: acta cognitionum, epistulas omnes denique ad provinciam adtinentes. Te iuvabunt tuisque . . . .[2] <ut> adsidue <tu omnia> munera obires . . . .[3] <cum ho>nore provinciales tractare, ut verum sit quod antiqui veteres dixerunt, *τοῦ αὐτοῦ εἶναι καὶ παίζειν καὶ σπουδάζειν*. Valerianus . . . . bonus si . . . . studebam . . . .[4] conclusus; nec me Valerianus noster videre potuit. A Dominis nostris Imperatoribus non propter aliud amari me opto, quam ut te quoque participem mei corporis et animi diligant: et cum bonitate eorum certus sum ita fore.

Quom tibi scriberem, paulo commodius valebam. Adhuc quidem eo tempore eram ex longissima valetudine, quam contra curam . . . . aeque . . . .
Ambr. 279 . . | . . male mulcavit, recitavi in senatu satis . . . .[5] <ut> repeterem, postularetur. Fac, mi Naucelli, valetudinis tuae curam agas, ut fortis ad nos venias. Dei praestabunt ut me quoque forti-

[1] From the Index (Naber, p. 172).
[2] About twenty-five letters missing.
[3] About ten letters lost.
[4] In these lacunae eight lines are lost.
[5] In the first gap ten letters are lost, in the second ten lines, and in the third three lines.

services, assured of the reality of our love . . . . With a friend I would wish all joys and sorrows shared . . . . it came to this that he was not only my dearest friend, but almost the single one who . . . .

? 162 A.D.

Fronto to Claudius Julianus, greeting.

I know not how it comes to pass . . . . all the provincials say; to do many things also more laboriously than the case itself requires: memoranda of the trials, lastly all letters which relate to the province. They will assist you . . . . that you should diligently perform all your duties . . . . treat the provincials with respect, that the saying of the classic ancients may be verified, that the same man can be both sportive and strenuous. Valerianus[1] . . . . ; nor was our friend Valerianus able to see me. I desire not to be loved by our Lords the Emperors[2] on any other terms than that you too the partner of my body and mind should be included in their love: and such is their good nature I feel sure that this will be so.

While writing to you, I feel a little better. I am still indeed at this time after my most protracted ill-health, which in spite of care . . . . roughly handled, I delivered in the Senate . . . . was asked to repeat it. Be sure, my Naucellius, to take care of your health, that you may be strong when you come to us. Please God

[1] Possibly the master of the emperor Pertinax (see Capit. *Vit. Pert.* 12).

[2] Marcus Antoninus and Lucius Verus (161–169).

culum invenias. Valerianus noster magnas ad te plagas rettulit, quas ab omnibus . . . .[1] gravius eum tractavi quam Stratonabian aut Pyrallum.[2] Stragula mihi linea sculpta† quae germani . . . .[3]

Ad M. Caes. ii. 16 (Naber, p. 37).

<Domino meo>.

Ambr. 104, following 105? . . . . <praedam> | abripere terrae, ut dicitur, immo cellae filios: tantam de thesauris Antonini pecuniam prodigi quam nescio quae ista altilis alumna accipiet, unde nihil Egatheus acceperit. Quanti vero rumores adversi, quantae querimoniae exorientur bonis lege Falcidia distractis? Lineam istam famosam atque celebratam ceteraque tantae pecuniae ornamenta quis emet? Tua uxor si emerit, praedam invasisse et minimo aere eripuisse dicetur, eoque minus ad eos quibus legatum erat pervenisse.

[1] Two lines lost. [2] These two words are not certain.
[3] Perhaps ten lines are lost here.

---

[1] From the fragmentary nature of the evidence, it is not easy to understand the legal points in the case alluded to in these three letters. Matidia, the great-aunt of Marcus and Faustina, had made them her heirs, but whether they were her natural heirs is not known. The *codicilli* were informal documents added to the will, in which directions were given to the heir as to certain gifts to be distributed by him. These were cancelled by Matidia, but certain interested parties tried to pass them off as valid. Fronto is afraid that Marcus will, for fear of benefiting himself, let them stand, in which case they might absorb more than the three-fourths of the whole property contrary to the Falcidian law,

you will find me too a little stronger. Our friend Valerianus has told you the great blows, which from all (quarters) . . . . I have treated him more firmly than Stratonabia or Pyrallus. A linen covering . . . .

Fronto to Marcus Antoninus as Emperor

162 A.D.

To my Lord.[1]

. . . . that children of the earth, as the saying goes, or rather of the gutter, should snatch the booty: that so much wealth from the treasuries of Antoninus should be thrown away for that pampered protégée, whoever she is, to get, so that Egatheus[2] will get nothing. What unfriendly comments however, what grumblings will arise, when the goods have been dispersed under the Falcidian Law? That celebrated string of pearls,[3] which everyone talks of, and all the other ornaments of such value, who will buy them? If your wife buys them, she will be said to have pounced upon the spoil and snatched them away at a very small price, and that so much the less had come to the legatees under the

which stipulated that the heir must receive at least one-fourth of the whole inheritance. Marcus could either refuse to act as heir, or decide against the codicils, and so bring the gifts mentioned in them into his own share as residuary legatee, or let the codicils stand in spite of the seals being broken (*cp* his own decision in *Dig.* xxviii. 4, 3, and Gaius, ii. 120 and 151). It is most likely that he took the second course, though he may also have carried out the cancelled provisions.

[2] See *Corp. Insc. Lat.* vi. 8440: *T. Aurelius Egatheus Imp. Antonini Aug. Lib. a Codicillis.*

[3] Possibly alluded to by Scaevola, one of the *amici*, in *Dig.* xxxv. 2, 36.

At non emet haec ornamenta Faustina. Quis igitur emet margarita, quae filiabus tuis legata sunt? Iis margaritis collos filiarum tuarum despoliabis ut cuius tandem ingluvies turgida ornetur?

An hereditas Matidiae a vobis non adibitur? Summo genere, summis opibus nobilissima femina de vobis optime merita intestata obierit? Ita prorsus eveniet ut cui funus publicum decreveris ei ademeris testamentum. Adhuc usque in omnibus causis iustum te et gravem et sanctum iudicem exhibuisti: ab uxorisne tuae causa prave iudicare inchoabis? Tum tu quidem ignem imitaberis, si proximos
Ambr. 103 am|bures, longinquis lucebis.

Ad M. Caes. ii. 17 (Naber, p. 38).

R<ESCRIPTUM> magistro meo.

Ergo magister meus iam nobis et patronus erit? Equidem possum securus esse, quom duas res animo meo carissimas secutus sim, rationem veram et sententiam tuam. Di velint ut semper, quod agam, secundo iudicio tuo, mi magister, agam.

Vides quid horae tibi rescribam. Nam post consultationem Amicorum in hoc tempus collegi sedulo ea quae nos moverant, ut Domino meo perscriberem faceremque cum nobis in isto quoque

will. But you will say Faustina will not buy these ornaments. Who then will buy the pearls, which were left to your daughters? You will rob the necks of your daughters of these pearls that they may grace whose goitred gorge may I ask?

Shall Matidia's inheritance not be taken up by you? Shall a most noble lady of the highest rank, of the greatest wealth, one who has deserved especially well of you, have thus died intestate? The precise result, therefore, will be, that you will have robbed of her will one to whom you have granted a public funeral. Hitherto in every cause without exception you have shewn yourself a just and weighty and righteous judge. Will you begin with your wife's case to give wrong judgment? Then will you indeed be like a fire, if you scorch those who are nearest and give light to those who are far off.[1]

THE EMPEROR MARCUS ANTONINUS TO FRONTO

162 A.D.

ANSWER to my master.

So my master will now be my advocate also! Of a truth I can feel easy in my mind, when I have followed the two guides dearest to my heart, right reason and your opinion. God grant that whatever I do I may always do with your favourable endorsement, my master.

You see how late I am writing my answer to you. For after a consultation with my Friends up to this moment, I have carefully collected all the points which weighed with us, so as to write fully to my Lord,[2] and make him our assessor in this business

[1] *cp.* Sallust in Suidas *s.v.* Athenodotus.

[2] Lucius Verus, who had gone to the Parthian war.

negotio praesentem. Tum demum θαρσήσω τοῖς βεβουλευμένοις, quom fuerint ab illo comprobata. Orationem, qua causam nostram defendisti, Faustinae confestim ostendam, et agam gratias ei quod mihi talis epistula tua legenda ex isto negotio nata est. Bone et optime magister, vale.

Ad Amicos, i. 14 (Naber, p. 183).

Aufidio Victorino genero <Fronto salutem>.

Ambr. 313, following 314 Ad obruzae tempus[1] . . . . | et Varianis alumnis masculis feminisque sestertium deciens[2] singulis reliquit usurarium potius quam proprium: nam quinquagena annua ab Augusta singulis dari iussit. Plerique omnes, qui eam curaverant, frustra fuerunt: ne librae quidem singulis ponderatae sunt. Ausi sunt tamen nonnulli, navi scilicet et strenui viri, codicillos, quos iam pridem Matidia inciderat, obsignare, quom illa sine sensu ullo iaceret. Ausi etiam sunt codicillos istos apud Dominum nostrum ut probe ac recte factos tueri et defendere. Nec sine metu fui, ne quid philosophia perversi suaderet. Quid ad eum de re scripserim, ut scires, exemplum litterarum misi tibi.

In oratione Bithyna, cuius partem legisse te scribis,

[1] From the Index, as read by Hauler (*Wien. Stud.* 33, pt. 1, p. 175). [2] Possibly *viciens* in the Codex.

---

[1] He chaffingly calls the letter a speech.

[2] This assaying of the gold (presumably the gold ornaments) was done by means of fire in a small flat vessel called a cupel.

also. Then only shall I have confidence in our decision, when it has been approved by him. The "speech[1]" in which you have advocated our cause, I will shew at once to Faustina, and will tender her thanks because as an outcome of that business it has been my lot to read such a letter from you. Good master, best of masters, farewell.

162 A.D.

FRONTO to Aufidius Victorinus his son-in-law.

At the time of the gold-test[2] . . . . and to her Varian protégés of either sex she left a million sesterces[3] apiece for them to enjoy as a life interest rather than for their own; for she directed that 50,000 sesterces[4] apiece should be given them every year by the Empress. Almost all those who had paid her court lost their labour: not a pound apiece was weighed out to them. Some of them however, brisk and smart fellows without a doubt, had the effrontery, while Matidia lay unconscious, to seal up the codicils, which she had annulled a long while before. They had the effrontery also to uphold and defend these codicils before our Lord as duly and truly executed. And I have not been without apprehension that Philosophy might lead him to a wrong decision. That you may know what I wrote to him on the subject, I send you a copy of my letter.

In my Bithynian speech, part of which you write

[3] About £20,000.

[4] About £500. It is not clear whether these *alumni* were children of an alimentary foundation, such as the *puellae Faustinianae*.

multa sunt nova addita, ut arbitror ego, non inornate, locus in primis de acta vita, quem tibi placiturum puto, si legeris quod in simili re M. Tullius pro L.[1] Sulla egregie scriptum reliquit: non ut par pari compares, sed ut aestimes nostrum mediocre ingenium quantum ab illo eximiae eloquentiae viro abludat.[2]

(Naber, p. 155.)

Ad Marcum Antoninum de Orationibus

<Antonino Augusto Fronto>.

Ambr. 382, following 387

1. . . . . | pauca subnectam fortasse inepta iniqua, nam rursus faxo magistrum me experiare. Neque ignoras omnem hanc magistrorum <turbam>[3] vanam propemodum et stolidam esse: parum eloquentiae et sapientiae nihil. Feres profecto bona venia veterem potestatem et nomen magistri me usurpantem denuo.

2. Fateor enim, quod res est, unam solam posse causam incidere, qua causa claudat aliquantum amor

[1] So Cod. by mistake for *P.*
[2] Haupt for Cod. *abluat* (Mai). *cp.* Hor. *Sat.* II. iii. 320.
[3] Mai. Query <*rem*>.

[1] Owing to the confusion in the leaves of the Codex and their partial illegibility, it is impossible to be quite sure of the position of the various parts of this tractate, and consequently of the thread of the argument. It is obviously connected with the similar letters *De Eloquentia* above, being like them an appeal to Marcus not to neglect eloquence for philosophy. Little seems lost at the beginning, and Fronto enters at once on an indictment of the false eloquence of Seneca and his school, whom he accuses of trickeries and tautology, taking Lucan especially as an instance of the latter fault. He compares their mannerisms to a harpist in a

that you have read, there are many fresh things introduced, not inelegantly as I fancy, particularly a passage on my past life, which I think will please you, if you read that excellent speech on a similar subject in defence of P. Sulla left us by M. Tullius: not that you should compare us as equals, but that you should recognise how far my mediocre talent falls short of that man of unapproachable eloquence.

On Speeches

? 163 A.D.

Fronto to Antoninus Augustus.

1. . . . . I will subjoin a few possibly unreasonable and unjust criticisms, for I will make you again have a taste of me as a master.[1] And you are aware that all this company of masters is more or less futile and fatuous—little enough of eloquence and of wisdom nought! You will I am sure bear with me for taking up anew my old-time authority and title of master.

2. For I confess, what is the fact, that only one thing could happen to cause any considerable set-back

cantata repeating a note again and again. He also charges such writers with meanness and slovenliness of diction, with effeminate fluency and preciosity. Turning to a speech lately delivered by Marcus, he praises him for his invention, and repeats (§ 8) what he had said in the *De Eloquentia* about clear and imperfect utterance. In connexion with this he refers to a treatise of Theodorus, which he had evidently used in his lessons. In § 9 an unfortunate gap obscures the trend of the argument, but we find him still discussing the Senecan style. From this he turns to the grandiloquence of a Gallic rhetor and his inappropriate use of Ennius. But the abrupt transition from Alexander to the Tiber is puzzling. In conclusion, he criticises severely an edict of Marcus and adds a warning against the debased style.

erga te meus—si eloquentiam neglegas. Neglegas tamen vero potius censeo quam prave excolas. Confusam eam ego eloquentiam, catachannae ritu[1] partim pineis[1] nucibus Catonis partim Senecae mollibus et febriculosis prunulis insitam, subvertendam censeo radicitus, immo vero, Plautino ut utar verbo,[2] *exradicitus*. Neque ignoro copiosum sententiis et redundantem hominem esse: verum sententias eius tolutares video nusquam quadripedo concitas[3] cursu ten<d>ere, nusquam pugnare,[4] nusquam maiestatem studere; ut Laberius *dictabolaria*, immo *dicteria*, potius eum quam dicta confingere.

3. Itane existimas graviores sententias et eadem de re apud Annaeum istum reperturum te quam apud Sergium? *Sed non modulatas aeque*: fateor; Ambr. 381 *neque ita* | *cordaces*: ita est; *neque ita tinnulas*: non nego. Quid vero, si prandium utrique adponatur, adpositas oleas alter digitis prendat, ad os adferat, ut manducandi ius fasque est ita dentibus subiciat, alter autem oleas suas in altum iaciat, ore aperto excipiat, ut calculos praestigiator, primoribus labris ostentet? Ea re profecto pueri laudent, convivae

[1] So Hauler in *Festschrift Theod. Gomperz*, p. 392.

[2] Brakman for Cod. *Plautino trato*. Stud. prefers *Plautinotato*, for which *cp.* Aul. Gell. iii. 3, *Plautinissimus*, and Lucian, *V. H.* ii. 19, Πλατωνικώτατος.

[3] For Cod. *concito*, which does not seem to be used like *concitato*. [4] Heindorf suggests *pungere*.

in my love for you, and that is, if you were to neglect eloquence. Yet indeed I would rather you neglected it than cultivated it in the wrong way. For as to that hybrid eloquence of the *catachanna*[1] type, grafted partly with Cato's pine-nuts,[2] partly with the soft and hectic plums of Seneca, it ought in my judgment to be plucked up by the roots, nay, to use a Plautine expression, *by the roots of the roots.* I am aware that he is a man who abounds in thoughts, aye bubbles over with them; but I see his thoughts go trot-trot, nowhere keep on their course under the spur at a free gallop, nowhere shew fight, nowhere aim at sublimity: like Laberius, he fashions *wit-bolts,* or rather *wit-flashes,* rather than wit-sayings.

3. Do you then suppose that you could find weightier thoughts and on the same subject in your Annaeus than in Sergius? *But (in Sergius)*[3] *not so rhythmical:* I grant it; *nor so sprightly:* it is so; *nor with such a ring:* I do not deny it. But what, if the same meal be set before two persons, and the one take up the olives set on the table with his fingers, carry them to his open mouth, let them come between his teeth for mastication in the decent and proper manner, while the other throw his olives into the air, catch them in his mouth, and shew them when caught, like a juggler his pebbles, with the tips of his lips. Schoolboys of course would clap the feat and the guests be amused, but the one will

[1] See i. p. 140.

[2] The plain, austere eloquence of Cato is compared to the fruit of the wild pine (Hauler refers to Cato, *R.R.* xlviii. 3), as contrasted with the soft, feverish style of Seneca.

[3] Sergius Flavius or Plautus a Stoic, who, says Quintilian (*Inst.* viii. 3), formed many new words, some very harsh.

delectentur; sed alter pudice prandierit, alter labellis gesticulatus erit.

At enim sunt quaedam in libris eius scite dicta, graviter quoque nonnulla. Etiam laminae interdum argentiolae cloacis inveniuntur; eane re cloacas purgandas redimemus?

4. Primum illud in isto genere dicendi vitium turpissimum, quod eandem sententiam milliens alio atque alio amictu indutam referunt. Ut histriones, quom palliolatim saltant, caudam cycni, capillum Veneris, Furiae flagellum, eodem pallio demonstrant: ita isti unam eandemque sententiam multimodis faciunt, ventilant, commutant, convertunt, eadem lacinia <varia> saltant,[1] refricant eandem unam sententiam saepius quam puellae olfactoria sucina.[2]

5. Dicendum est de fortuna aliquid? Omnes ibi

Ambr. 344: end of Quat. xxx.

Fortunas, Antiates, Praenesti|nas, Respicientes, balnearum etiam, Fortunas omnes cum pennis cum rotis cum gubernaculis reperias.

Unum exempli causa poetae prohoemium commemorabo, poetae eiusdem temporis eiusdemque nominis; fuit aeque Annaeus. Is initio carminis sui septem primis versibus nihil aliud quam *bella plus quam civilia* interpretatus est. N<umera>[3] replicet quot sententiis—*Iusque datum sceleri*: una sententia est; *in sua victrici conversum viscera*

[1] For Cod. *salutant*. Haupt suggests *eandem laciniam volutant*.

[2] Haupt for Cod. *olfactoriae*.

[3] Brakman.

have eaten his dinner decently, the other juggled with his lips.

You will say, there are certain things in his books cleverly expressed, some also with dignity. Yes, even little silver coins are sometimes found in sewers; are we on that account to contract for the cleaning of sewers?[1]

4. The first and most objectionable defect in that style of speech is the repetition of the same thought under one dress and another, times without number. As actors, when they dance clad in mantles, with one and the same mantle represent a swan's tail, the tresses of Venus, a Fury's scourge, so these writers make up the same thought in a thousand ways, flourish it, alter it, disguise it, with the same lappet dance diverse dances, rub up one and the same thought oftener than girls their perfumed amber.

5. Has something to be said about fortune? You will find there the whole gallery of Fortunes, Fortunes of Antium, of Praeneste, Fortunes Regardant,[2] Fortunes too of baths, all Fortunes with wings, with wheels, with rudders.

One prelude of a poem[3] I will quote by way of example from a poet of the same time and of the same name, an Annaeus like the other. In the first seven verses at the beginning of his poem he has done nothing but paraphrase the words *Wars worse than civil.* Count up the phrases in which he rings the changes on this—*and sanction granted to wrong:* phrase number one; *turning their conquering swords, in their own heart's blood to imbrue them:*

[1] Dryden, in his *Essay on Dramatic Poetry*, quotes the proverb *aurum ex stercore colligere.*

[2] *i.e.* ready to aid men; see Cic. *De Legg.* ii. 11, § 28.

[3] Lucan's *Pharsalia*, Book I. 2 ff.

<*dextra*>: iam haec altera est; *cognatasque acies:* tertia haec erit; *in commune nefas:* quartam numerat; *infestisque obvia signis signa:* accumulat quoque quintam; *pares aquilas:* sexta haec Herculis aerumna; *et pila minantia pilis:* septima—de Aiacis scuto corium. Annaee, quis finis erit? Aut si nullus finis nec modus servandus est, cur non addis *et similes lituos?* Addas licet *et carmina nota tubarum.* Sed et loricas et conos et balteos et omnem armorum supellectilem sequere.

6. Apollonius autem—non enim Homeri prohoemiorum par artificium est—Apollonius, inquam,
Ambr. 343 qui *Argonautas* scripsit, | quinque res <prorsus diversas diserte in> quattuor versibus narrat: κλέα φωτῶν, viros qui navigassent; οἳ Πόντοιο κατὰ στόμα, iter quo navigassent; βασιλῆος ἐφημοσύνῃ Πελίαο, cuius imperio navigassent; <χρύσειον> μετὰ κῶας, cui rei navigassent; ἐύζυγον ἤλασαν Ἀργώ, navem qua vecti essent.

Isti autem tam oratores quam poetae consimile faciunt atque[1] citharoedi solent unam aliquam vocalem litteram de Inone[2] vel de Aedone multis et variis accentibus <iter>are.[3]

7. Quid ego verborum sordes et illuvies? Quid verba modulate collocata <et> effeminate fluentia[4] . . . . Ibi igitur . . . . et aversantes <exami>nare

[1] Naber for Cod. *ut quae.*
[2] Peerlkamp for Mai's *Henme.*
[3] *Ibid.* Mai has <*cant*>*are.*
[4] This sentence is from the margin of Cod.

here we have a second; *kin against kin embattled:* that will be a third; *guilt that was shared by all:* he tells off his fourth; *and standards set against standards:* he piles up a fifth to boot; *eagles with eagles matched:* here's the sixth! why, this is a labour of Hercules; *and javelins poised against javelins:* a seventh! a bull's hide from the shield of Ajax. Wilt never be done, Annaeus? Or if no end or limit is ever to be kept, why not add *clarions also alike?* And you might go on, *and the well-known blare of the bugles.* Yes, and follow up with cuirasses and helmets and belts and all the paraphernalia of a soldier.

6. Apollonius, however—for Homer's openings are not equally skilful—Apollonius, I say, who wrote the *Argonautica,* describes five quite distinct facts explicitly in five lines: κλέα φωτῶν,[1] the heroes who sailed; οἳ Πόντοιο κατὰ στόμα, the route by which they sailed; βασιλῆος ἐφημοσύνῃ Πελίαο, at whose hest they sailed; χρύσειον μετὰ κῶας, on what quest they sailed; ἐύζυγον ἤλασαν Ἀργώ, the ship on which they were carried.

These writers, as well rhetoricians as poets, do just what harpers are wont to do, who dwell with many varied intonations on some single vowel from *Ino* or from *Aedon.*[2]

7. What shall I say of meanness and slovenliness in words? What of words rhythmically arranged and effeminately fluent? . . . . and from dislike regard with a critical eye

[1] Glories of heroes,—who by the Pontic strait,—as their monarch Pelias bade them,—seeking the Golden Fleece,—rowed forth in the well-built Argo.

[2] Musical plays so named from their subjects; but the names are by no means certain, and various others have been proposed instead.

hoc elegantiae[1] genus. <Uti> clipeo te Achillis in orationibus oportet, non parmulam ventilare neque hastulis histrionis ludere. Aquae de siphunculis concinnius saliunt quam de imbribus . . . . rem laudant . . . . quaerit . . . . quis istorum . . . . pandere . . . . apud . . . .

Ambr. 350 8. . . . . .[2] | *oculos convenientes* dixisti. Quis clamor iteratur![3] apparuit enim utrumque verbum quaesitum et inventum: quod ubi verbum invenisti, cavere pulchre scivisti. Impediti[4] voce dicuntur qui balbutiunt, et contrarium est soluta et expedita voce: multo melius apparuit *enodata*; quaesisse te arbitror ex eodem isto loco quod est ἀπὸ τοῦ ἐναντίου, quom imperfecta vox balbutientium sit, potuisse dici perfectam. Quae ignoras<se te . . . . quom>[5] *oculos convenientes* dixisti . . . .[6] improbatur hic locus ab . . . . <quia verbum varia> significatione est: Theodorus ἀπὸ τοῦ πολλαχῶς λέγεσθαι appellat. Nam convenire et decere et aptum esse et congruere Graeci ἡρμόσθαι appellant.

Non dubito alia item verba percensuisse. Nam, <quom> straboni oculi dispares sunt, potuisse te

[1] Eckst. prefers *eloquentiae*. *Uti* is from Mai.

[2] In the lacunae after *imbribus* about a quarter of a page would seem to be lost.

[3] Naber prefers *iteratus*.

[4] Query *impedita*.

[5] A little more than a line is lost. J. W. E. Pearce suggests *Quae ignoras <hinc saepe adhibenda sunt. Ex eo fonte igitur> oculos*, etc.

[6] Nine or ten letters lost.

this form of preciosity. In public speaking you have need to use the shield of Achilles, not wave a little targe or feint with the sham lances of the stage. Water gushes more daintily from little pipes than from the clouds . . . .

. . . .

8. . . . . You spoke of *harmonizing eyes*.[1] What applause, redoubled! for either word had been obviously sought after and found: and when you had found the word, you knew admirably how to use it with caution. Those who stammer[2] are said to have an impediment in their speech, and the contrary is the case with a speech free and unimpeded: much better clearly was your *tongue-untied*. And I think you have gone to that same passage for an expression "drawn from the contrary," that, since the utterance of stammerers is imperfect, it was possible to speak of a *perfect* utterance. That you should have been unaware of this . . . . when you said *harmonizing eyes* . . . . this passage is found fault with . . . . (because the word is of a varied) meaning: Theodorus calls it the "method from synonyms."[3] For the Greeks express to *agree*, to *fit*, to *suit*, to *harmonize* by the term ἡρμόσθαι (to be adapted).

I do not doubt that you passed in review other words also. For as in him who squints the eyes are not of a match, you could have called them equal or

[1] Marcus may have been alluding to himself and Lucius as the eyes of the state.

[2] See *De Eloquentia* above, 3, § 1.

[3] J. W. E. Pearce has suggested to me that this is the meaning of the words. A text-book on rhetoric by Theodorus seems referred to, by the rules of which Fronto judges the expressions quoted. There were two rhetoricians of this name, one of Gadara, the other of Byzantium. For the latter see Cic. *Brut.* 12 (*in arte subtilior*).

pares aut impares dicere; disconcinnos illos, hos concinnos dici potuisse; *convenientes* multo melius.

9. Dicas fortasse *quid in orationibus meis novicium, quid crispulum, quid luscum, quid purpurisso litum aut tumidum aut pollutum?* Nondum quicquam: sed vereor . . . .[1] eas promo . . . .[2]

10. Laudo Censoris factum, qui ludos talarios pro-
Ambr. 349 hibuit, | quod semet ipsum diceret, quom ea praeteriret, dignitati difficile servire, quin ad modum crotali aut cymbali pedem poneret. Tum praeterea multa sunt in isto genere dicendi sinceris similia, nisi quis diligenter examinat. *Iusque datum sceleri,*[3] M. Annaeus ait; contra Sallustius: *omne ius in validioribus esse.*

11. Gallicanus[4] quidam declamator, quom Macedones deliberarent, Alexandro morbo mortuo, an et Babylonem perverterent, *Quid si operas conduc<it>is leones?* inquit. Iste et superbe *Factum est*—eodem hoc verbo[5] Enni—*vobis lustra<tis>*[6] peroravit,[7] *factum est, factum est opus*[8] *inex<super>abile.* Tiberis est, Tusce,[9] Tiberis quem iubes claudi: Tiber amnis et dominus et fluentium circa regnator undarum;

[1] Six letters lost. [2] Three lines lost.
[3] Cod. adds *eo.*
[4] For all the following passage see Hauler, *Zeitschr. f. d. öst. Gymn.* lxi. pp. 673 ff.
[5] Over this word is written *in al(io) graviore sensu.*
[6] Or m[2] *ex alio: Quiritibus.* [7] Or m[2] *ex alio: exclamavit.*
[8] Over *opus* is written *tum facinus perfecta canalis,* and then *tali mole praestabilis.*
[9] Or possibly *Fauste* says Hauler. The Tuscan must have canalised the Tiber.

unequal, these accordant, those discordant; but *harmonizing* was much better.

9. Perhaps you will say *what is there in my speeches new-fangled, what artificial, what obscure, what patched with purple, what inflated or corrupt?* Nothing as yet;[1] but I fear . . . .

10. I praise the Censor's[2] act, who shut up the gaming houses because he himself, as he said, when he passed that way could scarce consult his dignity so far as to refrain from dancing to the sound of the castanets or cymbals. Then besides there are many things in that kind of oratory[3] not unlike the genuine thing, if one does not look carefully into it. *Sanction granted to wrong*, says M. Annaeus; on the other hand Sallust: *all right rests with the stronger.*

11. A certain Gallic rhetorician,[4] while the Macedonians on Alexander's death from disease were debating[5] whether they should utterly destroy Babylon also, says, *What if you hire lions to do your work?* Grandiosely too he[6] cries in his peroration, using the same word as Ennius, *By you citizens has been wrought, has been wrought a work unsurpassable.* It is the Tiber, O Tuscan,[7] the Tiber that thou biddest be penned in: the river Tiber, master and monarch of all

[1] This passage, if no other, makes impossible the suggestion of Mommsen that this treatise was written as late as 177. Fronto died, almost certainly, in 166 or 167.

[2] It is not known who the Censor was.

[3] The Senecan style.

[4] Probably not Favorinus, the Gallic orator of Hadrian's circle, who was a friend of Fronto's.

[5] *i.e.* in the orator's show speech on the subject.

[6] The Gallic orator.

[7] Who the Tuscan was who canalised the Tiber is not clear, nor whether the whole of this is not another extract from the rhetorician.

Ennius *<Factum 'st>: pos<t> aqüam*[1] *<iam> consistit isti fluvius qui <est> omnibu' princeps,*[2] *qui sub ovilia*[3] ait.

Peritia opus est ut vestem interpolem a sincera discernas. Itaque tutissimum est lectionibus eiusmodi abstinere. Facilis ad lubrica lapsus est.

12. Unum edictum tuum memini me animadvertisse, quo periculose scripseris vel indigna defecto aliquo libro. Huius edicti initium est: *Florere in suis actibus inlibatam iuventutem.* Quid hoc est, Ambr. 352 Marce? Hoc | nempe dicere vis, cupere te Italica oppida frequentari copia iuniorum. Quid in primo versu et verbo primo facit *florere?* Quid significat *inlibatam iuventutem?* Quid sibi volunt ambitus isti et circumitiones? Alia quoque eodem edicto sunt eiusmodi. Revertere potius ad verba apta et propria et suo suco imbuta. Scabies porrigo ex eiusmodi libris concipitur. Monetam illam veterem sectator. Plumbei nummi et cuiuscemodi[4] adulterini in istis recentibus nummis saepius inveniuntur quam in vetustis, quibus signatus est Perperna vel Treba<nius> . . . . Quid igitur? Non malim mihi

[1] m² *postquam.* Above these words is written *sensu* (or *versu*) *duro pressi*, and above that *retro ad arida.*

[2] For this line the Codex also gives *Retro iam substat fluvius*, etc., and *Constitit is fluvius qui est princeps omnium aquarum.*

[3] Over these words are written *Urbis Romae saxis Palatini inhabitasse feruntur.*

[4] Kluss. would read *cuiusquemodi.*

circumfluent waters;[1] Ennius says: *'Twas wrought: after its flood now | stayed at the spot stood still that stream that is queen of all rivers, | which underneath the Ovilia*[2] (flows).

There is skill needed to distinguish a patched dress from a sound one. So the safest course is to eschew all such citations. It is easy to slip on the ice.

12. One edict of yours I remember to have noticed, in which you hazardously wrote what would be even unworthy of some faulty book. The edict begins: *That there should flourish on their holdings*[3] *unimpaired youth.* What is this, Marcus? What you wish to say is doubtless that you desire to see the Italian towns stocked with a plentiful supply of young men. What is *florere* doing in the first line and as the first word? What is meant by *unimpaired*[4] *youth?* What is the object of these inversions and circumlocutions? Other faults of a similar kind are to be found in the same edict. Hark back rather to words that are suitable and appropriate and juicy with their own sap. The itch and the scurf are caught from books of that kind.[5] Cleave to the old mintage. Coins of lead and debased metal of every kind are oftener met with in our recent issues than in the archaic ones which are stamped with the names of Perperna or Trebanius[6] . . . . What then? Am I not to prefer

[1] *cp.* Verg. *Aen.* viii. 77. He probably followed Ennius.

[2] The *Ovilia* was a place in the Campus Martius where the voting at the elections took place.

[3] *Actus*, a certain measure of land (see Plin. *N.H.* xviii. 17).

[4] Marcus (*Ad Caes.* i. 2 and v. 7) uses the word *illibatus* of *corpus* and *salus*, coupling it with *incolumis* in the latter case. Pius uses it in a rescript (*Inst. Iust.* i. 8, 2) with *potestas*. It appears, therefore, that its use with a personal subject was objectionable. [5] That is, like Seneca's.

[6] See Index.

nummum Antonini aut Commodi aut Pii? Polluta <ista> et contaminata et varia et maculosa maculosioraque quam nutricis pallium. Omni ergo opera, si possit <fieri>,[1] linguam communem reddas; verbum aliquod requiras non fictum a te, nam id quidem absurdum est, sed usurpatum concinnius aut congruentius aut accommodatius.

13. *Tantum antiquitatis curaeque maioribus pro Italica gente fuit*, Sallustius ait. *Antiquitas* verbum usitatum, sed nusquam isto sensu usurpatum,[2] neque ideo probe placitum. Nam volgo dicitur, quod potius sit, antiquius esse. Inde prorsus[3] ipsa <a> Sallustio
Ambr. 351 derivata: et | quoniam minus clarum quod et minus usitatum verbum est, insequenti verbo interpretatus est, *antiquitatis curaeque.*

Hoc modo . . . . municipes sacrorum . . . . actus . . . . Quid . . . . vale . . . . poculum. In ore[4] plebis ad hoc pervolgatum est usque hoc genus verborum; Accius, Plautus, Sallustius saepenumero, etiam raro Tullius <usurpat> . . . .[5]

[1] Mai. He marks the word *communem* as doubtful.
[2] For this passage see Hauler, *Wien. Stud.* 32, pt. 2.
[3] Cod. *pro . . s.* Brakman prefers *probes.*
[4] m[1] *aures.*
[5] The lacunae cover more than a column.

---

[1] This mention of Commodus is difficult. He was named Caesar in 166, but did not become emperor till 177. Though the father of Lucius Verus was Commodus, the latter could not have been called Commodus. Bourchier (*Class. Rev.* Nov.

for myself a coin of Antoninus or Commodus[1] or Pius? Those old words are stained and contaminated and discoloured and spotted, aye, more spotted than a nurse's apron. There is need, therefore, of all your pains to render your language, if possible, current coin; be ever on the look-out for some word, not one coined by you, for that, indeed, is an absurdity, but used by you more elegantly or more aptly or more happily than by others.[2]

13. Says Sallust: *Such reverent regard*[3] *and affection did our ancestors have for the Italian race.* This word *antiquitas* is often used, but nowhere employed in that sense,[4] and therefore is not properly correct. For it is commonly said that what is preferable is *antiquius.* Thence undoubtedly did Sallust derive his use of *antiquitas* itself; and, since a word that is less usual is also less clear, he interpreted it by means of the following word, *antiquitatis curaeque.*

In this way . . . .
. . . . In the mouths of the people words of this kind have hitherto always been in vogue; Accius, Plautus, Sallust very often, even occasionally Cicero, (use them) . . . .

1922) thinks Eolus of Ennius Verus may be meant. Perperna was consul 130 B.C. There is a coin of the *Gens Trebania* extant; see Eckhel, v. 326, possibly a coin of C. before 172 is meant.

[2] Fronto says: Follow the older writers. The Senecan style is as catching as the itch. There is purer metal in the older coins. What, not prefer a coin of Antoninus? Of course the older words are worn and discoloured with age and want careful handling to justify their use.

[3] From Sallust's *Hist.* Lib. I. says Hauler. Servius quotes the passage on Verg. *Georg.* ii. 209.

[4] Cicero seems to use it so.

Ad Verum Imp. ii. 2 (Naber, p. 129)

<Magistro meo salutem.>

Ambr 422, following Vat. 16 . . . .[1] <necessa>|rio correcta vel in tempore provisa vel celeriter curata vel sedulo instructa, praedicare ipse[2] apud te supersedi. Da verecundiae veniam, si urgentibus curis praepeditus negotia in manibus praeversus sum, speque tuae erga me benignissimae facilitatis interim in scribendo cessavi. Fiduciae amoris ignoscito, si piguit consilia me singularum rerum forsitan in dies mutanda sub incerto adhuc exitu dubia existimatione perscribere. Causam quaeso tam iustae cunctationis accipias. Cur igitur aliis quam tibi saepius? Ut breviter absolvam: quoniam quidem, nisi ita facerem, illi irascerentur, tu ignosceres; illi tacerent, tu flagitares:[3] illis officium officio repensabam, tibi amorem pro amore debebam.[4] An velles ad te quoque me litteras invitum querentem festinantem, quia necesse erat potius quam quia libebat, darem? Cur autem, inquies, non libebat? Quia nequedum quicquam eiusmodi effectum erat, ut te liberet ad gaudii societatem vocare. Curarum vero, quae me dies noctesque miserrimum habuere, et prope ad desperationem
Ambr. 421 summae rei per|duxere, facere participem hominem carissimum et quem semper laetum esse cuperem,

[1] The best part of a page is lost between the end of *Ad Verum*, ii. 1, and here. [2] Heindorf for Cod. *ipsa.*
[3] Mähly would read *flagitarent . . . taceres.*
[4] Heindorf for Cod. *debeam.*

---

[1] Verus is writing from Syria not long after his arrival at the seat of war, while the Parthians had not yet been definitely beaten.

M. CORNELIUS FRONTO

From Lucius Verus to Fronto

163 A.D.

To my master, greeting.

. . . . I have refrained from relating to you myself all that had necessarily to be set right or provided for in good time, or quickly remedied or carefully arranged.[1] Make allowance for my scrupulosity, if shackled with urgent cares I have dealt first with the business in hand and, counting on your good-natured indulgence towards me, have meanwhile given up writing. Pardon my reliance on our love if I have fought shy of describing my measures in detail, liable as they were to daily alteration and while the issue was still doubtful and all forecast precarious. Accept, I beseech you, the reason for so legitimate a delay. Why, then, write to others oftener than to you? To excuse myself shortly: because, in fact, did I not do so, they would be angry, you would forgive; they would give up writing, you would importune me; to them I rendered duty for duty, to you I owed love for love. Or would you wish me to write you also letters unwillingly, grumblingly, hurriedly, from necessity rather than from choice? Now why, you will say, not from choice? Because not even yet has anything been accomplished such as to make me wish to invite you to share in the joy. I did not care, I confess, to make one so very dear to me, and one whom I would wish to be always happy, a partner in anxieties which night and day made me utterly wretched,[2] and almost brought me to despair

[2] Nazarius (*Paneg.* xxiv. § 6) says that Varus in a panic offered the Parthian king terms which were scornfully rejected, but he means Lucius Verus: see p. 212.

fateor non libebat. Nec enim illud libebat, aliud dolere aliud loqui. Simulare Lucium quicquam adversus Frontonem! a quo ego prius multo simplicitatem verique[1] amorem quam loquendi polite disciplinam didicisse me praedico. Equidem pacto quoque, quod inter nos iampridem intercessit, satis me ad veniam impetrandam paratum esse arbitror. Denique, quamquam mihi lacessitus a me saepius numquam tamen rescripsisses, dolebam hercules sed pacti memoria non succensebam. Postremo quid plura? ne potius defendere me quam orare te videar: peccavi, fateor: adversum quem minime decuit: etiam id fateor. Sed tu melior esto. Satis poenarum lui, primum in eo ipso quod peccasse me sentio: mox quod tantis terris disiunctus, qui te in vestigio exorare potuissem, tot interea mensibus dum meas litteras accipis, dum ego tuas recipio, cura discruciabor. Adhibeo tibi deprecatores humanitatem ipsam, nam et delinquere humanum est et hominis

Ambr. 421 ends maxime proprium | ignoscere . . . .[2]

Ad Antoninum Imp. i. 3 (Naber, p. 101).

Vat. 90 *ad init.* | Domino meo Antonino Augusto.

Vidi pullulos tuos, quod quidem libentissime in vita mea viderim, tam simili facie tibi ut nihil sit

[1] Heindorf for Cod. *verum*.

[2] This word is from the margin of Cod. Mommsen says at least two leaves are lost between this word and the mutilated beginning of *Ad Verum*, ii. 3.

of success. Nor, indeed, did I care for the alternative, to feel one thing and utter another. What, Lucius to make pretences to Fronto! from whom I do not hesitate to say I have learnt simplicity and the love of truth far before the lesson of polite phrasing. Indeed, by the compact also, which has long subsisted between us, I think I am sufficiently qualified for receiving pardon. At all events, when in spite of repeated appeals from me you never wrote, I was sorry, by heaven, but, remembering our compact, not angry. Finally, why say more, that I seem not rather to justify myself than to entreat you? I have been in fault, I admit it; against the last person, too, that deserved it: that, too, I admit. But you must be better than I. I have suffered enough punishment, first in the very fact that I am conscious of my fault, then because, though face to face I could have won your pardon in a moment, I must now, separated as I am from you by such wide lands, be tortured with anxiety for so many intervening months until you get my letter and I get your answer back. I present to you as suppliants in my favour humanity herself, for even to offend is human, and it is man's peculiar privilege to pardon . . . .[1]

Fronto to Marcus

163 A.D.

To my Lord Antoninus Augustus.

I have seen your little chicks,[2] and a more welcome sight I shall never in my life see, so like in features to you that nothing can be more like than the

[1] A second *deprecator* was probably Marcus.

[2] The twins Lucius Aurelius Commodus and Antoninus Geminus, born at Lanuvium on August 31, 161. The latter died in 165.

hoc simili similius. Feci prorsus compendium itineris Lorium usque, compendium viae lubricae, compendium clivorum arduorum: tamen vidi te non exadvorsum modo sed locupletius, sive me ad dexteram sive ad laevam convertissem. Sunt autem dis iuvantibus colore satis salubri, clamore forti. Panem alter tenebat bene candidum, ut puer regius, alter autem cibarium, plane ut a philosopho prognatus. Deos quaeso sit salvos sator, salva sint sata, salva seges sit, quae tam similes procreat. Nam etiam voculas eorum audivi tam dulces tam venustas, ut orationis tuae lepidum illum et liquidum sonum nescio quo pacto in utriusque pipulo adgnoscerem. Iam tu igitur, nisi caves, superbiorem aliquanto me experiere; habeo enim quos pro te non oculis modo amem sed etiam auribus.

Ad Antoninum Imp. i. 4 (Naber, p. 101).

MAGISTRO meo salutem.

Vat. 89 Vidi filiolos meos, quom | eos vidisti; vidi et te, quom litteras tuas legerem. Oro te, mi magister, ama me ut amas; ama me sic etiam quo modo istos parvolos nostros amas: nondum omne dixi quod volo: ama me quo modo amasti. Haec ut scriberem, tuarum litterarum mira iucunditas produxit. Nam

[1] The author of *De Differentiis Vocabulorum*—possibly Fronto himself—explains *locuples* as a *copia locorum*. Fronto means that he has been able to see Marcus without going to

likeness. I have absolutely taken a journey by short cut quite to Lorium, a short cut of the slippery road, a short cut of the steep ascents: nevertheless I have seen you not only opposite to me but in more places than one,[1] whether I turned to the right hand or to the left. God be praised they have quite a healthy colour and strong lungs. One was holding a piece of white bread, like a little prince, the other a piece of black bread, quite in keeping with a philosopher's son. I beseech the Gods to bless the sower, bless the seed sown, bless the soil that bears a crop so true to stock. For even the sound of their little voices was so sweet, so winsome to my ear that I seemed, I know not how, to hear in the tiny piping[2] of either the clear and charming tones of your own utterance. Now therefore, if you do not take care, you will find me holding my head a good deal higher, for I have those whom I can love instead of you, not with eyes only but with ears also.

Marcus to Fronto

163 A.D.

To my master, greeting.

I saw my little sons, when you saw them; I saw you too, when I read your letter. I beseech you, my master, love me as you do love me; love me too even as you love those little ones of ours: I have not yet said all that I want to say: love me as you have loved me. The extraordinary delightfulness of your letter has led me to write this. For as to its

Lorium, where he apparently was, in the faces of his two children.

[2] *cp.* "Thy small pipe," Shaks. *Tw. N.* i. 4, 32.

de elegantia quid dicam? nisi te Latine loqui, nos ceteros neque Graece neque Latine. Domino meo fratri peto scriptites. Valde volt ut hoc a te impetrem: desideria autem illius intemperantem me et violentum faciunt. Vale mi iucundissime magister. Nepotem tuum saluta.

Ad Antoninum Imp. i. 5 (Naber, p. 102).

ANTONINO AUGUSTO Domino meo.

1. *Ante gestum, post relatum,* aiunt qui tabulas sedulo conficiunt. Idem verbum epistulae huic opportunum est, quae litteris tuis nuper ad me scriptis nunc demum respondet. Causa morae fuit quod, quom rescribere instituissem, quaedam menti meae se offerebant non *supino,* ut dicitur, *rostro* scribenda. Dein senatus dies intercessit, et in senatu labor eo gravior perceptus, quod cum gaudio simul altius penetraverat, ita ut cum sole ventus. Nunc haec epistula, quod non suo tempore praesto

Vat. 96 | adfuerit, veniam in dilationibus[1] usitatam poscit *ne fraudi sit.*

2. Quom accepi litteras tuas, ita rescribere coeperam—*Ama me ut amas,* inquis. Huic verbo respondere paulo verbis pluribus in animo est; prolixius enim rescribere tibi tempore illo solebam, quo

[1] Kiessling for Cod. *relationibus.*

---

[1] Fronto seems to mean that his reply, or payment of his debt, was not made at once but followed later, as the entry in the ledger follows the transaction.

style what can I say? except that you talk Latin while the rest of us talk neither Latin nor Greek. Write often, I pray you, to the Lord my brother. He especially wishes me to get this from you. His wishes, however, make me unreasonable and exacting. Farewell, my most delightful of masters. Give my love to your grandson.

Fronto to Marcus

163 A.D.

To my Lord Antoninus Augustus.

1. *First done, then entered,*[1] say they who keep their books carefully. The same saying is applicable to this letter, which now at last answers your recent one to me. The reason of the delay has been that, when I made up my mind to write, some things came into my mind, which could not be written down *beak in air,* as the saying is. Then intervened the sitting of the Senate, and the labour it entailed was felt the more heavily in that, being simultaneous with my joy, it had taken deeper hold of me, just as the wind when combined with the sun.[2] Now this letter, as it was not forthcoming at its due time, asks the indulgence usual in postponements, *that it be without prejudice.*

2. When I received your letter, I began my answer thus—*Love me as you do love me,* you say: I propose to answer this phrase somewhat less briefly. For I used to answer your letters more at length in

[2] Does Fronto mean that as the wind finds freer entrance to our bodies when the sun has caused us to lay aside our wraps, so toil makes itself more felt when joy has relaxed our energies?

amatum te a me satis compertum tibi esse tute ostendis. Vide, quaeso, ne temet ipse defraudes et detrimentum amoris ultro poscas: amplius enim tanto amari te a me velim credas mihi, quanto omnibus in rebus potior est certus praesens fructus quam futuri spes incerta. Egone qui indolem ingenii tui in germine etiam tum et in herba et in flore dilexerim, nunc frugem ipsam maturae virtutis nonne multo multoque amplius diligam? Tum ego stolidissimus habear agrestium omnium omniumque aratorum, si mihi cariora sint sata messibus. Ego vero <eorum> quae optavi quaeque vovi compos, optatorum votorumque meorum damnatus atque multatus sum: in eam multam duplicatum amorem tuum defero,[1] non, ut antiquitus multas inrogari mos fuit, mille minus dimidio. Assae nutricis est infantem magis diligere
Vat. 95 quam adultum; succensere etiam | pubertati stulta nutrix solet, puerum de gremio sibi abductum et campo aut foro traditum. Litteratores etiam isti discipulos suos, quoad puerilia discunt et mercedem pendunt, magis diligunt. Ego quom ad curam cultumque ingenii tui accessi, hunc te speravi fore qui nunc es; in haec tua tempora amorem meum intendi. Lucebat in pueritia tua virtus insita, luce-

[1] Boissonade for Cod. *desero*.

---

[1] Cato (see Aul. Gell. vii. 3, 37) mentions this old law, under which the fine for certain offences was limited to half a man's property less 1,000 (asses). Fronto says that, all his wishes and prayers for Marcus having been abundantly ful-

those days when, as you yourself shew, you were sufficiently assured of my love for you. Look, I beseech you, that you do not rob yourself, and of your own accord demand a diminution of love, for I would have you believe that you are so much more fully loved by me now, as in all things a present certain fruition exceeds an uncertain hope in the future. Shall not I, who loved the native quality of your genius even then, when in bud and in leaf and in flower, love now far far more deeply the very fruit of your matured excellence? Then should I be deemed the most blockish of all country swains and all ploughmen, if I valued what was sown above what was harvested. I indeed, being granted all that I wished and prayed for, have been cast and fined in my very wishes and prayers: to meet that fine I put in my doubled love for you, not, as was the custom in old time for fines to be inflicted, at the rate of half less a thousand (asses).[1] A dry-nurse commonly loves a baby more than an older child; a foolish nurse is even prone to be angry with adolescence for taking away her boy from her arms and giving him over to the playground or the forum. Your instructors of youth too love their pupils more while they learn boyhood's lessons and pay their fees. When I was called to the care and cultivation of your natural powers, I hoped you would be what you now are; I carried my love on to these your present days. Conspicuous in your boyhood was your innate excellence; even more conspicuous was

filled, he is bound now to perform his part of the bargain and pay the fine due. To meet this liability he tenders his doubled love for Marcus, and does not, as was the old custom, pay with less than half his assets.

bat etiam magis in adulescentia: sed ita ut quom serenus dies inluculascit lumine inchoato. Nunc iam virtus integra orbe splendido exorta est et radiis disseminata: et[1] tu me ad pristinam illam mensuram luciscentis amoris tui revocas, et iubes matutina dilucula lucere meridie! Audi, quaeso, quanto ampliore nunc sis virtute quam antea fueris, quo facilius credas, quanto amplius amoris merearis et poscere desinas tantumdem.

3. Ut a pietate contendere te tibimet incipiam, obsequia erga patrem tua pristina commemorabo, eaque cum praesentibus officiis comparabo. Quis ignorat, ubi pater tuus minus valeret, te iuxta cum eo carere balneo, vino aqua etiam et cibo temet deducere solitum? Nulla unquam te neque
Vat. 95 ends with Quat. xii. somni neque vigiliae neque cibi | neque itineris tua tempora habuisse sed patris temporibus inservisse[2] . . . .

Ad Marcum Imp. i. 6–10, Index only (Naber, p. 93).

Vat. 83 ***ad init.*** <MAGISTRO meo salutem> | Minus valui, mi magister . . . .

<ANTONINO AUGUSTO Domino meo> Si ambulare iam <poteris>[3] . . . .

<MAGISTRO meo salutem> Festino, mi magister, <scribere> . . . .

[1] Klussmann for Cod. *est.*
[2] The last nine words are from the margin of Cod., except that there the verbs are given in the indicative.
[3] Or perhaps *potero.*

it in your youth; but in such a way as when a cloudless day begins to break with newly-dawning light. Now already your full excellence has risen with dazzling disc and spread its rays on every side: and yet you call me back to that bygone measure of my dawning love for you, and bid the morning twilight shine at noonday! Hear, I pray you, how much enhanced beyond your former is your present excellence, that you may more easily understand how much larger a measure of love you deserve, while you cease to claim only as much.

3. To begin my comparison of yourself to yourself with your dutifulness, I will mention your bygone devotion to your father,[1] and contrast it with your present attention to duty. Who does not know that, when your father was unwell, you used to discontinue baths in order to keep him company, deny yourself wine, even water and food; that you never studied your own convenience in the matter of sleep or waking or food or exercise, but sacrificed everything to your father's convenience? . . . .

Five Letters between Marcus and Fronto of which only the opening Words Remain

163 A.D.

To my master, greeting. I have been unwell, my master . . . .

To my Lord Antoninus Augustus. If you can walk yet . . . .

To my master, greeting. I hasten to write, my master . . . .

[1] His adoptive father Pius. Marcus's *pietas* is also mentioned Capit. v. § 8, vii. § 2, and Dio, lxxi. 35.

<ANTONINO AUGUSTO Domino meo> Non reticebo . . . .

<MAGISTRO meo salutem> Ego, mi magister, ...

Ad Antoninum Imp. ii. 3 (Naber, p. 106).

<MAGISTRO meo salutem.>

Vat. 144 from a new Quat. . . . . <quom nihil magis explo>|ratum atque expeditum sit, mi magister, quam tua clemens in officiis adversum te nostris interpretatio. Scribe[1] igitur Domino meo pollicenti tibi multas suas litteras comperisse te ex me quae mandavit. Tum cetera adfectionis et comitatis tuae subnecte, mi magister; nam in litteris tuis, ut aequom est, adquiescit.

Ego biduo isto, nisi quod nocturni somni cepi, nihil intervalli habui: quam ob rem nondum legere epistulam prolixiorem[2] Domino meo a te scriptam potui, sed crastinam opportunitatem avide prospicio. Vale mi iucundissime magister. Nepotem saluta.

Ad Verum Imp. ii. 1 (Naber, p. 119).

Ambr. 446, col. 2 *ad med.* | DOMINO meo Vero Augusto salutem.

1. Iam iam, Imperator, esto erga me ut voles utque tuus animus feret; vel tu me neglegito vel

[1] Naber for Cod. *scribo*. [2] The following letter.

---

[1] Lucius Verus, his colleague.

[2] This long letter to Lucius in Syria was written on the victorious conclusion of the Armenian portion of the great Parthian war, when Lucius received the title *Armeniacus*. Besides flattering Lucius on the military successes, he praises the eloquence of his despatch to the senate. The rest of the letter is a glorification of eloquence, in which he includes all

To my Lord Antoninus Augustus. I will not hide from you . . . .

To my master, greeting. I, my master . . . .

Marcus Antoninus to Fronto

To my master greeting. 163 A.D.

. . . . since nothing is more to be counted upon and more readily given, my master, than the kindly construction you put upon our services in respect to yourself. Write then to my Lord,[1] who promises you many letters in return, that you have received his message from me. Add also other tokens of your affection and good-nature, my master, for he rests on them, as he has every reason to do.

For the last two days I have had no respite except such sleep as I have got at night: consequently I have had no time as yet to read your lengthy letter to my Lord, but I greedily look forward to an opportunity of doing so to-morrow. Farewell, my most delightful of masters. Love to your grandson.

Fronto to Lucius Verus

To my Lord Verus Augustus, greeting.[2] 163 A.D.

1. From this moment, O Emperor, treat me as you please and as your feelings prompt you. Neglect

good literature, shewing its essential importance to the ruler and the general in the field. Unfortunately the letter is much mutilated, and many interesting passages are only partially intelligible. The last part is taken up with a comparison between Lucius's despatch and other historical documents of a similar character. The picture of the demoralised army is given again in the *Principia Historiae*, but the restoration of discipline was the work of Avidius Cassius and Martius Verus and the other generals.

etiam spernito, nihil denique honoris impertito, <in> postremis,[1] si videbitur, habeto. Nihil est ita durum aut ita iniurium, quod me[2] facere adversum, Ambr. 432 | si maxime velis, possis, quin ego ex te gaudiis amplissimis abundem.

Virtutes tuas bellicas et militaria facinora tua atque consulta me nunc laudare tu forsitan putes. Quibus ego rebus, tametsi sunt pulcherrimae in rem publicam imperiumque populi Romani, optimae amplissimae, tam<en> iis ego rebus laetandis virilem pro ceteris portionem voluptatis capio; ex eloquentia autem tua, quam scriptis ad senatum litteris declarasti, ego iam hic triumpho.

2. Recepi, recepi, habeoque teneoque omnem abs te cumulatam parem gratiam: possum iam de vita laeto animo excedere, magno operae meae pretio percepto magnoque monumento ad aeternam gloriam relicto. Magistrum me tuum fuisse aut sciunt omnes homines aut opinantur aut vobis credunt: quod equidem parcius mihimet adrogarem, nisi vos ultro praedicaretis: id quoniam vos praedicatis, ego nequeo negare.

3. Bellicae igitur tuae laudis et adoreae multos habes administros, multaque armatorum milia undique gentium accita victoriam tibi adnituntur et adiuvant: eloquentiae vir<tus>,[3] ausim dicere, meo

[1] Pearce *extremis*. [2] Klussmann for Cod. *mihi*.
[3] Hauler (*Wien. Stud.* 26, p. 344) gives this as the reading of the Codex for Mai's *vero*. Brakman gives *eloquentia tua*,

me, or even despise me, in a word shew me no honour, put me, if you will, with the lowest. There is nothing you can do against me, however much in earnest you are, so harsh or unjust, that you should not be for me the source of the most abounding joys.

Perhaps you may think that it is your warlike qualities and your military achievements and strategy that I am now praising. True, they are most glorious for the state and Empire of the Roman people, none better or more magnificent, yet in rejoicing over them I but take my individual share of delight proportionably with others; but in the case of your eloquence, of which you gave such plain evidence in your despatch to the Senate, it is I who triumph indeed.

2. I have received, I have received, and I have and hold a full return from you in like measure heaped high: I can now depart this life with a joyous heart, richly recompensed for my labours and leaving behind me a mighty monument to my lasting fame. That I was your master all men either know or suppose or believe from your lips: indeed, I should be shy of claiming this honour for myself did you not yourselves both proclaim it: since you do proclaim it, it is not for me to deny it.

3. In your military glory and success you have many instruments, and many thousands of armed men called up from every nation under heaven spend themselves and lend their aid to win victory for you: but your supremacy in eloquence has been gained, I may make bold to say, under my leadership, O

---

but as Mai and Hauler see the letters *v* and *r*, it seems as if the reading may be *eloquentia vero tua.*

Ambr. 431 ductu, Caesar, meoque auspicio parta[1] est . . | . .
Vat. 14 . . . . | . . spolia . . . . <regi>[2] Parthorum prompte et graviter respondisti. Scilicet hoc te a centurionibus vel primipilaribus, elegantissimis altercatoribus, didicisse? Dausara et Nicephor<i>um et Artaxata ductu auspicioque tuo armis capta sunt, sed arcem munitam et invictam et inexpugnabilem, quae in fratris tui pectore sita est, ad nomen *Armeniaci* quod recusaverat sumendum, quis alius quam tu, aut quibus aliis tu quam eloquentiae copiis adortus es? Comitem tibi ad impetrandum adscisti exercitum, sed loquentem exercitum oratione pugnantem. In ea tu parte litterarum tuarum, ut fratrem amantem decuit, sententiis magis crebris[3] et dulcibus usus es et verba modulatius collocasti; quas quom legerem—in senatu enim per valetudinem non potui adesse—quom eloquentia tua fratrem tuum urgeri viderem, ita cum tacitis cogitationibus meis compellabam: *Quid hoc rei est, Antonine? Nam tibi*
Vat. 18 *video nomen quod recusaveras acci|piendum esse et de sententia decedendum. Quid nunc meae, quid philosophorum litterae agunt? Litteris militis vincimur. Ecquid autem <parum>[4] pulchre scripsisse videtur? Numquod verbum insolens aut intempestivom? Aut num ego*

[1] m[2] has *nata*.
[2] Eight lines are lost from the beginning of Vat. 14.
[3] No convincing emendation of this unsatisfactory reading has been proposed. *cp.* however Cicero, quoted in Suet. *Caes.* 55.
[4] Klussmann.

---

[1] See ii. 213.
[2] Dausara was near Edessa and Nicephorium on the

Caesar, and under my auspices . . . . Your answer to the Parthian king[1] was prompt and weighty. Of course you learnt this from your centurions or front-rankers, those truly polished disputants! Dausara and Nicephorium and Artaxata[2] were taken by storm under your leadership and auspices, but that fortified and unconquered and impregnable citadel, which is planted in your brother's breast, against the assumption of the title *Armeniacus*,[3] which he had refused, who other than you assaulted, and you with what other weapons than those of eloquence? You called in as your ally in winning your way an army, but a vocal army fighting with words. In that part of your letter, as befitted a loving brother, your thoughts were more closely packed and took a tenderer cast, and you arranged your words more rhythmically. When I read them—for I was too unwell to be present in the Senate—and perceived your brother to be hard pressed by your eloquence, I thus apostrophized him in my unspoken thoughts: *What do you say to this, Antoninus? I see that you will have to take the title which you have declined, and retreat from your resolve. What is the use now of my letters, what of the letters of philosophers? We are outdone by a soldier's letter. Is there anything, think you, less than admirable in the writing? any unusual or unseasonable word? Or do I seem to you to have trained a vain-*

Upper Euphrates in Mesopotamia. Artaxata was the capital of Armenia.

[3] Capit. (*Vit. Mar.* ix. § 2) says this title was bestowed on both emperors after the successful campaign of Statius Priscus in Armenia in 163, but refused at first by Marcus. It appears on his coins late in 164, and he dropped it on the death of Lucius in 169.

tibi videor gloriosum militem erudisse? Quin, quod votis omnibus expetisti, habes fratrem fortem, "virum bonum dicendi peritum": eadem enim dicit ille quae tu, sed ea minus multis[1] *ille quam tu.*

4. Quom maxime haec ego mecum agitabam, orationi tuae successit Antonini oratio—Di boni, quam pulchra, quam vera multa! Plane dicta omnia et verba delenifica pietate et fide et amore et desiderio delibuta. Quid <ergo? Utrum>[2] inter duos ambos[3] meos, petitoremne an unde peteretur, magis laudarem? Antoninus erat cum imperio obsequens; tu autem, Luci, cum obsequio eras prae amore imperiosus. Eas ego orationes ambas quom dextra laevaque manu mea gestarem, amplior mihi et ornatior videbar daduchis Eleusinae faces gestantibus et regibus sceptra tenentibus et quindecimviris libros adeuntibus; deosque patrios ita comprecatus sum: *Hammo*
Vat. 29 *Iuppiter, te Liby<ae deum, oro>* . . | . . deorum etiam partim eloquentes se quam tacitos coli maluerunt . . . . contumacia ego . . . . sinit . . . . pervicacibus eloquentia incutiatur. Ne fulmen quidem aeque terreret nisi cum tonitru caderet. Ea ipsa tonandi potestas non Diti Patri neque Neptuno neque deis ceteris sed imperatori summo Iovi tradita est, ut fragoribus nubium et sonoribus procellarum,

[1] *sc. verbis.*
[2] Mai fills the gap with *agerem tum.* Brakman reads the Codex as *Quib<us> ver* . . .
[3] For the late-Latin reduplication *cp.* ii. 92, *antiqui veteres.* Klussmann would read *amicos.*

glorious soldier? Nay, you have what you have asked for in all your prayers, a brave brother, "a good man skilled in speaking." [1] *He says the same things as you, but expresses them more concisely than you.*

4. At the very moment, when I was turning this over in my mind, following yours came the speech of Antoninus—Good heavens, how many admirable things, how many true! Every saying, every word quite fascinating, steeped in loyal affection and trust and love and longing. What then? which of both my two friends, the petitioner or the petitioned, should I praise the more? Antoninus with all his imperial power was complaisant, but you, Lucius, with all your complaisance, were for very love imperious. Carrying those two speeches in my right hand and my left, methought I was more honoured and more richly adorned than the priests of Eleusis carrying their torches, and kings holding sceptres in their hands, and the quindecimvirs opening the Sacred Books; and thus did I make my prayer to my ancestral [2] Gods: *O Jupiter Ammon, I beseech thee, Libya's God* . . . . some of the Gods also preferred to be worshipped as speaking rather than as silent . . . . the obstinate be inoculated with eloquence. Even the levin-bolt would lose half its terror did it not fall to the accompaniment of thunder. That very power of thundering was not committed to Father Dis or to Neptune or to the other Gods, but to their sovran emperor Jove, that by the crashing of clouds and the roaring of storms,

[1] A phrase found in the Elder Seneca (*Controv.* i.) and Quint. (*Instit.* i. pr.). It apparently originated with Cato.
[2] Fronto was a native of Cirta.

Vat. 80 velut quibusdam caelestibus vocibus, altissimum | imperium a contemptu vindicaret.

5. Igitur si verum imperatorem generis humani quaeritis, eloquentia vestra[1] imperat, eloquentia mentibus dominatur. Ea metum incutit, amorem conciliat, industriam excitat, impudentiam extinguit, virtutem cohortatur, vitia confutat, suadet, mulcet, docet, consolatur. Denique provoco audacter et condicione vetere: omittite eloquentiam et imperate; orationes in senatu habere omittite et Armeniam subigite. Alii quoque duces ante vos Armeniam subegerunt; sed una mehercules tua epistula, una tui fratris de te tuisque virtutibus oratio nobilior ad gloriam et ad posteros celebratior erit quam plerique principum triumphi. Ventidius ille, postquam Parthos fudit fugavitque, ad victoriam suam praedicandam orationem a C. Sallustio mutuatus est, et Nerva facta sua in senatu verbis rogaticiis[2] commendavit. Item plerique ante parentes vestros propemodum infantes et elingues principes fuerunt, qui de rebus militiae a se gestis nihil magis loqui possent quam galeae loquuntur.

6. Postquam respublica a magistratibus annuis ad C. Caesarem et mox ad Augustum tralata est, Caesari
Ambr. 412, end of Quat. ii. quidem facultatem dicendi video | imperatoriam[3] fuisse, Augustum vero saeculi residua elegantia[4] et

[1] Here Fronto addresses both emperors.
[2] Margin of Cod. has *rogatariis*.
[3] Naber for Cod. *imperatorem*.
[4] Niebuhr for Cod. *residui eleganter*.

as by some voice from heaven, he might safeguard his supreme sovranty from contempt.

5. Therefore, if you seek a veritable sovran of the human race, it is your eloquence that is sovran, eloquence that sways men's minds. It inspires fear, wins love, is a spur to effort, puts shame to silence, exhorts to virtue, exposes vices, urges, soothes, teaches, consoles. In fine, I challenge boldly and on an old condition—give up eloquence and rule; give up making speeches in the Senate and subdue Armenia. Other leaders before you have subdued Armenia: but, by heaven, your single letter, your brother's single speech on you and your merits will be as regards fame more ennobling, and as regards posterity more talked of, than many a triumph of princes. The famous Ventidius,[1] when he had defeated and dispersed the Parthians, to proclaim his victory borrowed a speech from C. Sallustius; and Nerva commended his acts in the Senate with words requisitioned from others. Moreover, most of the emperors that preceded your progenitors were virtually dumb and inarticulate, and were no more able to speak of their military achievements than could their helmets.

6. When the Commonwealth had been transferred from yearly magistrates to C. Caesar and anon to Augustus, I perceive, indeed, that Caesar's gift of speech was that of an imperator,[2] while Augustus was, I think, master of but the dying elegance of his

[1] Ventidius Bassus was enslaved as a child in the Social war. As legatus of Antony fifty years later he defeated the Parthians, and attained the unique distinction of a triumph over them.

[2] *cp.* Suet. *Caes.* 55. Montaigne (i. 25) speaks of "the soldier-like eloquence, as Suetonius calleth that of Caesar."

Latinae linguae etiam tum integro lepore potius quam dicendi ubertate praeditum puto. Post Augustum nonnihil reliquiarum iam et vietarum et tabescentium Tiberio illi superfuisse. Imperatores autem deinceps ad Vespasianum usque eiusmodi omnes ut non minus verborum puderet, quam pigeret morum et misereret facinorum.

7. Quod quis dicat, *non enim didicerant*, cur ergo imperabant? Aut imperarent gestu censeo, ut histriones; aut nutu ut muti; aut per interpretem ut barbari. Quis eorum oratione sua aut senatum adfari, quis edictum, quis epistulam suismet verbis componere potuit? Quasi phrenitis morbus quibus implicitus est, aliena eloquentes imperitabant; ut tibiae sine ore alieno mutae erant.

8. Imperium autem non potestatis tantummodo vocabulum sed etiam orationis[1] est: quippe vis imperandi iubendo vetandoque exercetur. Nisi bene facta laudet, nisi perperam gesta reprehendat, nisi hortetur ad virtutem, nisi a vitiis deterreat, nomen suum deserat et imperator frustra appelletur . . . .

Ambr. 411 | partum[2] subdere nefarium, falsam pugnam deferre militare flagitium, testimonium falsum dicere capital visum est . . . .

9. . . . . veteris eloquentiae colorem adumbratum ostendit Hadriana oratio[3] . . . . Osiris . . . .

[1] The marginal gloss is: <*de*> *imperatore quoad sciens esse debet et litterarum.*

[2] For the whole of this passage see Hauler, *Wien. Stud.* 25, pt. 1, pp. 162 ff. He says that he is reserving many other restorations in this letter for his forthcoming edition.

[3] From the margin of Cod.

times and such charm as the Latin tongue still retained unimpaired, rather than of opulent diction. After Augustus a few relics only, withered already and decaying, were left over for the notorious Tiberius. But his successors without a break to Vespasian were all of such a kind as to make us no less ashamed of their speaking than disgusted with their characters and sorry for their acts.[1]

7. But should one say *yes, for they had not been taught*, why, then, did they bear rule? That they might exercise it, I presume, either by gestures, like actors, or with signs like the dumb, or through an interpreter like foreigners. Which of them could address people or Senate in a speech of his own? which draw up an edict or a rescript in his own words? They ruled but as the mouthpiece of others, like men in the phrensy of delirium: they were as pipes that are only vocal with another's breath.

8. Now sovranty is a word that connotes not only power but also speech, since the exercise of sovranty practically consists in bidding and forbidding. If he did not praise good actions, if he did not blame evil doings, if he did not exhort to virtue, if he did not warn off from vice, a ruler would belie his name and be called sovran to no purpose . . . . to foist in a changeling was accounted abominable, to publish a false bulletin a military crime, to give false witness a capital offence . . . .

9. . . . . Hadrian's speech affects a spurious pretence of ancient eloquence[2] . . . . Osiris

[1] But Josephus (*Hist. of Jews*, xix. 3, 5) and Tacitus (*Ann.* xiii. 5) speak highly of the eloquence of Gaius (*i.e.* Caligula).

[2] For Hadrian's rococo tastes see Spart. *Hadr.* xvi. 5.

scilicet de facundiae mulo taceo: lyrae impar appel-
Ambr. 420 latur . . . . | apparem, non darem . . . . deus . . . . at allatum est.

10. Plerisque etiam indignis[1] paternus locus imperium per manus detulit: haud secus quam pullis, quibus omnia generis insignia ab ovo iam insita[2] sunt, cristae et plumae et cantus et vigiliae, regum pueris in utero matris summa iam potestas destinata est: opstetricis manu imperium adipiscuntur . . . .

11. Inter Romulum et Remum diversis montibus augur<antes aves de> rerum summa iudicaverunt. Et regnum Persarum . . . . equom . . . . seponet . . . . non cursu sed <equorum> priore hinnitu[3] . . . . paratus non . . . . aquilae et . . . . non si . . . .

Ambr. 420, col. 2, line 11 12. | Insidiis saepe aliorum et coniurationibus ademptum aliis imperium ad alios delatum scimus. Sed neque inventa eloquentia potest adimi neque morte adempta in alium transferri.[4] Tecum frater
Ambr. 419 tuus iuste probatis[5] facta Romuli . . . . | . . . .
Ambr. 418 . . . . | . . . .

13. *Iam Cato Hispaniam recuperabat, iam Gracchus locabat Asiam et Karthaginem viritim dividebat*[6] . . . .

[1] For Cod *indionus.*

[2] The margin gives *praesto* for this word.

[3] From the margin, but it is not clear where the sentence belongs. Naber gives further fragments from the text of Cod.: *e.g.* <*princi*>*patus* <*rerum Romanarum*> . . . . *prior* (Brakman *priorem*) *nemo.*

[4] For what follows see Hauler, *Wien. Stud.* 33, Pt. 1.

[5] Query *probat ea.* Brakman reads the first three words of the sentence as *Ego miratus tuo.*

. . . . of course I pass over the mule of eloquence:[1] he is labelled as no expert at the lyre . . . .

10. To many even unworthy sons the father's place has handed down the sovranty: just as chicks have all the marks of their kind present in them even from the egg, namely combs and feathers and crowing and wakeful ways, so for the sons of kings even in their mother's womb is supreme power destined: they receive the sovranty at the midwife's hand . . . .

11. Between Romulus and Remus, as they took the auguries on separate hills, birds decided the question of sovranty, and one of the Persian kings (is said in old days to have gained) the kingdom not by a race but by priority in the neighing of his horse.[2] . . . .

12. We know that the plots and conspiracies of others have often deprived one man of his sovranty and handed it over to another. But eloquence when once found can neither be taken away, nor when taken away by death be transferred to another. With you your brother approves these deeds of Romulus . . . .

13. *Cato was already recovering Spain, Gracchus already farming Asia and parcelling Carthage out among individual settlers* . . . . Now, Marcus Tullius was

[1] There was a proverb ὄνος λύρας, "an ass at the lyre." *cp.* Lucian, *De Merc. Cond.* 25: *Dial. Meretr.* 14; *Adv. Ind.* 4.

[2] I have given the probable meaning of the mutilated passage, according to Naber's view of it; *cp.* Min. Felix, *Octavius*, xviii. 6, and see Herod. iii. 84.

[6] From the margin, and quoted, says Hauler, from Sallust, who he asserts is mentioned in the previous lacuna.

Iam M. Tullius summum supremumque os Romanae Ambr. 417 linguae fuit[1] . . . . | . . . . vellet, Cicero autem modulatius; vos utriusque gratiam sectantes meam moderantis viam vaditis.[2]

14. Extant epistulae utraque lingua partim ab ducibus ipsis conscriptae, partim a scriptoribus historiarum vel annalium compositae, ut illa Thucydidis nobilissima Niciae ducis epistula ex Sicilia missa; item apud Gaium Sallustium ad Arsacen regem Mithridatis auxilium implorantis litterae criminosae; et Cn. Pompeii ad senatum de stipendio litterae graves; et Adherbalis apud Cirtas astu[3] obsessi invidiosae litterae; verum omnes, uti res postulabat, breves nec ullam rerum gestarum expeditionem continentes. In hunc autem modum, quo scripsisti tu, extant Catuli litterae, quibus res a se iacturis atque damnis gestas ut lauro merendas[4] historici exemplo exposuit; verum turgent <ea> elate prolata teneris prope verbis. Historia tamen potius splendide perscribenda; si ad senatum perscriberetur, etiam caute. Pollio Asinius iubilatus *Consiliorum* suorum si in formam epistulae contulisset necessario brevius et expeditius et den-

[1] From the margin.
[2] For this passage see Hauler, *Versam. d. deutsch. Philol.* 50, and *Wien. Stud.* 31, Pt. 1.
[3] Query *arte* (= *arcte*).
[4] We seem to require *ornandas* (Pearce) or *laurum merentes.*

the chiefest and supreme mouthpiece of the Roman tongue . . . . but Cicero more rhythmically:[1] both of you, aspiring to the charm of either, go the way that I guide you.

14. There are extant letters in both languages, partly written by actual leaders, partly composed by the writers of histories or annals, such as that most memorable letter in Thucydides of the general Nicias[2] sent from Sicily; also in Gaius Sallustius, the letter full of invective from Mithridates to Arsaces[3] the king, entreating his help; and the dignified despatch of Gnaeus Pompeius to the Senate touching his soldiers' pay;[4] and the recriminatory letter of Adherbal while treacherously beleaguered at Cirta;[5] but all, as the occasion required, short and without any description of events. In the style, however, of your letter there is extant a despatch of Catulus, in which he has set forth in the historical manner his own exploits, chequered with losses and failure, as deserving of the laurel crown. But there is a touch of bombast in these high-flown periods, couched in words almost plaintive.[6] History, however, should rather be written in the grand style and, if written for the Senate, with restraint as well. If Asinius Pollio had thrown the jubilations of his *Counsels* into the form of a letter, in a style necessarily terser, readier, and more compact, even if here and

[1] He is being contrasted probably with Cato.
[2] Thuc. vii. 11–16. [3] Sallust, *Hist.* iv.
[4] *ibid. Hist.* iii. The letter was from Spain; see Plutarch, *Life of Sertorius, ad fin.*
[5] *ibid. Bell. Jug.* 24. If *arte* be read, translate *straitly.*
[6] *cp.* Cic. *Brut.* 132, where he speaks of Catulus' book *De Consulatu et de rebus gestis suis* as written *molli et Xenophonteo genere sermonis.*

sius, si quod interdum respondit[1] inornatius, scripsisset melius.†

15. Tuae litterae et eloquentes sunt ut oratoris,
Ambr. 408 stre|nuae ut ducis, graves ut ad senatum, ut de re militari non redundantes. Nam neque . . . . eius . . . . de . . . . brevitatis . . . . coartatis . . . . fuit. Quis imperator, <ali>quid[2] ad senatum quom debet loqui, epistulam scriberet? Eaque tibi facultas . . . . de quibus scribendum erat quom . . . . dum . . . . se denique . . . . cum iam . . . . vita sicut prius quamquam prov . . . . ad populum dicere et . . . . quod . . . . vos . . . . exercitus insuper aut . . . . meo non ipse . . . . vel quod . . . . nos . . . . vel quod Sohaemo potius quam Vologaeso regnum Armeniae dedisset; aut quod Pacorum regno privasset; nonne[3] oratione huiusmodi explicari vis atque Nepos de re Numantina id epistula eo minore vi; *Bello insupra undique viri e nationibus adducti Hispaniae aderant*
Ambr. 407 . . . | operam gestantes . . . . scriptae . . . .

16. . . . . *Summum eloquentiae genus est de sublim-*
Ambr. 406 *ibus magnifice, de tenuibus frugaliter dicere*[4] . . . . | . . . . solitatim . . . .
Ambr. 405 . . . . | . . ego hac re . . . .

[1] Pearce suggests *res poscit.* We should at least expect *respondisset.* [2] Niebuhr.

[3] What follows is Hauler's restoration of the text from the Codex.

[4] From the margin of Cod. The words are Cicero's (*Orat.* 29). *Solitatim* is also from the margin.

---

[1] For Pollio's style see Seneca, *Ep.* 100, 7. Marcus took a dislike to this author; see i. p. 140.

there he did make some answer with a want of finish, he would have written better.[1]

15. Your letter is both eloquent, as being an orator's, strenuous, as being a general's, dignified, as to the Senate, and, as on a matter military, not overloaded. For neither . . . .

. . . . What imperator, when it is his duty to say something to the Senate, would write a letter? You, having no opportunity (of speaking to them) . . . . about which you had to write . . . .

. . . .

. . . .

. . . . that he had given the kingdom of Armenia to Sohaemus[2] rather than to Vologaesus; or that he had deprived Pacorus[3] of his kingdom; do you not wish this to be set forth in a speech after the manner in which Nepos on the Numantine affair described it in a letter so much less forcibly, thus: *in the above-mentioned war men drawn from all the nations of Spain were present* . . . .

16. *The supremest eloquence is to speak of sublime things in the grand style, of homely things in simple language* . . . .

. . . .

[2] A coin of Lucius, A.D. 164, with legend *Rex Armeniis datus* (Cohen, iii. 189, Plate 1), shews us Lucius giving Sohaemus the crown. He had been driven from his kingdom by the Parthians, and became senator and consul at Rome; for which see Photius, 94.

[3] A sarcophagus with an inscription by this Aurelius Pacorus to his brother is extant. See *Corp. Inscr. Graec.* 3559. Vologaesus had made him King of Armenia.

vicum . . . . ubi . . . . eos apud . . . . ab elo<quentia> . . . . viso . . . . neque officii obses . . . . quam philosopham . . . . nihil . . . . quidem . . . . sumpsit se . . . . valeat. Hinc quae . . . . magis minusve . . . . ut principio increpandum; ut post principia . . . . ubi gradus . . . . habenis eloquentia per . . . .[1] quando . . . .

17. Etiam Viriathus etiam Spartacus belli scientes et manu prompti fuere. Sed enim omnes universos, quicumque post Romam conditam oratores extiterunt, illos etiam quos in *Bruto* Cicero eloquentiae civitate gregatim donavit, si numerare velis, vix trecentorum numerum complebis, quom[2] ex una Fabiorum familia trecenti milites fortissimi pro patria dimicantes uno die occubuerint. Non gentium multa milia . . . . sub pellibus . . . . unum
Ambr. 414 etiam . . . . quem tu . . . . . . | . . asinus[3]
. . . . ad summam eloquentiae . . . . ubi res postulat, ... sive de re submittere[4] <orationem>
Ambr. 418 . . . . . . | . . frustra sed ad . . . . fidei commemoratae. Ceteros ars ac . . . . opes . . . . quo . . . . binos egenum meminisse.[5]

18. His te consiliis, Imperator, a prima pueritia tua non circus[6] profecto nec lorica sed libri et litterarum disciplina imbuebant. Quom multa eiusmodi consiliosa exempla in historiis et in orationibus lectitares, ad rem militarem magistra eloquentia usus es.

[1] Fourteen letters, of which the last three are *-dum.*
[2] Mai for Cod. *quod.* [3] From the margin.
[4] These four words are from the margin.
[5] These fragments from the beginning of 414 represent eighteen lines. [6] Cornel. suggests *clipeus.* Possibly *cassis.*

. . . .
. . . .
. . . .
. . . .
. . . .
. . . .
. . . .

17. Even Viriathus[1] and even Spartacus[2] were skilled in war and quick to strike. But indeed, if you wish to count up the full tale of all the orators, as many as have existed since the foundation of Rome, including those whom Cicero in his *Brutus* endowed wholesale with the franchise of eloquence, you will scarcely make up the number of three hundred all told, while from one family of the Fabii there fell fighting for their country in one day three hundred soldiers, the bravest of the brave. Not of races many thousands . . . .
. . . . to the height of eloquence . . . . where the subject calls for it . . . . or to speak on a matter in a lower key
. . . .

18. It was surely, Imperator, not the circus or the breastplate that instilled these wise ideas into you from your earliest boyhood, but books and training in letters. When you read many instances of this kind, fruitful of wise suggestion, in histories and speeches, you used eloquence as your mistress in the art of war.

[1] A Lusitanian guerilla chief (147 B.C.) who defied the Romans for many years.

[2] A Thracian slave and gladiator who raised an insurrection and held out in Italy itself for two years. 73–71 B.C.

19. Exercitus tibi traditus erat luxuria et lascivia et otio diutino corruptus. Milites Antiochiae adsidue plaudere histrionibus consueti, saepius in nemore[1] vicinae ganeae quam sub signis habiti. Equi incuria horridi, equites volsi: raro brachium aut crus militum hirsutum. Ad hoc vestiti melius quam armati, adeo ut vir gravis et veteris disciplinae Laelianus Pontius loricas partim eorum digitis primoribus scinderet;
Vat. 15 equos pulvillis instratos animadverteret; | iussu eius cornicula consecta, a sedilibus equitum pluma quasi anseribus devolsa. Pauci militum equum sublimitus insilire, ceteri aegre calce genu poplite erepere;[2] haud multi vibrantes hastas, pars maior sine vi et vigore tamquam lanceas[3] iacere. Alea in castris frequens, somnus pernox aut in vino vigilia.

20. Huiuscemodi milites quibus imperiis contineres et ad frugem atque industriam converteres, nonne te Hannibalis duritia, Africani disciplina, Metelli exempla historiis perscripta docuerunt? Ipsum hoc tuum a te diutina prudentia consultum, quod non ante signis conlatis manum cum hostibus conseruisti quam levibus proeliis et minutis victoriis militem

1 Cornel. suggests *nidore*, from Cic. *In Pis.* 6.
2 Klussmann for Cod. *repere.*
3 Jordan for Cod. *laneas.*

---

1 *cp.* below, *Princ. Hist. ad med.* and *Ad Am.* i. 6.
2 *cp.* Lucian, *De Salt.*: οἱ Ἀντιοχεῖς . . . πόλις ὄρχησιν μάλιστα πρεσβεύουσα.

19. The army you took over was demoralized with luxury and immorality[1] and prolonged idleness. The soldiers at Antioch[2] were wont to spend their time clapping actors, and were more often found in the nearest café-garden than in the ranks. Horses shaggy from neglect, but every hair plucked from their riders: a rare sight was a soldier with arm or leg hairy. Withal the men better clothed than armed, so much so that Pontius Laelianus,[3] a man of character and a disciplinarian of the old school, in some cases ripped up their cuirasses with his finger-tips; he found horses saddled with cushions, and by his orders the little pommels on them were slit open and the down plucked from their pillions as from geese. Few of the soldiers could vault upon their steeds, the rest scrambled clumsily up by dint of heel or knee or ham; not many could make their spears hurtle, most tossed them like toy lances without verve and vigour. Gambling was rife in camp: sleep night-long, or, if a watch was kept, it was over the wine-cups.

20. By what disciplinary measures you were to break-in soldiers of this stamp and make them serviceable and strenuous did you not learn from the dourness of Hannibal, the stern discipline of Africanus, the exemplary methods of Metellus,[4] of which histories are full? This very precaution of yours, a lesson drawn from long study, not to engage the enemy in a pitched battle until you had seasoned your men with skirmishes and minor successes—did you

[3] We know his *cursus honorum* from *Corp. Inscr. Lat.* vi. 1549.

[4] Probably Q. Caecilius Metellus, called *Numidicus*, who conducted the war against Jugurtha in 109 B.C.; see below, Sallust, quoted *Ad Anton.* ii. 6.

imbueres, nonne Cato docuit orator idem et imperator summus? Ipsa subieci Catonis verba, in quibus consiliorum tuorum expressa vestigia cerneres: *Interea unamquamque turmam manipulum cohortem temptabam, quid facere possent: proeliis levibus*[1] *spectabam cuiusmodi quisque esset: si quis strenue fecerat, donabam honeste, ut alii idem vellent, atque in contione verbis multis laudabam. Interea aliquot pauca castra feci, sed ubi anni*
Vat. 16 *tempus venit, castra hiberna <constitui>* . . . . | . . Catonis imaginem de senatu proferri solitam memoriae traditum est: si ob militaria facinora, cur non Camilli? cur non Capitolini? cur non Curii aliorumque ducum?[2] . . . .

Ad Verum Imp. ii. 7 (Naber, p. 133).

| VERO AUGUSTO Domino meo.

Ambr. 433, *ad init.* 1. Quanta et quam vetus familiaritas mihi intercedebat cum Gavio Claro meminisse te, Domine, arbitror. Ita saepe de eo apud te ex animi mei sententia sum fabulatus. Nec ab re esse puto memorem te tamen admonere.

2. A prima aetate sua me curavit Gavius Clarus familiariter non modo iis officiis, quibus senator aetate et loco minor maiorem gradu atque natu senatorem probe colit ac promeretur; sed paulatim amicitia

[1] Mai for Cod. *lenibus*.
[2] All this from *Catonis* is from the margin of Cod. A gloss also adds *tres triumphi de Africanis* (Mai).

not learn it from Cato, a man equally consummate as orator and as commander? I subjoin Cato's very words, in which you can detect the express counterpart of your measures: *Meanwhile I tested each separate squadron, maniple, cohort, to gauge its capabilities. By little combats I found out the calibre of each man: if a soldier had done gallant service I rewarded him handsomely, that others might have a mind to the same, and in my address to the soldiers I was profuse in his praise. Meanwhile I made a few encampments here and there, but when the season of the year came round, I established winter quarters*[1] . . . . tradition tells us that Cato's bust used to be carried forth from the Senate: if by reason of his military exploits, why not the bust of Camillus? why not of Capitolinus? why not of Curius and other generals? . . . .

Fronto to Lucius Verus

To my Lord Verus Augustus. 163 A.D.

1. How great and long-standing is the intimacy which subsisted between me and Gavius Clarus is well known, I think, my Lord, to you. So often have I spoken of him from the fulness of my heart before you. Nor does it seem to me amiss to remind you of this, well as you remember it.

2. From his earliest years Gavius Clarus devoted himself to me as a personal friend, not only in those good offices with which a senator, lesser in age and rank, rightly honours and deserves well of another senator, higher in rank and older than himself. But gradually our friendship reached such a

[1] From an unknown work of Cato.

nostra eo processit ut neque illum pigeret nec me puderet ea illum oboedire mihi, quae clientes, quae liberti fideles ac laboriosi obsequuntur: nulla hoc aut mea insolentia aut illius adulatione; sed mutua caritas nostra et amor verus ademit utrique nostrum in officiis moderandis omnem detrectationem. Quid ego memorem negotia in foro nostra minima maximaque ab eo curata? aut domi quom[1] uspiam recte
Ambr. 424 clausum aut opsignatum aut curatum aut confectum | quid velim, me uni huic mandasse et concredisse.

3. Sed, quod alumnus meus aegre toleraret, valetudini meae curandae ita semper studuit, tantam omni tempore etiam operam dedit, ut excubaret etiam aegro mihi et, ubi meis ego uti manibus per valetudinem non possem, manu sua cibos ad os meum adferret. Postremo, si quid humanitus, absente Victorino et domino fratre meo, mihi accidisset, huic iusta corpori meo curanda mandavi. Praesentibus etiam illis ab hoc potissimum corpus meum contrectari volui, quo minus doloris ad fratrem et generum meum ex contactu ullo corporis mei perveniret.

4. Haec mihi cum Gavio Claro iura sunt. Iam ego, si res familiaris mihi largior esset, ne quid ad senatoris munia facile toleranda deesset, omni <ei>[2] ope subvenirem; neque umquam ego huius negotii causa eum trans mare proficisci paterer. Nunc et

[1] Haupt for Cod. *quod*. [2] Heindorf.

stage that, without dislike on his part or shame on mine, he could pay me the deference of a client, the respect that is shewn by faithful and diligent freedmen : this not from any arrogance on my part or servility on his, but our mutual affection and genuine love did away with any reluctance for either of us in the regulation of our duties. What need for me to mention his attention to my affairs in the forum, the least equally with the greatest; or at home, when I wished anything anywhere duly closed or sealed or attended to or completed, how I entrusted and confided it to him alone.

3. But, though my foster child would hardly shew such complaisance, he always devoted such attention to my health, was so unsparing, too, at all times of himself, that when I was sick he even sat up with me, and when rheumatism deprived me of the use of my hands he was wont to put the food to my mouth with his own hand. Lastly, I commissioned him to see to it that my body had its due rites, if in the absence of Victorinus and my good brother anything happened to me such as must to all men. Even if they should be on the spot, I wished my body to be handled by him rather than by any other, that my brother and my son-in-law might be spared the pain of touching my body.

4. These are the terms on which Gavius Clarus and I stand. Now, if my means were more ample, I would help him to the utmost of my power to enable him to discharge the duties of a senator in comfort, nor should I ever allow him to cross the sea on his present errand. As it is, both the moderate

nostrae res haud copiosae et huius paupertas artior me compulerunt, ut eum invitum expellerem in Suriam ad legata, quae ei in testamento hominis amicissimi obvenerunt, persequenda.

5. Quae paupertas Claro meo nulla ipsius culpa
Ambr. 423 optigit, | sed neque paterna ulla neque materna bona fruenda percepit: eaque fine heres patris fuit, ut creditoribus paternis aegre satisfaceret. Ceterum parsimonia et officiis et frugalitate onera quaestoria et aedilicia et praetoria perfunctus est. Cui[1] quidem per absentiam eius divus pater vester sumptum praeturae de fisco vestro quom expendisset, ubi primum in Urbem Clarus reconciliata sibi valetudine rediit, omne fisco vestro persolvit.

6. Nihil isto homine officiosius est, nihil modestius, nihil verecundius; liberalis etiam, si quid mihi credis, et in tanta tenuitate, quantum res patitur, largus. Simplicitas, castitas, veritas, fides Romana plane, φιλοστοργία vero nescio an Romana; quippe qui nihil minus in tota mea vita Romae repperi quam hominem sincere φιλόστοργον: ut putem, quia reapse nemo est[2] Romae φιλόστοργος, ne nomen quidem huic virtuti esse Romanum.

7. Hunc tibi, Domine, quantis possum precibus

[1] Heindorf for Cod. *cum*. [2] Naber for Cod. *sit*.

nature of my means[1] and his straitened circumstances have forced me to banish him against his will into Syria to secure the legacies which have come to him under the will of a very dear friend.

5. This want of means has been the lot of my friend Clarus from no fault of his own, for he received no benefit from either his father's or his mother's estate; the only result of his being his father's heir was that he found difficulty in paying his father's creditors. But by economy and attention to duty and frugality he discharged all his obligations as quaestor, aedile, and praetor, and whereas your deified father paid out from your privy purse[2] the expenses of his praetorship in his absence, as soon as ever Clarus recovered his health and came back to Rome he paid in the whole amount to the imperial treasury.

6. Nothing can be more conscientious than the man, nothing more reasonable, nothing more unassuming; generous also, if I am any authority, and considering the slenderness of his resources as open-handed as his means permit. His characteristics, simplicity, continence, truthfulness, an honour plainly Roman, a warmth of affection,[3] however, possibly not Roman, for there is nothing of which my whole life through I have seen less at Rome than a man unfeignedly φιλόστοργος. The reason why there is not even a word for this virtue in our language must, I imagine, be, that in reality no one at Rome has any warm affection.

7. This is the man, my Lord, whom I commend to

[1] Yet according to Aul. Gellius he could spend more than £3,000 on a bath (Gell xix. 10, § 4).

[2] *cp* Capit. *Pii Vit.* viii. 4.

[3] Especially between parents and children. See i. p. 281 and Marcus, *Thoughts*, i. 11, and Justinian, *Inst.* ii. 18 pr.

commendo. Si umquam me amasti sive amaturus umquam es, hunc a me fidei tuae atque opi traditum tuearis peto. Quaeras fortasse quid pro eo <ut facias rogare velim> . . . .

Ad Antoninum Imp. ii. 4 (Naber, p. 106).

Vat. 144, col. 2 | Magistro meo salutem.

Quom salubritas ruris huius me delectaret, sentiebam non mediocre illud mihi deesse, uti de tua quoque bona valetudine certus essem, mi magister. Id uti suppleas, deos oro. Rusticatio autem nostra μετὰ πολιτείας prorsus negotium illud est vitae togatae. Quid quaeris? hanc ipsam epistulam paululum me pergere non sinunt instantes curae, quarum vacatio noctis demum aliqua parte contingit. Vale mi iucundissime magister.

Vat. 143 Ciceronis epistulas, si forte | electas totas vel dimidiatas habes, impertias, vel mone quas potissimum legendas mihi censeas ad facultatem sermonis fovendam.

Ad Antoninum Imp. ii. 5 (Naber, p. 107).

Domino meo.

Quintus hic dies est ut correptus sum dolore membrorum omnium, praecipue autem cervicum et inguinum. Memini me excerpsisse ex Ciceronis epistulis ea dumtaxat, quibus inesset aliqua de eloquentia vel philosophia vel de republica disputatio;

you with the strongest appeal possible. If ever you have loved me, or wish ever to love me, I beg that you will befriend him whom I commit to your trust and protection. Perhaps you will ask what I wish you to do for him . . . .

Marcus Antoninus to Fronto

To my master, greeting. 163 A.D.

While enjoying this health-giving country air, I feel there is one great thing lacking, the assurance that you also are in good health, my master. That you make good that defect is my prayer to the Gods. But this country holiday of mine saddled with state business is, in fact, your busy city life still. In a word I cannot go on with this very letter for a line or two owing to pressing duties, from which I enjoy a respite only for a part of the night. Farewell, my most delightful of masters.

If you have any selected letters of Cicero, either entire or in extracts, lend me them or tell me which you think I ought particularly to read to improve my command of language.

Fronto to Marcus Antoninus

To my Lord. 163 A.D.

This is the fifth day since I have been seized with pain in all my limbs, but especially in my neck and groin. As far as I remember I have extracted from Cicero's letters only those passages in which there was some discussion about eloquence or philosophy or politics; besides, if there seemed to be

praeterea si quid eleganti[1] aut verbo notabili dictum videretur, excerpsi. Quae in usu meo ad manum erant excerpta, misi tibi. Tres libros, duos ad Brutum, unum ad Axium, describi iubebis, si quid rei esse videbitur, et remittes mihi, nam exemplares eorum excerptorum nullos feci. Omnes autem Ciceronis epistulas legendas censeo, mea sententia vel magis quam omnes eius orationes. Epistulis Ciceronis nihil est perfectius.

Ad Antoninum Imp. ii. 6 (Naber, p. 107).

Domino meo Fronto.

Vat. 157 1. . . . . <facili>|tatem[2] historiae aptam neque illam moderationem orationi accommodatam; figuras etiam, quas Graeci σχήματα vocant, illum historiae, hunc orationi congruentes adhibuisse; Sallustium antithetis honeste compositis usum: *alieni appetens, sui profusus; satis eloquentiae, sapientiae parum*; paronomasia etiam non absurda neque frivola sed proba et eleganti: *Simulator ac dissimulator;* Tullium vero commotissima[3] et familiari oratoribus figura usum, quam scriptores artium ἐπαναφορὰν vocant . . . .[4]

2. *Quis clarioribus viris quodam tempore iucundior? quis turpioribus coniunctior? quis civis meliorum partium*

[1] Query *elegantius.*

[2] Or <*uber*>*tatem.* There is a gap in the Codex here of twelve pages, says Naber, the last being Vat. 158. The fragments he gives at the beginning of the letter do not seem to belong to it.

[3] Naber: Mai reads *commodissima.*

[4] Four lines are lost.

any choice expression or striking word I have extracted it. Such of these as were by me for my own use I have sent to you. You might, if you think it worth while, have the three books, two to Brutus and one to Axius, copied and return them to me, as of these particular extracts I have made no copies. All Cicero's letters, however, should, I think, be read—in my opinion, even more than his speeches. There is nothing more perfect than Cicero's letters.

Fronto to Marcus Antoninus

Fronto to my Lord.[1] 163 A.D.

1. . . . . a facility adapted to history, and not that restraint which is suitable for oratory; that these authors[2] employed figures of speech also, which the Greeks call σχήματα, the former those which are in keeping with history, the latter with oratory; that Sallust made use of antithesis happily arranged: *greedy of another's wealth, lavish of his own; eloquence enough, too little wisdom;*[3] of word-echo, too, and that not ridiculous or trivial but judicious and in good taste: *expert in simulation and dissimulation;*[4] that Tullius, however, made use of a most passionate figure, and one well known to orators, which grammarians call *epanaphora* . . . .[5]

2. *Who on occasion more delightful to our nobler men? Who more intimate with the baser? Who at*

[1] This letter, contrasting the characteristics of history and oratory in the matter of style, preserves for us long extracts from Sallust which would have been greatly appreciated if Sallust's works had been totally lost. It has not been thought necessary here to give the extracts in full.

[2] Sallust and Cicero. [3] Sallust, *Catil.* 5.

[4] Sallust, *ibid.* [5] *i.e.* repetition of an emphatic word.

aliquando? quis tetrior hostis huic civitati? quis in voluptatibus inquinatior? quis in laboribus patientior? quis in rapacitate avarior? quis in largitione effusior? Et octo[1] deinceps ab eodem isto verbo sententiae inchoantur. Si videbitur, id quoque animadvertito et cum animo tuo cogitato,[2] an pro cetero ornatu ac
Vat. 167? tumultu me|dium illud inculpatum sit, *cum omnibus communicare quod habebat;* nam mihi paulo hoc volgatius et ieiunius videtur.

3. Non <prorsus ineptum> post illa Sallustii et Tullii de Catilina <quod> L. Antoni<us> <. . . .>utus[3] ait putabam ostendere: *<quem exercitum> praeter veteranum <alacri ardo>re magna pars iuventutis sequebatur.* Idcirco hoc in schemate tu faceres idem quod pictor, qui numquam equom pinge<re conatus esset> pro . . . .[4] pingit . . . .

4. Iugurthae forma huiusmodi est:

Qui ubi primum adolevit, pollens viribus, decora facie, sed multo maxime ingenio validus, non se luxu neque inertiae corrumpendum dedit, sed uti mos gentis illius est, equitare iaculari cursu cum aequalibus certare; et quom omnes gloria anteiret, omnibus tamen carus esse. Ad hoc pleraque tempora in venando agere, leonem atque alias feras primus aut in primis ferire, plurimum facere, minimum de se loqui.[5] . . . . *Nam Iugurtha, ut erat*

[1] For Cod. *porro*: if this be kept, read *quot porro*.

[2] Klussmann for *quod animadvertit de te . . . citato* (Mai and Naber).

[3] Query *L. Annaeus Cornutus*, a historian of Livy's time, who is confused by Suidas with the philosopher of the same name. [4] About a hundred letters are lost.

[5] First extract to *loqui* is complete. Of the second from *Nam Iugurtha* only about one-sixth is given.

times on the good side in politics? Who a fouler enemy to this state? Who more polluted in his pleasures? Who more enduring in his labours? Who more greedy in his rapacity? Who more lavish in his prodigality? Even eight sentences in succession begin with the same word. Notice this also, if you will, and turn it over in your mind whether, compared to all the embellishment and passion, that neutral phrase—*to share what he had with all*[1]—be not a blemish; for to me this seems a little too dry and commonplace.

3. After those passages of Tullius and Sallust on Catiline I thought it not wholly irrelevant to exhibit what L. Antonius . . . . says: *whom besides a veteran army a great part of the young men followed with eager enthusiasm.* Therefore, in using this figure you would do just what a painter, who had never tried to paint a horse . . . .

4. The sketch of Jugurtha is as follows:

As soon as he grew up, endowed with bodily strength, a handsome person, but above all with a powerful intellect, he did not give himself up to the seductions of luxury and idleness, but, as is the way with that nation, rode, threw the dart, and challenged his peers in the race; and though he outstripped all in glory, yet was he a favourite with all. Besides he spent much time in the chase and was the first, or among the first, to strike the lion or other wild beasts, and doing the most he still said the least about himself.[2] . . . . *For Jugurtha, possessed as he was of a vigorous*

[1] Cicero, *Pro Cael.* 6. The passage continues: *Illa vero iudices, in illo homine mirabilia fuerunt, comprehendere multos amicitia, tueri obsequio; cum omnibus communicare quod habebat; servire temporibus omnium suorum*, etc.

[2] Sallust, *Jug.* 6, § 1.

Ambr. 82 *imp|igro atque acri ingenio, ubi naturam P. Scipionis, qui tum Romanis imperator erat et morem hostium cognovit . . . . magis quam honesti.*[1]

5. Artes imperatoriae honore summo habitae . . . quid . . . . sperent ab per . . . . tibi natura . . . . is . . . . qui tum . . . . rem . . . . omnia.[2]

Ambr. 81 6. |Ne agri quidem forma praetereunda:

Mare saevum, importuosum; ager frugum fertilis, bonus pecori, arbori infecundus; caelo terraque penuria aquarum. Genus hominum salubri corpore, velox, patiens laborum; ac plerosque senectus dissolvit, nisi qui ferro aut bestiis interiere, nam morbus haud saepe quem<quam> superat. Ad hoc malefici generis plurima animalia.

7. Tum ille persequitur non inscite:

In regnum Adherbalis animum intendit: ipse acer, bellicosus, at is quem petebat quietus, imbellis, placido ingenio, opportunus iniuriae, metuens magis quam metuendus.

8. Hoc de consulis peritia:

Nam in consule nostro multae bonaeque artes et animi et corporis erant, quas omnes avaritia praepediebat; patiens laborum,[3] *acri ingenio, satis providens, belli haud ignarus, firmissimus contra pericula et insidias.*[4]

9. Milites deinde corrupti:

Exercitus imperatori traditur a Spurio Albino proconsule iners, imbellis, neque periculi neque laboris patiens, lingua quam manu promptior, praedator ex sociis et ipsa

[1] For all these Sallust extracts see Hauler, *Rhein. Mus.* 54, Pt. 2 (1899), pp. 161–170. The extract from *Nam* covers four pages (Naber).

[2] Naber says Ambr. 82 begins at *Artes.*

[3] Cod. *laboris.* [4] m^2 of Cod. for *invidias.*

and eager character, when he came to know the temper of P. Scipio, who was then the Roman general, and the ways of the enemy . . . . rather than respected.[1]

5. The qualities of a general held in the highest honour . . . .
. . . .

6. Nor must the sketch of the country be left out:

The sea is stormy and harbourless; the country fruitful in grain, good for cattle, but not kindly for trees; there is a scarcity of water from rain or springs. The inhabitants are healthy in body, active, inured to toil; the majority succumb to old age, unless they perish by violence or wild beasts, for disease seldom claims a victim. It must be added that noxious animals abound.[2]

7. Then he goes on as follows with no little skill:

He turned his thoughts to Adherbal's kingdom: himself daring, warlike, but he whom he was to assail quiet, unwarlike, of a gentle disposition, at the mercy of any attack, the victim rather than the cause of fear.[3]

8. This of the consul's generalship:

For our consul had many excellent endowments of body and mind, but avarice was a clog upon them all: he was inured to toils, enterprising in character, but wary enough, no novice in war, and undaunted in the face of danger and surprises.[4]

9. Then the demoralized soldiery:

The army handed over to the general, Spurius Albinus the proconsul, was without energy or warlike spirit, inured neither to danger nor toil, quicker with a word than a blow, spoiler of the allies and itself the spoil of the

[1] Sallust, *Jug.* 7, § 4–8, § 1.
[2] *ibid.* 17, § 5.
[3] *ibid.* 20 §§ 1 and 2.
[4] *ibid.* 28, § 5.

Ambr. 95 *praeda hostium, sine imperio | et modestia habitus. Ita imperatori novo plus ex malis moribus sollicitudinis, quam ex copia militum auxilii aut spei bonae accedebat.*

10. Effeminatio:

Nam Albinus, Auli fratris exercitusque clade perculsus, postquam decreverat non egredi provincia quantum temporis aestivorum in imperio fuit, plerumque milites stativis castris habebat, nisi quom odor aut pabuli egestas locum mutare subegerat. Sed neque muniebantur castra, neque more militiae vigiliae deducebantur; uti cuique libebat, ab signis aberat. Lixae permixti militibus diu noctuque vagabantur et palantes agros vastare, villas expugnare, pecoris et mancipiorum praedas certantes agere, eaque mutare cum mercatoribus vino advecticio et aliis talibus; praeterea frumentum datum publice[1] *vendere, panem in dies mercari; postremo quaecumque dici aut fingi queunt ignaviae luxuriaeque probra, ea in illo exercitu cuncta fuere et alia amplius. Sed in ea difficultate Metellum nec minus quam in rebus hostilibus magnum et sapientem virum fuisse comperior, tanta temperantia inter ambitio-*
Ambr. 96 *nem saevit|iamque moderatum*[2] . . . . *exercitum brevi confirmavit.*[3]

11. Tum forma Marii:

Per idem tempus Uticae forte C. Mario per hostias dis supplicante, magna atque mirabilia portendi haruspex dixerat: proinde quae animo agitabat fretus dis ageret:

[1] Sallust has *publice datum.*

[2] In the passage here omitted the Codex has *nec miles hastatus aut gregarius* where Sallust has only *ne miles gregarius.*

[3] Of this extract rather more than one-half is given.

enemy, kept in no obedience or discipline. So by their bad morale they brought their new commander more anxiety than they gave him support or confidence by their numbers.[1]

10. Growth of effeminacy:

For Albinus, dismayed by the disaster to his brother Aulus and his army, resolved not to stir out of his province for such time of summer campaigning as he was in command, and kept the soldiers for the most part in a stationary camp, except when the stench or want of forage compelled a move. But the camp was not fortified, nor regular watches posted according to the rules of war; the soldier absented himself from duty as he pleased. Camp-followers mingled with the soldiers and went in and out day and night, and wandered about robbing the countryside, forcing their way into the farm-houses, vying with one another in carrying off cattle and slaves, which they exchanged with the dealers for imported wine and other such-like things; not content with this, they sold the state allowance of corn and bought bread for daily consumption: in a word, all the evil effects of idleness and luxury, which can be expressed or imagined, were to be met with in that army, and others besides. But in these difficult circumstances I find that Metellus proved himself a great and wise man no less than in the field, so just a mean did he keep between a pandering to popularity and undue severity . . . . and in a short time he restored the discipline of the army.[2]

11. Then a sketch of Marius:

About the same time when Marius, who chanced to be at Utica, was sacrificing to the Gods, the diviner had announced that "great and wondrous things were presaged; let him therefore rely on the Gods and carry

[1] Sallust, *Jug.* 44, § 1.
[2] *ibid.* 44, § 4 to end of 45.

fortunam quam saepissime experiretur; cuncta prospere eventura. At illum iam antea consulatus ingens cupido
Ambr. ? page *exagitabat* | . . . . *petere non audebat.*[1]

12. Animo . . . .

Simul consul quasi nullo imposito omnia providere; apud omnes adesse, laudare, increpare merentia. Ipse armatus intentusque item milites cogebat; neque secus atque iter facere, castra munire, excubitum in portas cohortis ex legionibus, pro castris equites auxiliarios mittere; praeterea alios super vallum in munimentis locare, vigilias ipse circumire, non diffidentia futuri, quae imperavisset, quam uti militibus exaequatus cum imperatore labor
Ambr. 89 *volentibus esset:* . . . . | . . . . *bene atque decore gesta.*[2]

13. Sed forma ea imperatoris: perlege et voluptaria[3] . . . .:

Sed in his erat Sempronia, quae multa saepe virilis audaciae facinora commiserat. Haec mulier genere atque forma, praeterea viro liberis satis fortunata fuit; Graecis litteris et Latinis docta; psallere saltare elegantius quam necesse est probae; multa alia quae instrumenta luxuriae sunt. Sed ei cariora . . . . *quam peteretur.*[4]

[1] About one-third of this extract is given.
[2] About two-thirds of this extract are given.
[3] The margin has *volup atiua.*
[4] About one-half of this extract is given.

through what he had in mind: let him put fortune to the touch as often as he would; all would turn out well." Now, for a long time past Marius had been fired with an intense desire to be consul . . . . had not ventured to sue for the consulship.[1]

12. . . . .

At the same time the consul, as though no duty was delegated, saw to everything himself, was present everywhere, giving praise, giving blame where due. Himself armed and alert, he forced his soldiers to be so likewise; and he shewed no less caution in fortifying camps and in posting at the gates a watch from the legionaries of the cohort, and in front of the camp from the auxiliary cavalry, than in making marches; he stationed others besides above the rampart in entrenchments, and went the rounds of the watch in person, not so much from any doubt that what he had ordered would be done, as that the soldiers might endure cheerfully toils which they saw shared by their leader: . . . . conducted with dignity and success.[2]

13. But that is the sketch of a commander: listen to some things also in a more sensuous strain:

Among these was Sempronia, who had done many deeds that often shewed the daring of a man. Here was a woman sufficiently happy in her birth and her beauty, not to mention in her husband and children; she was learned in Greek and Latin literature; she could sing and dance more attractively than was required by an honest woman; and there were many other things which minister to luxury. But she valued everything more . . . . than solicited by them.[3]

[1] Sallust, *Jug.* 63, §§ 1–7.
[2] *ibid.* 100, §§ 3–5.
[3] *ibid. Cat.* 25.

14. *Quibus rebus permota civitas atque immutata nobis facies; ex summa laetitia*[1] *lasciviaque, quae diuturna quies pepererat, repente omnes tristitia invasit; festinare, trepidare, neque loco nec homini cuiquam satis credere; neque bellum gerere neque pacem habere: suo quisque metu pericula metiri. Ad hoc mulieres, quibus reipublicae*
Ambr. 90 *magnitudine belli timor insolitus, adflic|tare sese, manus supplices ad caelum tendere, miserari parvos liberos, rogitare omnia, omni rumore*[2] *pavere, adripere omnia, superbia atque deliciis omissis sibi patriaeque diffidere.*

15. Forma, qua flagitia disciplinae plebis describuntur:

Nam semper in civitate, quis opes nullae sunt, bonis invident, malos extollunt, vetera odere, nova exoptant; odio suarum rerum mutari omnia student; turba atque seditionibus sine cura aluntur; quoniam egestas facile sine damno habetur.[3]

. . . .

Ad Amicos, i. 7 (Naber, p. 179).

Ambr. 321 *ad init* | Fronto Aufidio Victorino salutem.

Antoninus Aquila vir doctus est et facundus. Quod tu dicas, *Audistine eum declamitantem?* Non

[1] m[1] *luxuria.*

[2] *Omni rumore* and *adripere omnia* are not found in our Sallust.

[3] This letter, says Hauler (*Rhein. Mus.* 54, Pt. 2, p. 161), is followed by an undeciphered letter of thanks from Marcus. To this apparently belong the fragments given by Naber (p. 111; Ambr. 89, col. 2): *misisti . . . nonus . . . sed quem*

14. *By these events the state was stirred to its depths, and the face of the city transformed for us: from the height of luxury and licentiousness, the outcome of a long-standing peace, all were suddenly seized with gloom; there was hurry, there was confusion, and no place, no person, was quite trusted; they were not at war, they were not enjoying peace; each man made his own alarm the measure of his danger. Moreover the women, unused to the fear of war, by reason of the greatness of the state, worried themselves, raised suppliant hands to heaven, bemoaned their little children, questioned everything, quaked at every rumour, snatched at every bit of news, and forgetting their pride and their pleasures, were despondent for themselves and their country.*[1]

15. Sketch of the insubordination of the people and their excesses:

For in a state those who have no wealth of their own invariably envy the better classes, glorify the bad, hate what is old, hanker after change; from discontent with their own condition, they are eager for a revolution; disorder and public discord provide them with subsistence without any effort of their own, since poverty is easily maintained without loss.[2]

. . . .

? 164 A.D.

FRONTO to Aufidius Victorinus, greeting.

Antoninus Aquila[3] is a learned man and an eloquent. But should you say, *Have you heard him*

[1] Sallust, *Cat.* 31, §§ 1–3. [2] *ibid.* 37, § 3.

[3] An eminent rhetorician of Galatia; see Philost. *Vit. Soph.* ii., under Chrestus.

. . . *sal<utem>*. It may have reference to the letters which follow *Ad Antoninum*, ii. 7 and 8.

mediusfidius ipse audivi, sed credidi affirmantibus id doctissimis et honestissimis et mihi carissimis viris, quos et iudicare recte posse et ex animi sententia testimonium perhibere certe scio.

Velim, Domine, ut adiuves eum quo facilius in civitate aliqua istius provinciae publice instituendis adulescentibus adsciscatur. Impense istud a te peto: fautum[1] enim Aquilae volo honoris eorum causa, qui pro eo studiose laborant; nec ita ei studerent profecto, nisi dignum tanto studio arbitrarentur; nec nisi facundiam eius magno opere probarent, tibi eum commendari tanto opere postularent, quom te gravissimum et prudentissimum iudicem cum aliarum rerum tum vel praecipue eloquentiae sciant. Ego vero etiam nomini[2] hominis faveo, ut sit ῥητόρων ἄριστος, quoniam quidem Aquila appellatur.

Ad Amicos, i. 12 (Naber, p. 181).

<Fronto> Aufidio Victorino genero <salutem>.

Ambr. 324, following 319 Litteras quas, domine,[3] . . . . <dei, si haec>[4] | meremur, et mihi filium et tibi uxorem, ut recte

[1] Heindorf for Cod. *factum*.
[2] Heindorf for Cod. *nomine*, which, however, the margin of Cod. supports, having the note *faveo illa re*.
[3] These words are from the Index (Cod. Ambr. 337; Naber, p. 172).
[4] Two pages are missing from the Codex between the last legible word of *Ad Amicos*, i. 11 (*aliter*) and *meremur* here.

declaim? no, of a truth, I myself have not, but I take it in trust on the assurance of the most learned and honourable men and very dear friends of mine, who I am perfectly certain are both able to judge correctly, and bear witness to what they really think.

I would wish you, honoured son,[1] to use your influence to get him an appointment as public instructor of youth in some state within your province.[2] I ask this earnestly of you, for I would have favour shewn to Aquila for their sake who interest themselves so diligently in his behalf, and they would surely not so interest themselves for him, did they not think him worthy of such great interest; nor unless they greatly approved of his eloquence, would they make such a point of his being recommended to you, knowing you to be a most serious and competent judge as well of other things as especially of eloquence. I however have faith in the man's very name, shewing him to be the prince of orators, since indeed he is called Aquila.

? 164 A.D.

FRONTO to Aufidius Victorinus his son-in-law, greeting.

The letter, honoured son, which . . . . The Gods, if we deserve it, will deal kindly with my

[1] This conventional use of *Domine* (cp. *Domine frater*, p. 244, and even, if the MS. is correct, *domine magister*, *Ad Ant.* ii. 1), is ridiculed in an epigram of the *Anthologia Palatina*, x. 44.

[2] Victorinus, the son-in-law of Fronto, was appointed legatus of Germany about 162.

proveniat, favebunt et familiam nostram liberis ac nepotibus augebunt et eos, qui ex te geniti sunt eruntque, tui similes praestabunt. Cum isto quidem sive Victorino nostro sive Frontone cotidianae mihi lites et iurgia intercedunt. Quom tu nullam umquam mercedem ullius rei agendae dicendaeve a quoquam postularis, Fronto iste nullum verbum prius neque frequentius congarrit quam hoc *DA*: ego contra quod possum, aut chartulas ei aut tabellas porrigo, quarum rerum petitorem eum esse cupio. Nonnulla tamen et aviti ingenii signa ostendit. Uvarum avidissimus est; primum denique hunc cibum degluttivit, nec cessavit per totos paene dies aut lingua lambere uvam aut labris saviari ac gingivis lacessere ac ludificari. Avicularum etiam cupidissimus est; pullis gallinarum columbarum passerum oblectatur, quo studio me a prima infantia devinctum fuisse saepe audivi ex eis qui mihi educatores[1] aut magistri fuerunt. Senex autem quanto perdicum studio[2] tenear, nemo est qui me leviter noverit quin sciat. Nullum est enim factum meum dictumve quod clam ceteris esse velim; quin cuius rei mihimet ipse conscius sim, ceteros quoque omnes iuxta mecum scire velim . . . .[3]

[1] For Cod. *educatores*. [2] *cp.* i. p. 239.
[3] Apparently very little is lost.

---

[1] The same person, viz. Gratia, who was possibly with child. The son here mentioned must be the consul of 199 A.D., who set up an inscription to his son of the same

daughter and your wife,[1] that all may go well, and will bless our household with children and grandchildren, and will see to it that those, who have been and shall yet be born of you, shall be like you. Daily tiffs indeed and disagreements I have with our little Victorinus or our little Fronto. While you never ask any reward[2] of any one for act or speech, your little Fronto prattles no word more readily or more constantly than this *Da* (*Give*). I on my part do my best to supply him with scraps of paper and little tablets, things which I wish him to want. Some signs, however, even of his grandfather's characteristics he does shew. He is very fond of grapes: it was the very first food he sucked down, and for whole days almost he did not cease licking a grape with his tongue or kissing it with his lips and mumbling it with his gums and amusing himself with it. He is also devoted to little birds; he delights in chickens, young pigeons, and sparrows. I have often heard from those who were my tutors and masters that I had from my earliest infancy a passion for such things. As for my penchant, however, for partridges in my old age, there is no one who knows me ever so slightly but is aware of that. For there is no deed or word of mine that I would wish to keep secret from others. Nay, whatever there be in my heart of hearts I would wish all others to know as well as myself . . . .

name: M · AUFIDIO · FRONTONI · PRONEPOTI · M · CORNELII · FRONTONIS · ORATORIS · CONSULIS · MAGISTRI · IMPERATORUM · LUCI · ET · ANTONINI · NEPOTI · AUFIDI · VICTORINI · PRAEFECTI · URBI · BIS · CONSULIS · FRONTO · CONSUL · FILIO · DULCISSIMO · (*Corp. Inscr. Lat.* xi. 6334).

[2] See Dio, lxxii. 11.

Ad Amicos, i. 13 (Naber, p. 182).

Ambr. 328

| <FRONTO> Aufidio Victorino genero <salutem>.

Graviter oculos dolui[1] . . . . Nullus dolor aut <cruciatus>[2] . . . . lateris aut internatii oriebantur. Internatium[3] Graeci ἱερὸν ὀστοῦν, Suetonius Tranquillus *spinam sacram* appellat. Ego me neque Graecum neque Latinum vocabulum ullius membri nosse mallem, dum istius doloris expers vitam degerem.

Ad Amicos, ii. 6 (Naber, p. 191).

ARRIO ANTONINO <Fronto salutem>.

Ambr. 290, col. 1, line 6 (Brakman); Naber says 287, following 288

Multum amicorum[4] . . . . | eram. Demonstratus est mihi a doctis et multum mihi familiaribus viris, quorum apud me voluntas ipsorum merito valet plurimum. Igitur, si me amas, tantum Volumnio tribue honoris facultatisque amicitiae tuae amplectendae, οἱ γὰρ φίλτατοι ἄνδρες conciliaverunt eum mihi. Igitur tam comi amicitia accipias velim quam ille volebat, Menoetiadi ζωρότερον δὲ κέραιρε quom imperabat.

[1] From the Index (Naber, p. 172; Ambr. 338). Several lines are lost.

[2] Brakman reads this word on the margin of the Codex, and instead of *aut alq* (doubtful).

[3] An emendation by Haupt (*Hermes*, i. 23) for Mai's *inter nativum*. The *sacred bone* was the lowest vertebra of the spine. In *Anthol. Pal.* xi. 38 it means "skull."

[4] From the Index (Naber, p. 189; Cod. Ambr. 277). The first part of the letter is lost in the gap that follows *Ad Amicos*, ii. 4. This gap contained pp. 339 and 338.

M. CORNELIUS FRONTO

? 164 A.D.

Fronto to Aufidius Victorinus his son-in-law, greeting.[1]

I have had severe pain in the eyes . . . . No pain or lumbago in the side or back came on. The Greeks call the back-bone ἱερὸν ὀστοῦν (the sacred bone): Suetonius Tranquillus calls it the *sacred spine*. For my part I would gladly not know the Greek or Latin name of a single member, if I could only live without pain in it.

? 164 A.D.

Fronto to Arrius Antoninus,[2] greeting.

. . . . He has been brought to my notice by learned men and close friends of my own, whose personal wishes rightly have the greatest weight with me. Therefore, if you love me, accord to Volumnius so much respect and opportunity of gaining your friendship, for very dear friends have enlisted my sympathy for him. Therefore I would ask you to welcome him with such kindly friendship as the great Achilles wished to shew, when he bid the son of Menoetius *mix the wine stronger*.[3]

[1] Publ. Consentius, in his *Ars Grammatica*, p. 2031, 16 (Putsch), quotes from Fronto, *et illae vestrae Athenae Dorocorthoro* (Rheims), words which were probably contained in a letter to Victorinus in his province.

[2] An interesting personality and a relative, probably, of Pius. We have his *cursus honorum* in an inscription set up by the municipality of Concordia (*Corp. Inscr. Lat.* v. 1874). There is an inscription also set up to him at Cirta (see Dessau, 1119). Tertullian (*Ad Scap.* 5) gives us an interesting anecdote of him in connection with a persecution of Christians in Asia Minor, 184–5.

[3] Hom. *Il.* ix. 203. The son of Menoetius was Patroclus. Plutarch (*Symp.* v. 4) discusses the meaning of these words. See also Athen. x. 6. The usual texts of Homer read κέραιε.

Ad Amicos, ii. 7 (Naber, p. 192).

Arrio Antonino <Fronto salutem>.

1. Have mi, domine fili carissime. Sicut eos qui dicta factaque tua <in> administranda provincia maximis laudibus ferunt, laetus ac libens audio, ita si quis quid remurmurat aut deprecatur, multo scrupulosius ausculto, et quo quicque modo gesseris aut iudicaveris requiro, ut qui existimationi tuae famaeque iuxta quam meae consultum cupiam.

2. Volumnius Serenus Concordiensis, si nihil in eis, quae commemorat, aut[1] verae rei demsit aut addidit, iure meritoque utetur me apud te vel patrono vel precatore. Quodsi ultra epistulae modum videbor progressus, eo eveniet | quod ea res postulat ut cum epistula coniuncta sit quaedam causidicatio. Ambr. 287? (Naber, 290)

3. Rem omnem ita, ut mihi Volumnius exposuit, proponam: simul et unumquidque verumne sit rogabo.

Estne lege coloniae Concordiensium cautum, nequis scribam faxit nisi eum quem decurionem quoque recte facere possit? Fueruntne omnes et

[1] Klussmann for Cod. *commemorarunt.*

---

[1] This letter is important for our knowledge of the status of a decurio, or municipal senator. It shews that these were elected by the whole body. The exact merits of the case at issue are obscured by the mutilation of the letter. We know from a law still preserved in the *Digest* that a decurio temporarily exiled for an offence not involving *infamia* might on his return take up his old position, but, if not a

? 164 A.D.

FRONTO to Arrius Antoninus, greeting.[1]

1. Health to my honoured and most dear son! just as I listen with willing and welcoming ears to those who are loudest in praise of your words and deeds in the administration of your province, so, if anyone grumbles at all or carps at it, I give him a much more critical hearing and require every detail of your acts and decisions, as one who would safeguard your reputation and good name equally with my own.

2. Volumnius Serenus of Concordia,[2] if in what he tells me he has subtracted nothing from the truth, nor added anything to it, has every right and claim to my services as his advocate and intercessor before you. But if I seem to overstep the limits of a letter, the reason will be, that the facts of the case require some legal advocacy to be mixed up with the letter.

3. I will set forth the whole matter as Volumnius has stated it to me, and ask you at the same time as to each point, whether it is true.

Is it provided by the charter of the Colony of Concordia,[2] that no one be made a notary except he be eligible also for the office of municipal senator?

senator previously, he could only become one with the emperor's express permission. By excluding Volumnius even for a time from the senate, Antoninus might seem to affix upon him the stigma of infamy. Fronto argues that there can be no doubt he was a senator before his exile. We learn from this letter also that the decurions had to pay for their privileges. The case came under the cognizance of Antoninus as *juridicus per Italiam regionis Transpadanae* (see inscription quoted under the previous letter).

[2] In Venetia.

sunt ad hoc locorum, quibus umquam scriptus publicus Concordiae <de>latus [1] est, decuriones?

Factusne est Volumnius decreto ordinis scriba et decurio? Pensiones plurimas ad quartam usque ob decurionatum dependitne?

Ususne est per quinque et quadraginta annos omnibus decurionum praemiis commodisque, cenis <in> publicis, in curia, in spectaculis? Cenavitne seditne ut decurio, censuitne?

Si quo usus fuit publice legando, legatusne est Volumnius saepenumero? Estne Volumnio legato semper [2] viaticum publicum decretum.

Item legationis de re frumentaria gratis a Volumnio susceptae estne in commentariis publicis descripta commemoratio?

4. Si omnia ista, quae supra dixi, ita decreta, ita depensa, ita gesta sunt, quid [3] est cur dubites post
Ambr. 289 quinque et | quadraginta annos sitne decurio, qui
scriba fuerit, pecuniam ob decurionatum intulerit,
commoda decurionatus usurpaverit, munia functus
Ambr. 295, <fuerit> [4]? Et quid est, mi fili, quid est quod ista
Brakman (Naber, 296) probari tibi planius [5] velis? Quoniam quae . . . . [6] |
Col. 2 . . . . <commo>|dis, pecuniam intulerit, munia
fecerit.

5. Post ista ultro citroque a me rogata atque responsa, nonne etiam praeiudicium . . . . [7] delatus est Volumnius quasi in curiam inrumperet, quom ei ius [8] introeundae curiae non esset ut relegato, quod

[1] Klussmann. [2] Heindorf for Cod. *per*.
[3] Cod. *id*. [4] Or query *fecerit* for *functus*.
[5] For Cod. *plenius*, a form which Fronto repudiates (p. 183).

Have they all been and are they all senators, who up till now have ever been given the post of notary public at Concordia?

Was Volumnius elected notary and senator by a resolution of the local senate? and has he made as many as four payments in respect of his senatorship?

Has he enjoyed for five and forty years all the rewards and privileges attaching to senators, at public banquets, in the senate-house, at shows? Has he dined, has he sat, has he voted as a senator?

In the case of public deputations has Volumnius been often chosen to be a deputy? Have his expenses as deputy always been voted to Volumnius from the public chest?

Again is there in the municipal registers record of a deputation on the corn supply undertaken by Volumnius at his own charges?

4. If all this that I have mentioned above has been so decreed, so paid, so done, how can you be in doubt after five and forty years whether he is a senator, who has been a notary, has paid in money in respect of his being senator, has enjoyed the privileges of being senator, has discharged its duties? And what is there, my son, what is there that you would wish more plainly proved? Since . . . . (has enjoyed) the privileges, paid-in moneys, discharged duties.

5. After these questions and answers of mine backwards and forwards, is it not also a begging of the question . . . . Volumnius has been accused of forcing his way into the senate illegally, since as a man temporarily banished he had no right to enter

[6] Thirty-seven and a half lines are lost.
[7] Five lines lost. [8] Niebuhr for Cod. *eius*.

neque ante exilium pro decurionatu omnem pecuniam neque ullam posterius intulisset. Quae cum longissimis temporibus forent perorata, Lollius Urbicus causa inspecta nihil adversus Volumnium statuit;
Ambr. 296 (Naber, 295) sed loco . . . . | . . . . sed pro . . . . istum . . . . num . . . . debet . . . . defenderit . . . . pro honore ratis, non video qui possit asse . . non insitus.†

Quid, quod imperatores nostri in Isidori Lysiae causa ita constituerunt?[1] . . . . aut . . . . an
Ambr. 304 legatio . . . . . . | . . tus . . . . simul per . . . . ignominia . . . . inuritur sempiterna[2] . . . .

Non idem dedecus est homini solitario ignominia feriri, quantum dedecus est plena liberis ac nepotibus domo infamia notari, cuius infamiae aspergo inquinat simul multos et dedecorat. Sicut non eadem clades est in proeliis unum equitem obtruncari et triremem frangi. Tur . . . .[3] armato . . . . et . . . . remis vero . . . . perierit . . . .[4]

6. Leges pleraeque poenam sanciverunt, ne quis arborem felicem succidisset. <Haec> quaenam est arboris felicitas? Rami scilicet[5] fecundi et frugiferi, bacis pomisque onusti. Nemo cannam quamvis proceram, nemo harundinem dixerit felicem. Aequiusne est arboribus honori atque tutelae poma et bacas esse quam hominibus liberos nepotesque?

[1] Eighteen lines are illegible here.
[2] From the margin of Cod.
[3] Seven lines are lost. [4] Eight lines lost.
[5] Eckstein for unintelligible letters in Cod.

---

[1] He was *praef. urb.* in 152 and following years, when this case would have come before him. We know that he condemned certain Christians, named Ptolemaeus and Lucius, to death (Justin, *Apol.* ii. §§ 1 and 2). He was also governor

it; in that neither before his exile had he paid in all the money for his senatorship nor any since. When all this had been argued out in the lengthiest of proceedings, Lollius Urbicus,[1] after examining the case, made no decree against Volumnius; but in place of . . . .
reckoned in proportion to the honour, I do not see . . . .

What again of the similar decision of our Emperors[2] in the case of Isidorus Lysias? . . . . is branded with indelible infamy . . . .

The disgrace is not the same for a single man to receive the stigma of ignominy, as is the disgrace for a house full of children and grandchildren to be stained with infamy, for this bespattering with infamy defiles and disgraces many at once. Just as the loss is not the same in wars if a single horseman be cut down or a trireme be rammed . . . .

6. Many laws[3] have fixed a penalty for cutting down "happy" trees.[4] What is this happiness of a tree? Is it not flourishing and fruit-bearing branches laden with berries and fruit? No one ever called a reed, however tall, no one ever called a bamboo happy. Is it more right that fruits and berries should count as an honour and safeguard for trees than children and grandchildren for men? . . . .

of Britain, defeated the Brigantes, a Yorkshire tribe, and completed the Wall of Antoninus between the Forth and the Clyde. See *Corp. Inscr. Lat.* x. 419 (*Add.*).

[2] Marcus and Verus. Nothing further is known of the case of Lysias. [3] *Digest*, xlvii. 7, 2; Gaius, iv. 2, etc.

[4] *Felices arbores Cato dixit quae fructum ferunt*, Paul. ex Fest. p. 92.

Ambr. 303 . . . . | . . . . globus equitum Romanorum, pars curiae in uno homine dehonestatur . . . . Raro umquam tot simul capita de caelo tacta sunt, quot tu condemnasti . . . .

7. Ille qui esse quam videri bonus maluit, fortunis parum prosperis usus est . . . . Verum est eum, qui opinionem virtutis neglegat, ipsam quoque neglegere virtutem . . . . Nec quisquam bonas artes magno opere studet adipisci, quas adeptus necne sit non studet scire[1] . . . . donicum . . . . de sententia . . . . cumulare . . . . verbum quod in sententia . . . . curia . . . . cur . . . . miror . . . . principio . . . . sin repudium dare et Gneus[2] orbari possit, id dubito. Namque id quod longum sit posse interdum fieri longius, altum altius, numerosum numerosius. Haec et eiusmodi verba video admittere aliquod augendi laxamentum, pleno autem plenius nihil fieri posse. Nam poculum profecto si
Ambr. 304 plenum sit, | magis compleri frustra postules, nisi effuderis. Enimvero quom omnibus negotiis artata sint tempora <et huic quidem> tempus alterum, <illi>[3] coniunctum alterum, reputes cum animo tuo an ista causa tempus argumenti probandi careat. Antequam decurio . . . . per <curiam> creari debuit: creatus est; ubi creatus est, usurpare honorem debuit: multifariam usurpavit; postquam usurpavit, pensionibus inferre pecuniam debuit: quater intulit; munia decurionatus <facere debuit: fecit>; . . . . et esset . . . . quidem . . . . labrum sum . . . . et tanto redemptas[4] parum valent, quidquid huc additum fuerit, frustra abunda-

[1] These five sentences are from the margin of the Codex.
[2] Buttm. would read *gnatis*.
[3] Heindorf would read *an in ista causa careas*.
[4] Klussmann for Cod. *tanta redentas*.

. . . . a troop of Roman cavalry, a part of the senate is dishonoured in the person of one man . . . . scarcely ever have so many men lost their lives physically by lightning as will lose theirs civilly by your decision . . . .

7. He, who has preferred being to seeming good, has enjoyed far from prosperous fortune . . . . Certain it is that he who cares not to be thought virtuous does not care to be virtuous either . . . . Nor is there anyone who is greatly interested in acquiring the noble arts that is not interested to know whether he has acquired them . . . . but if he can grant a divorce and Gnaeus can be bereaved—that is what I doubt. For what is long can on occasion become longer, what is deep, deeper, what is numerous, more numerous. These and similar words I see admit of some latitude of increase, but nothing can become fuller than full. For surely if a cup be full, it would be useless to ask for it to be filled still more, unless you emptied some of it. For indeed, since in all business time is limited, and one time is closely associated with this business and another with that, consider in your own mind whether this case lacks the time for proving the point urged. Before that . . . . he ought to have been elected senator by the senate: he was elected; when elected he ought to have exercised his rights: he did exercise them in many ways; after exercising them he ought to have paid in money by fixed instalments: he did pay this in four times; he ought to have discharged the duties of senatorship: he did discharge them; . . . . whatever is added to this will be a superfluity.

bit. Nam ubi quae ad fidem sat esse oportet, satis iudici non sunt, nullus finis est ambiguitatis. Ut rectam ingressis viam certus itineris est finis ac modus, errantibus aut peragrare facilius est quam pervenire . . . . minores sis . . . .

Ambr. 301 8. | Nunc aut . . . . alter . . . . tentant . . . . quantum est, nisi quod sunt . . . . lenissimum mansuetissimum doctissimum piissimum in causa non dicam bona—finge enim ambigua—tanto natu senem prohibuisse curia *interim.*

Cui aetati omnium vacatio munerum data est, aetatem <eam> nulla lex, si sacramento adigantur . . . . mei tua et aut igno<minia> . . . .[1] seni septuaginta annos egresso insignem maculam infligis, quando, oro te, abolendam? Quantulum enim vitae reliquum est ad exuendam infamiam et pristinam dignitatem sperandam. Hoc quod vocas *interim,* quanti<sper>[2] sperabit? Si tantisper dum spirat,[3] paulisper sperabit. Quis segeti torridae messem procrastinat? Nec non quis vindemiam maturam ac distillantem propellit?[4] Aut sa<ne>[5] quis tempus prorogat pomis mitibus aut floribus marcescentibus
Ambr. 300 aut facibus | ardentibus? aptum[6] soli <nas>centi verbum est *interim,* occid<enti> *confestim.* Vellem sicut tu senem differs, ita aetas quoque differret . . . . adulescentiae iuventuti prolixa vitae curricula data sunt, sicut diebus et noctibus interdum licet

[1] Three lines are lost. [2] Heindorf.
[3] Rob. Ellis for Mai's doubtful *dedisset.*
[4] The margin has *differt.*
[5] For Naber's *nec non.* [6] For Cod. *etiam.*

For when the judge is not satisfied with what ought to be sufficient to convince, there is no limit to uncertainty. As for one who starts on the right road a journey has a fixed destination and limit, so for those who get off the path it is easier to roam than to get home . . . .

8. . . . . to have shut out from the senate *meanwhile*, in a case I will not call a good one—let us call it doubtful—a man of such advanced age, most kindly, most gentle, most learned, most dutiful.

That age,[1] which is entitled to exemption from all duties, no law, if they are bound by a military oath . . . . on an old man past his seventieth year you inflict a signal stain, and when, I ask, is it to be effaced? For how brief is the life left him for shaking off his dishonour and looking forward to regaining his former rank. This that you call the *meanwhile*, how long can he expect to hope for it? If as long as he breathes, it will be but a brief time for hope. Who delays to put the sickle to the sun-browned cornfield? and who defers the vintage when the grapes are ripe and dropping their juice? Who in fact loses time when fruits are mellowing, flowers fading, and torches burning down? *Meanwhile* is a word that fits the rising sun, for the setting sun the word is *at once*. Would that old age might put the old man off as you do . . . . Before youth, before manhood lies many a lengthy lap of life, just as days and nights may sometimes

[1] No one who had reached fifty-five could be forced to become a decurion; see *Digest*, l. 2, 2, 8.

esse longis: senectus crepusculum est, quod longum esse non potest . . . . metienda sunt . . . . debet.

9. Proculus . . . . biennium illud . . . . est . . . . homini seni quidquid interim fit iuxta interim[1] fit . . . . poenam inrogatam . . . . praevertit, et quinquennium in triennium artavit. Namque meum . . . . late tum . . . . omnium facit
Ambr. 299 . . . . Clementer . . . . . . | . .[2] Proculus homo ingenio ad cetera remisso et delicato sed in sententiis dicundis ad puniendum paullo ut <opinor pro>[3]nior et infestior . . . . Plerique ad cetera visi minime serii, in iudicando tamen asperi fuere; scilicet ut pro severitate, qua carebant, obtentui saevitiam subornarent.

10. Biennium tunc de . . . . demum Volumnio pro . . . . nunc . . . . biennium vita . . . . agi a te . . . . <ex sent>entia tua res . . . . detrahi ignominiam <libe>ris nepotibus genero[4] adfinibus, quibus . . . . domi patrem fratresque reliqueris. Subleva misericordia aetatem familiarem tibi et
Ambr. 298 patritam . . . . et rescindas | . . . . interim . . . . vel tutus eum si vita . . . . vel dolor . . . . decurio . . . . pec<unia> . . . . te . . . . meum . . . . in te . . . . qui . . . . omnem pro decurionatu pecuniam dependisset. Sibi . . . . num, fili, ... ni . . . . quae . . . . quidem interdum facias <velim>.

[1] Ehrenthal would read *interitum*, but the word is repeated in the margin.

[2] Nine lines lost at the beginning of the page.

[3] Schwierczina is responsible for *opinor* and Alan for *pronior*.

[4] Klussmann for Cod. *genere*.

be long. Old age is a twilight that cannot last . . . . must be measured . . . .

9. Proculus[1] . . . . that two years period . . . . for an old man whatever is meanwhile means but a mean while . . . . quashed the penalty and shortened the five years to three. For . . . . Proculus, a man of a disposition in all other respects easy-going and pleasure-loving, yet in passing sentence was, I think, a little too ready to punish, and too severe . . . . Many who have seemed in other matters far from taking things seriously, yet have been harsh on the bench, wishing no doubt to hide their real lack of severity under a cloak of ruthlessness put on for the purpose.

10. The two years then . . . . at last for Volumnius . . . . his children, grand-children, son-in-law, and relations to be freed from infamy, for whom . . . . you will leave father and brothers at home. Relieve by your compassion an age which you know so well in your home and in your father . . . . and cancel . . . . that *meanwhile* . . . . had paid all the money for his senatorship . . . .

[1] There was a notable jurist named Proculus quoted in the *Digest*. A Cornelius Proculus is also mentioned in the *Digest* as the recipient of a rescript from Marcus and Verus.

Ad Amicos, ii. 8 (Naber, p. 199).

<FRONTO> Arrio Antonino <salutem>.

Gratulor mihi plerisque hominibus . . . .[1] esse . . . .[2] esse me a te non secus quam parentem observari. Eo fit ut ad me decurrant plurimi, qui tuam gratiam cupiunt. Quos ego non temere nec sine dilectu audio sed probe petentibus suffragium meum impertio. Iis vero qui parum probe quid a te impetratum velint, <pos>se[3] denego. Ut a me potius ill<um> . . . . te repulsam[4] Baburiana . . . . nos . . . . sua . . . . sita . . . . caros mihi viros et magno opere iis obsequi cupiam, ita tamen ut
Ambr. 297 <sum>ma[5] | mihi ac potissima sit iustitiae tuae ratio . . . .[6] tuae humanitati congruens videbatur; desiderium Baburianae[7] commendandum tibi recepi, et quam possum studiosissime commendo . . . . ego per . . . . de opere extruendo . . . . extructum. Videbatur . . . . defendi . . . . pronuntiasti quid ad . . . . quo . . . . agas quod fuit tradendum, superest quod a te . . . . in pauca conferam.

Sententiae tuae Baburiana non aequo animo sed prompto etiam et paene <libente animo obtemperavit>[8] . . . . Quid igitur postulat, quod non ambitiosum concessu, Baburianae vero <magno opere>[9] iucundum impetratu fuerit . . . . <di>cunt a . . . . quae de sententia tua usurarum . . . . penditur

[1] Six letters are missing. The preceding words are partly from the Index (Ambr. 277; Naber, p 189).

[2] Three lines are lost. [3] Naber *esse*: Klussmann *ipse*.

[4] So Niebuhr, but Naber prints *erctul. . . .*

[5] Schwierczina prefers *prima*.

[6] Two lines lost. [7] Cod. *Baburiani*.

[8] The gap is of about thirty letters. Possibly *modo* has fallen out or should replace *animo*. [9] Naber.

? 164 A.D.

FRONTO to Arrius Antoninus, greeting.[1]

I congratulate myself that for most men it is . . . . that I am looked up to by you quite as a parent. Consequently very many who desire your favour have recourse to me. I do not give them a hearing at haphazard and without circumspection, but I lend my support to those whose petition is honest. To those, however, who wish to obtain some dishonest advantage from you, I say *Impossible*. That Baburiana should rather from me . . . . men dear to me and I would most gladly oblige them, only so far however as is compatible above and before all with a regard for your justice . . . . It seemed in keeping with your humane disposition[2]; I took upon myself to commend Baburiana's wish to you, and I do commend it most heartily . . . . with regard to constructing the work . . . .

. . . .

Baburiana bowed to your decision not resignedly only but even promptly and almost willingly . . . . What then does she ask which would not be worth your while to grant, and at the same time very much to Baburiana's interest to obtain . . . . payment of interest in accordance with your decision

[1] This letter seems to refer to a contract for a public building, for part of which Baburiana was responsible. Arrius had found some fault with this, or had fined B. for the work not being finished in time.

[2] *Humanitas* was beginning about this time to get the meaning *humanity*. See Aul. Gell. xiii. 16; *Digest*, xliv. 37, etc.

. . . . extruendo adiungatur . . . .[1] quondam petita. Contulisse . . . . infamia multata videtur. Id populo quoque . . . .[2]

Ad Amicos, i. 8 (Naber, p. 179).

FRONTO Passieno Rufo salutem.

Ambr. 320, following 321 Aemilius Pius cum studio|rum elegantia tum morum eximia probitate mihi carus est. Commendo eum tibi, frater. Nec ignoro nullum adhuc inter nos mutuo scriptitantium[3] usum fuisse, quamquam ego te optimum virum bonarumque artium sectatorem communium amicorum fama cognossem, et tu fortasse aliquid de me secundi rumoris acceperis. Sed nullum pulchrius amicitiae copulandae <tempus>[4] reperire potui quam adulescentis optimi conciliandi tibi occasionem. Ama eum, oro te. Cum ipsius causa hoc peto, tum mea quoque. Nam me etiam magis amabis si cum Pio familiarius egeris. Novit enim Pius nostra omnia et in primis quam cupidissimus sim amicitiarum cum eiusmodi viris, qualis tu es, copulandarum.

Ad Amicos, i. 6 (Naber, p. 178).

Ambr. 322, col. 1 *ad fin.* | FRONTO Avidio Cassio salutem.

Iunius Maximus tribunus, qui laureatas adtulit litteras, non publico tantum munere strenue, sed

[1] Seven or eight lines are lost.
[2] Two pages are lost before the next letter (*III viris et Decurionibus*), Ambr. 306.
[3] Heindorf for Cod. *scribtitantem*. [4] Mai.

---

[1] There was another letter to Arrius in the Codex, but we have only its title in the Index (Naber, p. 189; Ambr. 277 or 292) and the first two words, *Valerianus Clitianus*.

. . . . attached to the construction of the work . . . .[1]

Fronto to Passienus Rufus,[2] greeting. ? 164 A.D.

Aemilius Pius[3] is endeared to me both by the refinement of his tastes and the absolute integrity of his character. I commend him to you, my brother. I am not unaware that hitherto we have not been on the terms of correspondents, though I have known of you through common friends as an excellent man and a lover of the noble arts, and you perhaps have heard me well spoken of. Yet I could find no fairer prospect of establishing a close friendship with you than the occasion of recommending to your favour an excellent young man. Love him, I beseech you: I ask this for his sake, but also for my own. For you will love me too the more, the more intimate with Pius you become. Pius knows all my heart, and how very much I desire to enter into close friendship with such men as yourself.

Fronto to Avidius Cassius,[4] greeting. 165 A.D.

Junius Maximus the tribune, who brought the laurelled[5] letter, not only discharged his public

[2] Possibly consul in 149, and, if so, proconsul about 164, for at this time about fifteen years separated the two offices

[3] Probably a pupil of Fronto's.

[4] The ablest general in the Parthian war. He afterwards, in 175, revolted against Marcus, and after a six months' dream of empire was assassinated.

[5] In token of victory on the successful termination of the Parthian war. So in the Peninsular war our coaches ran down through the country decked with laurel when a victory had been won.

privato erga te officio amice functus est; ita de
laboribus et consiliis tuis et industria et vigilantia
praedicator ubique frequentissimus extitit. Ad me
quidem minus valentem quom in suburbanam villam
venisset, numquam cessavit in vesperum usque fabulas nectere itinerum tuorum et disciplinae ad priscum morem institutae ac retentae; tum in agmine
ducendo et manu conserenda strenuissimi vigoris
tui et consultissimae opportunitatis; prorsus ut
nullus miles Plautinus de suis quam hic de tuis
virtutibus gloriose praedicaret: nisi quod Plautus
de suo milite cum lepore, hic de te cum amore et
Ambr. 321 cum summa fide |. Dignus est quem diligas et
suffragiis tuis ornes. Tuae propriae gloriae addideris, quantum dignitati praedicatoris tu adstruxeris.

Ad Amicos, i. 19 (Naber, p. 186).

Ambr. 279 col. 1 | <Fronto> Fulviano <salutem>.

Ego integer epistularum[1] . . . . Munus hoc ab
ineunte aetate infrequens habui et paene neglectum;
nec quisquam est hominum, nisi me fallo, qui rarius
quam ego scripserit ad amicos aut rescripserit, nec
quisquam de[2] <quo minus> quam <de me> . . . .
Ambr. 282 noscitur . . . . | den[3] . . . . ultro citroque tibi
<facul>tas est . . . . te . . . . tamen . . . .

[1] From the Index (Naber, p. 172; Cod. Ambr. 337). See Hauler (*Wien. Stud.* 33, Pt. 1, p. 175). I follow Brakman in placing here the following sentence, which Naber gives to *Ad Amicos*, i. 18.

mission with despatch, but also his private duty towards you with friendship, so unfailingly did he appear everywhere as the eulogist of your labours and measures and industry and vigilance. Indeed, when he came to me in my villa near the city, when I was far from well, he never ceased till nightfall telling tale after tale of your expeditions and of the discipline which you had restored and maintained up to the ancient standard; then of your unremitting vigour on the march and unerring instinct for the right moment for battle. In very truth no soldier of Plautus[1] so vaingloriously eulogized his own merits as he did yours, only that Plautus in the case of his soldier spoke with pleasantry, while of you Maximus spoke with affection and the utmost loyalty. He deserves your love, and to profit by your patronage. Whatever you do to enhance the honour of your eulogist will redound to your own glory.

165 A.D.

FRONTO to Fulvianus, greeting.

In the matter of letters when I was vigorous . . . . From my earliest days I have paid but fitful attention to this duty and almost neglected it; and if I mistake not, there is no man who has written to his friends or answered their letters less often than myself, nor anyone . . . . You have an opportunity of (sending)

[1] The *Miles Gloriosus.*

---

[2] To the end of the page six lines are lost.
[3] Query <*mittendi*>.

amicis et comitibus . . . . hic . . . . possi . . . .
Ambr. 281 quod . . . . non . . . . post . . . . quae . . . . | neque duco, neque umquam querar. Quid igitur? Nonne illud quoque evenire solet, ut is, qui diu amaverit quempiam, subito vel levitate morum vel copia novorum amicorum desinat amare? Scis saepenumero hoc satis multis usu venisse, sed non nostrae mensurae hominibus . . . . hoc . . . . alias . . . . amicis . . . .[1] diligentiae . . . .[2] nostrae mediocritas retinet.

Ad Verum Imp. ii. 3 (Naber, p. 131).

<Magistro meo.>[3]

Ambr. 436, following 421 . . . . | illi suis litteris subdiderunt. Ea vero quae post meam profectionem gesta sunt ex litteris a<d> me scriptis a negotio cuique praepositis ducibus cognosces. Earum exemplaria Sallustius noster, nunc Fulvianus, dabit. Ego vero, ut et consiliorum meorum rationes commemorare possis, meas quoque litteras, quibus quidquid gerendum esset demonstratur, mittam tibi. Quodsi picturas quoque quasdam desideraveris, poteris a Fulviano accipere. Et quidem quo magis te quasi in rem praesentem inducerem, mandavi Cassio Avidio Martioque Vero commentarios quosdam mihi facerent, quos tibi mittam, et quibus[4] mores hominum et sensum[5] eorum cognosces. Quodsi me quoque voles aliquem commentarium facere, designa mihi qualem velis

[1] In these lacunae five lines are included. [2] One word.

[3] Niebuhr annexes this letter to *Ad Verum*, ii. 10, which seems very unlikely. Mai suggests that it may be part of *Ad Verum*, ii. 2, which is impossible from the contents of it.

backwards and forwards . . . . to friends and companions . . . . nor do I think so, nor shall I ever complain. What then? Is not this often the case that one, who has long loved another, suddenly, whether from fickleness of character or by reason of the quantity of his new friends, gives up loving? You know that this has constantly occurred to quite a number of people, but not to persons of our type . . . .

Lucius Verus to Fronto

165 A.D.

To my master, greeting.

. . . . they subjoined to their letters. What was done, however, after I had set out you can learn from the despatches sent me by the commanders entrusted with each business. Our friend Sallustius, now called Fulvianus, will provide you with copies of them. But that you may be able also to give the reasons for my measures, I will send you my own letters as well, in which all that had to be done is clearly set forth. But if you want some sort of pictures besides, you can get them from Fulvianus. And to bring you into closer touch with the reality, I have directed Avidius Cassius and Martius Verus to draw up some memoranda for me, which I will send you, and you will be quite able from them to gauge the character of the men and their capacity, but if you wish me also to draw up a memorandum, instruct me as to the form of it

[4] Naber <*tu*>.
[5] So Cod. anticipated by Heindorf.

faciam, et ut iubes faciam. Quidvis enim subire paratus sum, dum a te res nostrae illustrentur. Plane non contempseris et orationes ad senatum et adlocutiones nostras ad exercitum. Mittam tibi et sermones meos cum barbaris habitos. Multum haec tibi conferent.

Unam rem volo non quidem demonstrare disci-
Ambr. 435 pulus magistro, | sed existimandam dare. Circa causas et initia belli diu commoraberis, et etiam ea quae nobis absentibus male gesta sunt. Tarde ad nostra venies. Porro necessarium puto, quanto ante meum adventum superiores Parthi fuerint, dilucere, ut quantum nos egerimus appareat. An igitur debeas, quomodo πεντηκονταετίαν Θουκυδίδης explicuit, illa omnia corripere, an vero paulo altius[1] dicere, nec tamen ita ut mox nostra dispandere, ipse dispicies.

In summa meae res gestae tantae sunt, quantae sunt scilicet, quoiquoimodi[2] sunt: tantae autem videbuntur, quantas tu eas videri voles.

(Naber, p. 202, *ad init. Principia Historiae.*)

<Domino meo Antonino Augusto.>

. . . . | des adesse dies . . . . in elogiis te
Ambr. 276, following 264 and 263 . . . . nime legas quod . . . . magni . . . .[3] et

[1] Heindorf *latius*.
[2] A locative used as genitive of quality.
[3] There are twenty-four lines lost at the beginning of this letter.

---

[1] From the defeat of Xerxes to the Peloponnesian war. Thuc. i. 89 ff.

which you prefer, and I will follow your directions. I am ready to fall in with any suggestions as long as my exploits are set in a bright light by you. Of course you will not overlook my speeches to the Senate and harangues to the army. I will send you also my parleys with the enemy. These will be of great assistance to you.

One thing I wish not indeed to point out to you—the pupil to his master—but to offer for your consideration, that you should dwell at length on the causes and early stages of the war, and especially our ill success in my absence. Do not be in a hurry to come to my share. Further, I think it essential to make quite clear the great superiority of the Parthians before my arrival, that the magnitude of my achievements may be manifest. Whether, then, you should give only a sketch of all this, as Thucydides did in his *Narrative of the Fifty Years' War*,[1] or go a little more deeply into the subject without however expatiating upon it, as you would upon mine in the sequel, it is for you to decide.

In short, my achievements, whatsoever their character, are no greater, of course, than they actually are, but they can be made to seem as great as you would have them seem.[2]

FRONTO TO MARCUS ANTONINUS

To my Lord Antoninus Augustus.[3] 165 A.D.

. . . .

. . . . and to the great exploits

[2] *cp.* Cic. *Ad Fam* v. 12, a letter which Lucius seems to imitate. See also Pliny to Tacitus (vii. 33).

[3] This is evidently a covering letter to Marcus with the *Principia Historiae*. The fuller account of the war was possibly, owing to Fronto's death in 166 or 167, unless Lucian (*Quomodo Hist.*, 19) refers to Fronto, never written.

fratris tui magnis rebus gestis historia non[1] indiligenter scripta nonnihil studii et rumoris additura[2] sit, sicut ignem quamvis magnum vel levis aura, si adflaverit, adiuverit.

Ubi primum frater tuus commentarium miserit, rem copiose scribere adgrediemur, si tamen hoc quod
Ambr. 275 gusto mittimus non displicebit . . . . . . | . .[3]

(Naber, p. 202.)

Principia Historiae

<Ad Lucium Verum Imp.>

Ambr. 275 1. . . | . . . . . .[4] tantas res a te gestas, quantas Achilles gessisse cuperet et Homerus scripsisse . . . . ab orationibus . . . . nis . . . . <pror>sus vereor nequa novitate aut insolentia . . . . rem cantibus et modis absonum quid modulatu et cantu cecinerim . . . .[5]

Ambr. 266 2. | . . . . Sallustius . . . :[6] *Eorum profecto uberrima ingenia frustra fuissent, ni magnificis sese rebus scribendis occupassent, itemque nisi pro magnitudine rerum gestarum scriptorum quoque ingenia congruerent* . . . .

[1] Instead of *non in-* Hauler (41 *Vers. d. deut. Phil.* 1895, pp. 78 ff.) reads *consilio et*.
[2] Klussmann for *auctura* (Mai).
[3] Four and a half lines lost.
[4] For Hauler's new readings in this tractate see *Versam.* 41 *d. deut. Phil.* pp. 78 ff and *Wien. Stud.* 38, pp. 166 ff.
[5] All the above is from the margin of the Codex.
[6] The margin adds *Homerum dicit.*

---

[1] A preface to the history of the Parthian war which Fronto was to write from materials supplied to him by Lucius. This we may presume would have had considerable

of your brother a history written in no perfunctory spirit would be likely to add some interest and celebrity, just as the blowing even of a light breeze can fan a fire however great.

As soon as your brother sends me his memoranda, I will undertake the writing of a full account, provided however that this, which I send as a foretaste, finds favour . . . .

Preamble to History[1]

Fronto to Lucius Verus. 165 A.D.

1\. . . . . these great exploits wrought by you such as Achilles himself would fain have wrought and Homer written . . . . I am quite afraid that through some novelty and unusualness . . . . I shall have sung something not accordant with songs and measures . . . .

2\. . . . . Sallust . . . : *In fact their natural gifts, however rich, would have been of no avail had they not concerned themselves with the writing of their splendid achievements, and likewise were not their talents as writers on a par with the greatness of the deeds* . . . .

historical value. This preamble covered twenty-eight pages of the Codex. Fronto praises Lucius extravagantly, setting him even above the great Trajan. But much of the eulogy is mere rhetoric, and he seems to have had his eye on a rhetorical commonplace, Livy's sketch of Hannibal. The piece is too mutilated for us to be able to judge Fronto's performance fairly, but his account of the virtues and exploits of Lucius does not tally with what we learn of him elsewhere. Lucian may be referring to Fronto in his *Quom. Hist. Scrib.* § 19, where he ridicules the contemporary historians of the Parthian war, when he speaks of ἄλλος τις ἀοίδιμος ἐπὶ λόγων δυνάμει.

Ambr. 265 . . | . . Herculi aerumnae celebres, si <non re>[1] etiam, disciplinae[2] . . . .

3. Enimvero fandi agendique laudibus longe praestantibus omnium Cato Porcius . . . . Rei factae mater natura: in navium adparatu . . . . deus alitis pinnas, ut eas effingeret homo natura tuenda: remus ergo de natura[3] . . . .

Catus ita Cato[4]<dat> Agrigentinis aratra, oppidatim statuis ornandus, qui prima acta h<ominum atque> Latini nominis subolem et Italicarum origines <urbium et ab>originum pueritias illustravit
Ambr. 268 . . . . . . | . . Xenophon hic sub Cyro voluntaria stipendia fecit . . . . quantum a stipendiis otii
In the following gap come Ambr. 267, 269, 270 datum in venando occupatur . . . .[5] | . . . .

Ambr. 272 4. | . . . . Imperium populi Romani a Traiano imperatore trans flumina hostilia porrectum . . . . principa<tum> cum pueri . . . . et mihi . . . . Liberum amanti et[6] inculpatum silentium. Namque ceteri mortales praesenti die mentiuntur; scriptorum mendacia tam culpam quam memoriam merent
Ambr. 271 sempiternam . . . . | . . . . humani . . . . tute . . . . fida . . . . comminisci . . . . parem. Nam praesenti die minuunt . . . . immo non est . . . . gens . . . . certum est . . . . fratre[7] . . . .

[1] Mai.

[2] This sentence and all those which are in the next section are from the margin of Cod.

[3] Hauler gives *Apollo deus . . . . tueri dare. Ius ergo.* Mai has *deus* and *tuendi eius.* For *Apollo* some verb seems required, and Pearce reads *accommodans*; he also suggested *tuenda* and *remus.*

[4] See Plutarch, *M. Cato ad init.*

The labours of Hercules famous, if not as facts also, (yet) by way of teaching . . . .

3. Indeed for speech and action alike the reputation of Porcius Cato stands far the highest of all . . . . Nature the mother of invention: in the equipment of ships God (supplied) the wings of a bird, for man to imitate them by having an eye on nature; the oar therefore is copied from nature . . . .

So the acute Cato, worthy of being honoured with statues in every city, gives the Agrigentines ploughs. He shed light on the earliest history of man and the races of the Italian name and the origins of the Italian cities and the childhood of the first inhabitants . . . . This Xenophon served campaigns as a volunteer under Cyrus . . . . All the leisure left to him from his campaigns he devoted to hunting . . . .

4. . . . . The Empire of the Roman People was advanced beyond the hostile rivers[1] by the Emperor Trajan . . . .

To the lover silence is free and carries no blame. For all other mortals tell present-day lies, but the lies of writers deserve a reprobation as everlasting as their memory . . . .

[1] Euphrates and Tigris.

[5] A marginal note on p. 269 of Cod. says a eulogy of Trajan was to be found on that page of the Codex. It is not clear whether Hauler found the words *a Traiano imperatore* in the text. [6] For Cod. *est*.

[7] The above fragments are from the margin, which also has *Ordo regnorum ante Romam* (Assyria, Persia, and Macedon).

Ambr. 262 5. | . . . . Macedonum opes torrentis modo magna vi ortae brevi die occiderunt: quorum unius humanae prolis aetate imperium extinctum est. Nam illa quae Alexandri comites familiaresque tenuerunt, praefecturae magis quam imperia appellandae . . . .

6. Nemini usquam oppidum neque tectum diutinum aut limen inveteratum, libertatem inopia sortiti, quia inopem subigendi[1] sterilis fructus laboris capitur . . . . vagi palantes, nullo itineris destinato fine non ad locum sed ad vesperum contenditur . . . .[2]

Ambr. 261 7. . . . . <direp>|tiones clades ediderunt, latronum potius quam hostium numero duco. Soli hominum Parthi adversus populum Romanum hostile nomen haud umquam contemnendum gesserunt: id satis demonstrat non Crassi modo clades et Antonii foeda fuga, sed etiam fortissimi imperatoris Traiani ductu legatus cum exercitu caesus et principis[3] ad triumphum decedentis haudquaquam secura nec incruenta[4] regressio.

8. Bella igitur duo maxima a duobus maximis imperatoribus adversus Parthos nostra memoria pari eventu bellata contendere inter se pro copiis cuiusque ducis et temporis[5] pergam: haud ignarus fortia

[1] Klussmann *subigenti.*
[2] The above three sentences are from the margin.
[3] Margin adds *ipsius* before *principis.*
[4] The margin has *et laudata.*
[5] Hauler, *Wien. Stud.* 24, Pt. 1, p. 529.

5. . . . . The power of the Macedonians swelling like a torrent with mighty force in a brief day fell away to nothing: and their empire was extinguished in the lifetime of a single generation. For those portions which were held by the companions and friends of Alexander deserve the name of satrapies rather than of kingdoms . . . .

6. Not one of them anywhere has a town or permanent dwelling or settled home: they owe their freedom to their poverty, for he who goes about to subjugate the poor gets but a barren return for his labour . . . . wandering, roving, with no fixed goal of their march, the end of which depends not on locality but on nightfall . . . .

7. . . . . (those nations whose) plundering raids have caused disasters I class as brigands rather than as enemies. The Parthians alone of mankind have sustained against the Roman People the rôle of enemy in a fashion never to be despised, as is sufficiently shewn, not only by the disaster to Crassus,[1] and the shameful flight of Antonius,[2] but by the slaughter of a general[3] with his army, under the leadership even of Trajan, the stoutest of Emperors, and by the retreat, by no means unharassed or without loss, of that emperor as he retired to celebrate his triumph.

8. I will proceed then to compare with one another, in respect to the forces of either leader and either occasion, the two most memorable wars against the Parthians fought with like success in our time, not forgetting withal that the doughty deeds

[1] At Charrae in Mesopotamia, B.C. 53.
[2] Mark Antony, in 36.
[3] Maximus, mentioned again below. See Dio, lxviii. 29, 30.

facinora viventium gravatius, mortuorum gratius, accipi; faveri praeteritis, invideri praesentibus. Namque invidia semper ad superstitem mordens adıt . . . . docebit ut . . . . Dempta visque extra posse
Ambr. 274 quo . . . . visui . . . . . .[1] . .|. . . . Ubi primum magnum ducem respublica poposcit, id est pensis p<arem> propositis, omnibus Arpinati paupertate aut Nursina duritia ortis ducibus bellicosior extitit . . . . Parthos Romano sanguine impiatos . . . .
Ambr. 278 orbant . . . . tranquillus[2] . . . .| oratoribus[3] . . . .
Ambr. 252: Quat. xxxvii. ends (Naber, xxxvi.) atque . . . . <hostem> | olim adversus Romanos intentum et infestum et instructum: bellis exercitatum <sane> ab insidiis ad . . . . dum . . . . in . . . . agit . . . . ratum, quom ad omne facinus audendum praeceps agebatur, nullo iam scelere quod atrocius auderet reliquo.

9. Tum praeterea e<x inst>ruend<o> . . . .[4] datum . . . . bellum . . . . <explo>randum . . . . Ad hoc . . . .[5] in bellum profectus est cum cognitis militibus hostem Parthum contemnentibus, sagittarum ictus post ingentia Dacorum falcibus inlata volnera despicatui habentibus. Multos militum imperator suo quemque nomine proprio atque castrensi et ioculari appellabat. Pigros . . . .[6] vel corniculo vel aereo vel partim . . . . cuiusque . . . . herede <usu> militari pensiones hostium spoliis feroces,†

[1] About sixteen lines are lost in these lacunae.
[2] All the above on p. 274 from the margin of Cod.
[3] In the margin here is a note, *Panegyricus Vologasi* (*i.e.* the Parthian king). [4] Nine letters.

of the living are listened to in a more grudging, of the dead in a more generous, spirit; that the past are regarded with partiality, the present with envy. For as long as a man lives snarling envy is ever at his side . . . .
As soon as ever the state called for a great leader, that is to say a man who was equal to the task before him, there appeared one who was more warlike than all the leaders reared in the needy homes of Arpinum[1] or the hardy ways of Nursia[2] . . . . Parthians stained with Roman blood . . . . an enemy of old, resolved and dangerous, and prepared to meet the Romans, trained in wars verily from ambush . . . . when he was hurried headlong into daring any wicked deed, no crime more outrageous being now left for him to dare.

9. Then besides . . . .
. . . .
He set out for the war with tried soldiers who held the Parthian enemy in contempt, making light of the impact of their arrows compared with the gaping wounds inflicted by the scythes of the Dacians. Numbers of his soldiers would the emperor[3] call each by his own name, aye, and by any humorous nickname of the camp. Those who hung back . . . . with a helmet decoration or bronze or partly . . . . by military custom payments proudly gained from spoils of the enemy such as, though victorious and celebrating

[1] Marius. [2] Vespasian.
[3] He is speaking of Trajan. See Pliny, *Paneg.* 15.

---

[a] Seven lines are lost from *datum*.
[b] From here to the end of p. 262 are thirteen lines.

Ambr. 251 quas saepe victor et triumphos celebra|ns viris legatis invidisset.[1]

10. Lucio Parthis aut dilectu novi Quirites sumendi fuerunt aut fortissimi ex subsignanis deligendi militibus tristi et molli militia corruptis. Namque post imperatorem Traianum disciplina propemodum exercitus carebant, Hadriano et amicis cogundis et facunde appellandis exercitibus satis impigro,[2] et in summa instrumentis bellorum; quin provincias manu Traiani captas variis bellis ac nunc[3] constituendas omittere maluit quam exercitu retinere. Eius itinerum monumenta videas per plurimas Asiae atque Europae urbes sita, cum alia multa tum sepulchra ex saxo formata.

Non solum in gelosas sed etiam in alias meridionalis sedis terras profectus est saluti his provinciis, quas trans Euphratis et Danuvii ripas sitas Traianus spe Moesiae et Asiae provinciae addere posse se imperio Romano adnexuerat. Has omnes provincias, Daciam et Parthis amissas partes, ultro restituit. Exercitus in Asia se pro scutis atque gladiis salibus sub pellibus delectare: ducem neminem umquam post eiusmodi vidit.

[1] For the whole of this passage see Hauler, *Serta Hartel.* 1896, p. 266. For *feroces* Brakman reads *teretes*, and for *spoliis*, *gratias*: query *paratas*. For *celebrans* m[1] has *emeritis*, which seems required as well as *celebrans*. I have read *quas* for Hauler's *quos* to make a translatable sentence.

[2] Hauler reads *inimicis* (against Mai and Brakman), with what meaning is not clear, and *ed* for *et*. Mai gave *suis*

triumphs, he had often grudged brave men, his generals (who had served him well).

10. Lucius had either to take new citizens by a levy for the Parthian war, or out of the reserve legionaries, demoralized by dull and lax service, choose the stoutest men. For after the Emperor Trajan's time the armies were almost destitute of military training, Hadrian being energetic enough in mobilizing his friends and eloquently addressing his armies and generally in the appliances of war. Moreover he preferred to give up,[1] rather than to hold with an army, the provinces which Trajan had taken in various wars, and which now required to be organized. Records of his progresses one can see set up in many a city of Asia and Europe, as well tombs[2] built of stone as many others.

He made his way not only into frozen lands, but also into others of a southern situation, to the advantage of those provinces which, lying beyond the Euphrates and the Danube, Trajan had annexed to the Roman Empire with the hope that he could add them to Moesia and the province of Asia. These entire provinces, Dacia and the parts lost by the Parthians, Hadrian voluntarily restored. His armies in Asia he amused with "sallies" in the camp instead of with swords and shields: a general the like of him the army never afterwards saw.

[1] See Spart. *Hadr.* 5 and Aug. *De Civ. Dei*, iv. 29.
[2] Such as the *Moles Hadriana* at Rome, and perhaps the tomb of Antinous in the Campus.

---

impigro sed a summa . . . . bellorum, where the *sed* seems to introduce a point in which Hadrian was deficient. With Hauler's reading we have to supply this deficiency mentally.
[3] Brakman. Hauler has *novo.*

11. A rebus—pari studio pacis—sane iustis retinuisse se fertur, plane vana apstinendo uni omnium Romanorum principum Numae regi aequiparandus.[1]
Ambr. 258 Pax | . . . . pertum est dat . . . . his <rem>-publicam sibi administrandam . . . . sis a patria . . . . nec belli adversus Parthos instaurandi amator existens,[2] ita longa desuetudine bellandi miles Romanus ad ignaviam redactus <est>. Nam cum omnibus vitae artibus tum praecipue rei militari desidia noxia est. Permultum etiam interest fortunam variam experiri et naviter milites in campo exercere.

12. Corruptissimi vero omnium Syriatici milites, seditiosi, contumaces, apud signa infrequentes, prae statutis[3] praesidiis vagi, exploratorum more palantes, de meridie ad posterum temulenti, ne armatu quidem sustinendo adsueti, sed impatientia laboris armis singillatim omittendis in velitum atque funditorum modum seminudi. Praeter huiuscemodi dedecora malis proeliis ita perculsi fuerunt, ut ad primum Parthorum conspectum terga verterent, tubas quasi fugae signum canentes audirent.

13. Tantam militaris disciplinae labem pro re Lucius coercuit, industria sua ad militandum exemplo
Ambr. 257 proposita. | Primus ipse in agmine haud saepius equo vehi quam pedibus fatisci; tam solem torridum

[1] A marginal note has *qualis et Antoninus fuit.* *cp.* Capit *Pius*, 25.

[2] This word is read with some doubt by Hauler.

[3] m[1] has *freti armis.* For all this passage see Hauler, *Wien. Stud.* 24, Pt. 1, p. 520 f.

11. The same devotion to peace is said to have withheld him from action absolutely justified, so that in his freedom from empty ambition he is clearly comparable in all the line of Roman Emperors to Numa alone.

Peace . . . . that the state should be governed by him . . . . nor being enamoured of a new war against the Parthians, so by long unfamiliarity with fighting the Roman soldier was reduced to a cowardly condition. For as to all the arts of life, so especially to the business of war, is sloth fatal. It is of the greatest importance also for soldiers to experience the ups and downs of fortune, and to take strenuous exercise in the open.

12. The most demoralized of all, however, were the Syrian soldiers, mutinous, disobedient, seldom with their units, straying in front of their prescribed posts, roving about like scouts, tipsy from noon one day to the next, unused even to carrying their arms, and, as from dislike of toil they left off one arm after another, like skirmishers and slingers half naked. Apart from scandals of this kind, they had been so cowed by unsuccessful battles as to turn their backs at the first sight of the Parthians and to listen for the trumpet as the signal for flight.

13. This great decay in military discipline Lucius took in hand as the case demanded, setting up his own energy in the service as a pattern.[1] Marching in person at the head of his troops, he tired himself with trudging on foot quite as often as he rode on horseback; he made no more of the blazing sun

[1] Mai compares Livy's description of Hannibal (xxi. 24) and Pliny's *Panegyric of Trajan*, 13.

facile quam diem serenum ferre; pulverem confertum pro nebulis pati, sudorem in armis ut in ludicris insuper habere, caput apertum soli et imbribus et grandini et nivibus neque vel[1] adversus tela munitum praebere; spectandis in campo militibus operam dare et aegros intervisere; non incuriose per militum contubernia transire, sed forte temere Syrorum munditias Pannoniorum inscitias introspicere[2]; de cultu cuiusque ingenium arbitrari. Sero ipse post decisa negotia lavatus[3]: mensa sobria, victu in castris plebeio: vinum loci, aquam temporis bibere: primam vigiliam facile vigilare, postremam iamdudum expergitus opperiri: labore magis quam otio laetari: otio ad laborem abuti: vacua militaribus tempora civilibus negotiis occupare. In penuria subita ramis nonnumquam et frondibus pro[4] supellectile usus est, caespitem interdum ut torum incubans. Somnum cepit labore paratum non silentio quaesitum. Graviora demum perverse facta severe animadvertit, leviora sciens dissimulavit: locum poenitendi reliquit. Nam
Ambr. 256 |delicta sua plerique, dum ignorari putant, corrigunt: ubi manifesta sciunt, impudentia obfirmantur . . . . certaminis fuga . . . . necessitatis . . . . <vol>uisset providere: per tot provincias, tot obsidionum proeliorum arcium stationum castellorum excidendorum aperta discrimina curas et consilia dispergere, non luxurias, ducenta tametsi profudit spolia[5]

[1] m[1] adds *se*: so Mai. [2] In Cod. follows *munditias*.
[3] m[1] *lavatu*: Naber reads *lavari*. [4] For Cod. *proprie*.
[5] From here to the end of Ambr. 256 fourteen lines.

than of a bright day; the choking dust he put up with like a mist; sweating under arms he minded as little as sweating at athletics; he left his head exposed to sun and shower and hail and snow, and unprotected even against missiles; he was careful to inspect the soldiers in the field, and go the round of the sick; he visited the soldiers' quarters with no unobservant eye; cast a casual but keen glance at the Syrians' dandy ways and the gaucheries of the Pannonians; from each man's manner of life he divined his character. After all his business done,[1] he took a belated bath himself: his table plain, his food the common camp-fare; his drink the wine of the locality, the water of the season; he keeps the first watch easily, for the last he is awake long beforehand and waiting; work is more to his taste than leisure, and his leisure he misuses for work: time not required for military duties he devotes to civil business. In a sudden emergency he has utilized boughs on occasion or leaves by way of bedding, stretching himself at times on the turf as his couch. The sleep he took was earned by toil, not wooed with silence. The more serious misdemeanours only did he punish severely, the more trifling ones he knew how not to see: he left room for repentance. For many a man corrects his own faults, while he thinks them unperceived; when he sees that they are known, he brazens them out[2] . . . . through so many provinces, so many open dangers of sieges, battles, citadels, ports, and fortresses stormed, he lavished care and counsels, not luxuries, though he showered upon them a

[1] Hor. *Ep* I. vii. 59.
[2] *cp.* Dio, lii. 34.

. . . . Num consentirem . . . . de legi<on>ibus
Ambr. 255 anxia fuit cura[1] . . . . . . | . . gnarus . . . . de
legioni<bus>[2] . . . . portare . . . . longior mora
. . . . imperator[3] . . . . quam ob rem . . . .
etiam tum iunioris decere . . . . quo minus ad
Ambr. 246 triumphum[4] . . . . habitus . . . . | spectes.[5]

14. Lucius consiliorum sollertia longe <praestantior> . . . . sciret catafractos similes esse beluis piscibus, eas eludere alto mari cernuantes . . . . in magnis persultare campestribus.[6] Equi lubrico instabiles, manus frigore inritae, arcus imbribus enerves . . . . Paucis ante diebus Lucius ad Volo-
Ambr. 245 gaesum | litteras ultro dederat, bellum si vellet condicionibus poneret; dum oblatam pacem spernit, barbarus male mulcatus est.

Ea re dilucide patet, quanta Lucio cura insita sit militum salutis, qui gloriae suae dispendio redimere cupiverit pacem incruentam. Traiano suam potiorem gloriam sanguine[7] militum futuram de ceteris eius studiis multi coniectant, nam saepe Parthorum legatos pacem precantes dimisisse inritos.

15. Iustitiae et clementiae fama apud barbaros sancta de Lucio: Traianus non omnibus aeque purgatus. Regnum fortunasque suas in fidem Lucii contulisse neminem paenituit; Traiano caedes Partham-

[1] These words from the margin. [2] *ibid.*
[3] A marginal note says: *cuiusmodi sunt hostes Parthi.*
[4] *ibid. panegy icus Traiani.*
[5] The margin has *de Parthorum belli more.*

thousand spoils . . . .
. . . .
. . . .
. . . .
. . . .

14. Lucius in the skilfulness of his measures far superior . . . . knew that the mail-clad troops were like finny monsters, that diving headlong in the deep sea they escape . . . . to prance about on the wide champaign. Horses without firm footing on the slippery ground, hands numbed with cold, bows limp with the rain . . . . A few days before Lucius of his own accord had sent a letter to Vologaesus to put an end to the war by agreement, if he would; but the barbarian, while he spurned the offer of peace, paid dearly for it.

This fact shews clearly how much Lucius had the lives of his soldiers at heart, ready as he was to purchase a bloodless peace at the price of his own glory. With Trajan, as many judge from the rest of his ambitions, his own glory was likely to have been dearer than the blood of his soldiers, for he often sent back disappointed the ambassadors of the Parthian king when they prayed for peace.

15. The reputation, too, of Lucius for justice and clemency[1] was unblemished among the barbarians. Trajan was not equally cleared in the eyes of all. No one had reason to repent having trusted his kingdom and fortunes to the good faith of Lucius: it is not easy to absolve Trajan from the murder of a suppliant

[1] The *bonitas* of Lucius is mentioned several times by the historians.

---

[6] These words are from Hauler. The margin has *Laus Traiani.* [7] Cod. *in sanguine.*

asiri<s> regis supplicis haud satis excusata. Nam etsi ultro vim coeptans tumultu orto merito interfectus est, meliore tamen Romanorum fama impune supplex abiisset quam iure supplicium luisset, namque talium facinorum causa facti latet, factum spectatur, longeque praestat secundo gentium rumore iniuriam neglegere quam adverso vindicare.

16. Bello Parthico utroque consulares viri duo
exercitum utrique ducentes obtruncati: Severianus
Ambr. 260 quidem Lucio ab urbe | necdum etiam tum profecto;
Appius[1] vero quom praesens Traianus Euphrati et
Tigridis portoria equorum et camelorum tribularet
retro ab Arbace[2] caesus est.

17. Illud eti<am commune ut>ri<que est vitio>[3] datum, histriones ex urbe in Suriam accisse. Sed profecto sicut arborum altissimas vehementius ventis quati videmus, ita virtutes maximas invidia criminosius in<sect>atur.[4] Ceterum bello an pace clarior Traianus existimandus sit, in ambiguo equidem pono,

[1] m^2 for *enim*; and over it *Santra*, a cognomen of Maximus (apparently).

[2] Cod. *Arbacer*, with *r* deleted. This and the two preceding words are from Hauler. He says that m^2 apparently reads *alatu* or *atatu* over the *ba*, meaning *Arbalatu* or *Arbalatuce*. He remarks that *Arsace* would be an easy conjecture. Over *retro* is *ad Balcia Tauri* (*i.e.* the eastern continuation of Taurus range).

[3] The additions are by Mai and Naber.

[4] So Naber. The margin has *incessit*.

king Parthamasirius.[1] For though by being the first to appeal to violence, he brought his fate upon himself in the outbreak that ensued, yet it would have been better for the good name of the Romans had a suppliant departed unharmed than been punished even justly; for in such deeds the reason of the act lies hid, the act itself is before the eyes, and it is far better to pass by an injury and have public opinion on your side than to avenge one and have it against you.

16. In either Parthian war a man of consular rank, in either case commanding an army, was put to the sword: Severianus[2] while Lucius had at the time not even left the city; Appius,[3] however, while Trajan was present in the East making more stringent the ferry dues for camels and horses on the Euphrates and Tigris, was slain by Arbaces[4] in rear of the Emperor.

17. This is also brought as a charge against both equally, that they sent for actors[5] from Rome into Syria. But assuredly as we see the tallest trees shaken the more violently by the winds, so envy attacks the greatest merits the more vindictively. For the rest, whether Trajan is to be accounted more illustrious in war or peace for my part I leave

[1] See Dio, lxviii. 17, Victor, xlviii. 10. But Pliny, *Paneg.* 16, defends Trajan.

[2] See Lucian, *Pseudomant.* 27, and *Quom. Hist. Scrib.* 21 and 25.

[3] Appius Maximus Santra (see Hauler, *Wien. Stud.* 38, 1916, p. 170). Fronto is blaming Trajan for attending to unimportant matters while his troops are attacked in the rear.

[4] According to Hauler's reading.

[5] See Capit. *Vit. Veri*, viii. §§ 10, 11, and for Trajan see Dio, lxviii. 24.

nisi quod armis etiam Spartacus et Viriathus aliquantum potuere, pacis artibus vix quisquam Traiano ad populum, si qui adaeque, acceptior extitit. Ipsa haec cum pri . . . .[1] ae nonne illis optrectationibus faces sunt? Ex summa civilis scientiae ratione sumpta videntur, ne histrionum quidem ceterorumque scenae aut circi aut harenae artificum indiligentem principem fuisse, ut qui sciret populum Romanum duabus praecipue rebus, annona et spectaculis, teneri; imperium non minus ludicris quam seriis probari; maiore damno seria, graviore invidia ludicra neglegi; minus acribus stimulis congiaria quam spectacula expeti;
Ambr. 259 congiari|is frumentariam modo plebem singillatim placari ac nominatim, spectaculis universum <populum conciliari>. Quod . . . . se oporteat . . . . namque ut famem . . . . plane . . . . Neptunum Martemque molestias illas sibi . . . . est arceant non . . . . magis aut . . . . avis vocem . . . . quam ludis spectaculorumque caerimoniis placari. Ei rei pompas et carpenta et tensas et exuvias a maioribus dicatas, elephantos, uros . . . . populus Romanus usus sit spectaculis deserti . . . . constrepi aut linguis pluribus ominari. Haec a me detrectationis refutandae causa memorata sunt.

18. Ceterum . . . . Lucius autem ipse, quoquo in

[1] Four letters only are missing. Query *cum praecipue* Pearce suggests *Comprobanda*.

undecided, only pointing out that even Spartacus and Viriathus had considerable ability in war, whereas for the arts of peace scarcely anyone has excelled if indeed anyone has equalled Trajan in popularity with the people. These very things . . . . are they not in the highest degree torches to these detractions? They seem to be based on the loftiest principles of political wisdom, that the Emperor did not neglect even actors and the other performers of the stage, the circus, or the amphitheatre, knowing as he did that the Roman People are held fast by two things above all, the corn-dole and the shows,[1] that the success of a government depends on amusements as much as more serious things; neglect of serious matters entails the greater loss, neglect of amusements the greater discontent; food-largess is a weaker incentive than shows; by largesses of food only the proletariat on the corn-register are conciliated singly and individually, whereas by the shows the whole populace is kept in good humour . . . .

. . . .

. . . .

. . . . than conciliated by games and the customary pageantry of the shows. Therefore processions and couches and sacred chariots and spoils dedicated by our ancestors, elephants, urochs[2] . . . . the Roman People has made use of shows . . . . the buzzing and predictions of many tongues. These things have been mentioned by me to refute detractors.

18. . . . . Lucius, however, himself, wherever

[1] *cp.* Juvenal, *Sat.* x. 78, *panem et circenses.*
[2] Added by Brakman from the Codex.

loco gestum quid foret, ad senatores scripsit litteris diserte ad significandum rerum[1] statum compositis, ut qui facundiam impenso studio restaurare (vellet)
Ambr. 250; Ambr. 249 . . . . | . . . . . <com>|parata si quis leget, seu proavus seu pronepos virtute praestare videbitur, comparationis quidem discrimen in familiae nomine permanebit.[2]

Ad Antoninum Imp. ii. 7 (Naber, p. 111).

Magistro meo.

Orationes desiderat sibi Dominus frater a me vel a te quam primum mitti. Sed ego malo, mi magister, tu mittas; easque ut in promptu haberes, exemplaria quae apud nos erant misi tibi. Ego mox
Ambr. 72, following 90 alia conficiam | quae . . . . e<x> eo . . . . sine in<genti> mora intercedente[3] alia mihi scripserit. Vale mi dulcissime magister. Nepotem saluta.

Ad Antoninum Imp. ii. 9 (Naber, p. 112).

Ambr. 72 *ad fin.* | Domino meo.

Has interea orationes mittito. In le<gendo> duas delig<am Domino fratri tuo mittendas>.[4]

[1] This word, according to Hauler, is doubtful. Query *belli*.

[2] In the Codex follow the words *Legi emendavi qui supra. Principia Historiae Frontonis.* [3] Heindorf for *intercedendo*.

[4] Additions by Alan to supply the four words Mai says are missing (so Naber); but in his 1823 edition Mai says half a column is lost.

After this letter follow two letters, *Domino meo* and *Magis-*

anything had been done, wrote to the Senate despatches expressly composed to describe the state of affairs, as one who had the rehabilitation of eloquence deeply at heart . . . . If any one reads the accounts side by side, as to whether the great-grandfather or the great-grandson shall appear to be first in merit, however the question of superiority be decided, the difference will only be a family matter

Marcus Antoninus to Fronto

To my master. 165 A.D.

The Lord my brother desires that the speeches should be sent to him as soon as possible by me or by you. I should prefer, my master, for you to send them, and that you might have them ready at hand I have sent you the copies I have by me. I shall soon get others made which . . . . without the interposition of any great delay, will write me others. Farewell, my sweetest of masters. My love to your grandson.

Fronto to Marcus Antoninus

To my Lord. 165 A.D.

Meanwhile send me the speeches. In looking them through I will choose two to be sent to your brother.

---

tro meo salutem, illegible except for a word here and there. They are contained on Ambr. 71 (Naber, p 112). Moreover the words, given by Naber, p. 107, at the beginning of *Ad Anton.* ii. 6 (Ambr. 143, col. 2), do not appear to belong to that letter, and I give them here as read by Brakman *Vel a* <*te*> *visum quanta sollicitudinem* <*mihi adferant*> . . . . *ita deo* . . . . *id ago* . . . . *explora diligentius*. They are from a letter of Fronto's and refer, perhaps, to his grief.

Ad Antoninum Imp. ii. 8 (Naber, p. 111).

DOMINO meo.

Pro cetera erga me benivolentia tua fecisti, quod orationum, quas frater tuus Dominus noster desideraverat, mittendarum me gratiam inire voluisti. Adiunxi ultro ego tertiam orationem pro Demostrato[1] Petiliano, de qua illa scripsi: *Adiunxi, inquam, orationem pro Demostrato, quam quom primum fratri tuo optuli, didici ex eo Asclepiodotum, qui oratione ista compelletur, a te non improbari. Quod ubi primum comperi, curavi equidem abolere orationem. Sed iam pervaserat in manus plurium quam ut aboleri posset. Sed quid fiat postea? Quid, inquam, fiat? nisi et Asclepiodotum, quia <tu> probasti,*[2] *mihi quoque fieri amicissimum, tam hercle quam est Herodes summus nunc meus, quamquam extet oratio.* Vale mi Domine dulcissime.

De Nepote Amisso, i. (Naber, p. 231).

Ambr. 149, col. 2 | MAGISTRO meo salutem.

Modo cognovi de casu. Quom autem in singulis articulorum tuorum doloribus torqueri soleam, mi magister, quid opinaris me pati quom animum doles? Nihil conturbato mihi aliud in mentem venit quam

[1] So Cod., Hauler, who says there are other variations in the preceding lines, which he does not record.
[2] See Hauler, *Wien. Stud.* 28, Pt. 1, p. 169.

---

[1] Demostratus appears twice as an accuser of Herodes in the year 142 (for the trial see i. 60 ff.), and again in 170, as we learn

Fronto to Marcus Antoninus

To my Lord. 165 A.D.

It is in keeping with all your other kindness towards me that you wish me to oblige my Lord your brother by sending him the speeches which he asked for. I have taken the liberty of adding a third speech, that for Demostratus Petilianus,[1] about which I have written to him as follows: *I have added the speech for Demostratus, but on submitting this to your brother*[2] *I learnt from him that Asclepiodotus, though he is taken to task in that speech, is not thought ill of by you. As soon as I was aware of this I did my best to have the speech suppressed. But it had already been circulated too widely to be called in. What is to be done next? What, I say, to be done, except that Asclepiodotus too since he has earned your approbation, should become a very dear friend of mine also, just as by heaven Herodes and I are now on the best of terms, in spite of the speech being extant.* Farewell, my most sweet Lord.

Marcus Antoninus to Fronto

To my master, greeting. 165 A.D

I have just heard of your misfortune. Suffering anguish as I do when a single joint of yours aches, my master, what pain do you think I feel when it is your heart that aches? Under the shock of the news I could think of nothing else than to ask you

from Philostratus, who also tells us that he wrote speeches against Herodes. The speech of Fronto here mentioned may also be the one against Herodes spoken of above (i. 65), but the allusion reads as if it were a recent one.

[2] *i.e.* Marcus.

rogare te ut conserves mihi dulcissimum magistrum, in quo plura solacia vitae huius habeo <quam> quae tibi tristitiae istius possunt ab ullo contingere.

Mea manu non scripsi, quia vesperi[1] loto tremebat etiam manus. Vale mi iucundissime magister.

De Nepote Amisso, ii. (Naber, p. 232).

Ambr. 150 Antonino Augusto | Fronto.

1. Multis huiusmodi maeroribus fortuna me per omnem vitam meam exercuit. Nam ut alia mea acerba omittam, quinque amisi liberos miserrima quidem condicione temporum meorum, nam quinque omnes unumquemque semper unicum amisi, has orbitatis vices perpessus, ut numquam mihi nisi orbato filius nasceretur. Ita semper sine ullo solacio residuo liberos amisi, cum recenti luctu procreavi.

2. Verum illos ego luctus toleravi fortius, quibus egomet ipse solus cruciabar. Namque meus animus meomet[2] dolori obnixus, oppositus quasi solitario certamine, unus uni par pari resistebat. At no<n iam> ego <uni> vel soli <obsto>, dolor e<nim> e dolore acri multiplicatur et cumulum luctuum meorum diutius ferre nequeo;[3] Victorini mei lacrimis tabesco, conliquesco. Saepe etiam expostulo cum deis immortalibus et fata iurgio compello.

[1] Charisius, *Ars Gram.* ii. 223, 26 (Kiel), quotes from the fifth book of letters *Ad Antoninum, at enim vesperi in triduum mittam.* Elsewhere Marcus always uses *vespera.*

[2] Haupt for Cod. *memet.*

[3] In this passage I follow Brakman, filling up the gaps as best I can.

to keep safe for me the sweetest of masters, in whom I find a greater solace for this life than you can find for your sorrow from any source.

I have not written with my own hand because after my bath in the evening even my hand was shaky. Farewell, my most delightful of masters.

On the loss of his Grandson[1]

165 A.D.

FRONTO to Antoninus Augustus.

1. With many sorrows of this kind has Fortune afflicted me all my life long. For, not to mention my other calamities, I have lost five children under the most distressing circumstances possible to myself. For I lost all five separately, in every case an only child, suffering this series of bereavements in such a way that I never had a child born to me except while bereaved of another. So I always lost children without any left to console me and with my grief fresh upon me I begat others.

2. But I bore with more fortitude those woes by which I myself alone was racked. For my mind, struggling with my own grief, matched as in a single combat man to man, equal with equal, made a stout resistance. But no longer do I withstand a single or solitary opponent, for grief upon bitter grief is multiplied and I can no longer bear the consummation of my woes, but as my Victorinus weeps, I waste away, I melt away along with him. Often I even find fault with the immortal Gods and upbraid the Fates with reproaches.[2]

[1] This grandson may be the one who died, aged three, in Germany (see *Ad Verum*, ii. 9, 10. below).

[2] See Marcus, *Thoughts*, ii. 2, 3; 13, 16; iv. 3, 32; vi. 49, etc.

3. Victorinum pietate mansuetudine veritate innocentia maxima, omnium denique optimarum artium praecipuum virum acerbissima morte filii adflictum, hoccine ullo modo aequum aut iustum fuit? Si
Ambr. 155 providentia res gubernantur, hoc idem[1] | recte provisum est? Si fato cuncta humana decernuntur, hoccine fato decerni debuit? Nullum ergo inter bonos ac malos fortunarum discrimen erit? Nulla deis[2] nulla fatis diiudicatio est, quali viro filius eripiatur? Facinorosus aliqui<s> et scelestus mortalis, quem ipsum numquam nasci melius foret, incolumes liberos educit, in morte sua superstites relinquit. Victorinus vir sanctus, cuius similes quam plurimos gigni optimum publicum fuerit, carissimo filio privatus est. Quae, malum, Providentia tam inique prospicit? Fata a fando appellata aiunt: hoccine est recte fari? Poetae autem colus et fila fatis adsignant: nulla profecto tam sit importuna et insciens lanifica, quae herili togae solidum et nodosum, servili autem subtile et tenue subtemen neverit. Bonos viros luctu adfici, malos re familiari incolumi frui, neque mensum neque pensum fatorum lanificum[3] duco.

4. Nisi forte alius quidem nos error iactat et

[1] m² *hoccine.*
[2] Niebuhr for Cod. *dies.*
[3] Ehrenthal *lanificium.*

3. Victorinus, a man of entire affection, gentleness, sincerity, and blamelessness,[1] a man, further, conspicuous for the noblest accomplishments to be thus afflicted by his son's most untimely death, was this in any sense just or fair? If Providence does govern the world, was this too rightly provided? If all human things are determined by Destiny, ought this to have been determined by Destiny? Shall there, then, be no distinction of fortunes between the good and the bad? Have the Gods, have the Destinies no power of discrimination as to what sort of man shall be robbed of his son? Some thoroughly vicious and abandoned wretch, who had far better himself never been born, rears his children safely and leaves them at his death to survive him.[2] Victorinus, a blameless man, is bereaved of his darling son, and yet it would have been in the highest interests of the state that as many as possible of his kind should be born. Why Providence—out upon it!—if it provides unfairly? The Destinies, they say, are called so from the word "to destine": is this to destine rightly? Now the poets assign to the Destinies distaffs and threads. Surely no spinner would be so perverse and unskilful as to spin for her master's toga a heavy and knotty yarn, but for a slave's dress a fine and delicate one. For good men to be stricken with sorrow while the bad enjoy every domestic felicity—such a spinning performance by the Destinies I hold to be neither by weight nor rate.[3]

4. Unless maybe quite another error throws us

[1] See Dio, lxxii. 11. [2] *cp.* Psalms, xvii. 14.

[3] Lit. *task weighed or measured.* It would almost do to translate it "neither in rhyme nor reason."

ignari rerum, quae mala sunt quasi prospera concupiscimus, contra quae bona sunt pro adversis aversamur, et mors ipsa, quae omnibus luctuosa videtur, pausam laborum adfert et sollicitudinum et
Ambr. 156 calamitatum miser|rimisque corporis vinculis liberatos ad tranquilla nos et amoena et omnibus bonis referta animarumque conciliabula travehit. Hoc ego ita esse facilius crediderim quam cuncta humana aut nulla aut iniqua providentia regi.

5. Quodsi mors gratulanda potius est hominibus quam lamentanda, quanto quisque eam natu minor adeptus est, tanto beatior et dis acceptior existimandus est, ocius corporis malis exutus, ocius ad honores liberae animae usurpandos excitus.[1] Quod tamen verum sit licet, parvi nostra refert qui desideramus amissos: nec quicquam nos animarum immortalitas consolatur, qui carissimis nostris dum vivimus caremus. Istum statum vocem formam auram[2] liberam quaerimus; faciem defunctorum miserandam maeremus, os obseratum, oculos eversos, colorem undique deletum. Si maxime esse animas immortales constet, erit hoc philosophis disserendi argumentum, non parentibus desiderandi remedium.

6. Sed utcumque sunt ista divinitus ordinata,

[1] For Cod. *exictus*.
[2] Or = *animam* (πνεῦμα).

out, and through ignorance of the facts we are coveting what is evil, as though it were to our advantage, and, on the other hand, turning away from what is good, as though it were to our harm,[1] whereas death itself, which seems grievous to all, brings rest from toil and care and trouble, and freeing us from these most wretched fetters of the body transports us to those serene and delightful assemblies of souls where all joys are to be found. I would more readily believe that this is so than that all human things are governed either by no Providence or by one that acts unfairly.[2]

5. But if death be rather a matter for welcome than for mourning, the younger each one attains to it the happier must he be accounted and the greater favourite of the Gods,[3] released as he will have been the sooner from the ills of the body, and the sooner called forth to inherit the privileges of an enfranchised soul. Yet all this, true though it be, makes little difference to us who long for our lost ones, nor does the immortality of souls bring us the slightest consolation, seeing that in this life we are bereft of our best-beloved ones. We miss the well-known gait, the voice, the features, the free air; we mourn over the pitiable face of the dead, the lips sealed, the eyes turned, the hue of life all fled. Be the immortality of the soul ever so established, that will be a theme for the disputations of philosophers, it will never assuage the yearning of a parent.

6. But however these things have been ordained

[1] *cp.* Marcus, *Thoughts*, iv. 58; ix. 2; x. 36.

[2] *ibid.* ii. 11; vi. 44.

[3] *cp.* the well-known fragment of Menander, ὃν οἱ θεοὶ φιλοῦσιν ἀποθνῄσκει νέος.

mihi quidem neutiquam diutinam adferent sollicitudinem, cui tam propinqua mors. Sive in aeternum
Ambr. 180 extinguimur, olim cupienti | mihi, tandem . . . . tu acerbiora . . . . neque arborum neque . . . . eodem tempore . . . . heres tuus . . . . ad vindemiam . . . . isto tempore . . . . asperius, nequi-
Ambr. 179 vi prae fletu | ac dolore. Meus etiam hic mi[1] dulcissimus nepos, quem ipse sinu meo educo, hic est profecto, qui me magis magisque lacerat et excruciat. Namque in huius facie illum amissum contemplor, exemplum oris imaginor, sonum vocis eundem animo fingo. Hanc sibi dolor meus picturam commentatur. Verum defuncti vultum ignorans, dum verisimilem coniecto, maceror.

7. Sapiet mea filia: viro omnium quantum est hominum optimo adquiescet: is eam consolabitur pariter lacrimando pariter suspirando <pariter>[2] loquendo pariter conticiscendo. Senex ego parens indigne consolabor; dignius enim foret ipsum me ante obiisse. Neque ulla poetarum carmina aut sapientium praecepta tantum promoverint ad luctum filiae meae sedandum et dolorem leniendum, quantum mariti vox[3] <ex> ore carissimo et pectore iunctissimo profecta.

8. Me autem consolatur aetas mea prope iam edita et morti proxima. Quae quom aderit, si noctis si lucis id tempus erit, caelum quidem consalutabo discedens et quae mihi conscius sum protestabor:
Ambr. 182 nihil in longo vitae meae spatio a me admissum |

[1] Heindorf for Cod. *huic me.* [2] Naber.
[3] Naber. Cod. has *uxor e carissimo pectore.*

from heaven, to me indeed, for whom death is so near, they can by no means bring any lasting perplexity. Whether we are annihilated for ever, as I once desired, at last . . . .
. . . . I was unable for grief and tears. Now it is even my darling grandson, whom I am bringing up myself in my own bosom, it is he, indeed, who more and more rends and racks my heart. For in his lineaments I behold the other whom I have lost, I seem to see a copy of his face and fancy that I hear the very echo of his voice. This is the picture that my grief conjures up of itself. But not knowing the dead child's face I fret myself away with imagining what he was like.

7. My daughter will be reasonable, she will rest upon her husband's love, and he is the best of men. He will comfort her by mingling his tears and sighs with hers, by speaking when she speaks and being silent when she is silent. It will scarce befit me, her aged father, to comfort her; for it were more fitting had I myself been the first to die. Nor would any poet's songs or philosopher's precepts avail so much to assuage my daughter's grief and soothe her pain as her husband's voice issuing from lips so dear and a heart so near her own.

8. My comfort, however, I find in my life being almost spent and death very near. When it comes, be its advent by night or by day, yet will I hail the heavens as I depart and what my conscience tells me I will testify,[1] that in my long span of life I have been guilty of nothing dishonourable, shameful, or

[1] Charisius, in his *Ars Grammatica*, quotes from Fronto's second book of letters to Antoninus: *Male me, Marce, praeteritae vitae meae paenitet.*

quod dedecori aut probro aut flagitio foret; nullum in aetate agunda avarum, nullum perfidum facinus meum extitisse; contraque multa liberaliter multa amice multa fideliter multa constanter saepe etiam cum periculo capitis consulta Cum fratre optimo concordissime vixi, quem patris vestri bonitate summos honores adeptum gaudeo, vestra vero amicitia satis quietum et multum securum video. Honores quos ipse adeptus sum numquam improbis rationibus concupivi. Animo potius quam corpori curando operam dedi. Studia doctrinae rei familiari meae praetuli. Pauperem me quam ope cuiusquam adiutum, postremo egere quam poscere malui.

9. Sumptu numquam prodigo fui, quaestu[1] interdum necessario. Verum dixi sedulo, verum audivi libenter. Potius duxi negligi quam blandiri, tacere quam fingere, infrequens amicus esse quam frequens adsentator. Pauca petii, non pauca merui. Quod cuique potui pro copia commodavi. Merentibus promptius, immerentibus audacius opem tuli. Neque me parum gratus quispiam repertus segniorem effecit ad beneficia quaecumque possem prompte imperti-

[1] Both text and margin have *quaestui*.

criminal; my whole life through there has not been on my side a single act of avarice or of treachery, but on the contrary many of generosity, many of friendship, many of good faith, many of loyalty, undertaken, too, often at the risk of my life. With the best of brothers I have lived in the utmost harmony, and I rejoice to see him raised by your father's kindness to the highest offices and resting in the friendship of both of you in all peace and security. The honours which I myself have attained[1] I never coveted to gain by unworthy means. I have devoted myself to the cultivation of my mind rather than my body. I have held the pursuit of learning higher than the acquisition of wealth. I preferred to be poor[2] rather than indebted to another's help, at the worst to be in want rather than to beg.

9. In expenditure I have never been extravagant, sometimes earned only enough to live upon. I have spoken the truth studiously, I have heard the truth gladly. I have held it better to be forgotten than to fawn, to be silent than insincere, to be a negligent friend than a diligent flatterer. It is little I have sought, not a little I have deserved. According to my means I have obliged every man. The deserving have found in me a readier, the undeserving a more quixotic, helper. Nor if I found anyone ungrateful, did that make me less willing to bestow upon him betimes all the services in my power; nor

[1] In a letter from the fourth book of letters *Ad Anton. Imp.*, quoted by Charisius, *Ars Grammatica*, ii. 197, 3 (Kiel), Fronto says *Satis abundeque honorum est quos mihi cotidiano tribuis*.

[2] He could not have been very poor; see Aul. Gellius, below.

Ambr. 181 enda. Neque ego umquam ingratis offensior | fui.
Eas quid<em> . . . .[1] mihi nec ob aeratos in re
. . . .[2] omnibus cum . . . . putavi . . . . cuperem
equidem . . . . male. Finem . . . . teneo . . . .
male . . . . quam . . . . Si nobis carere . . . .
operam. Sentio . . . . me proderes . . . . quam
Ambr. 196 leto colens et statu mentis | . . . . doleam . . . .
aliud . . . . reperto . . . . apud . . . . sana
Col. 1, line 7 mundum . . . . solvere . . . . | non est veritatis
nostra cum ii se indigere solacio. Dis placeat
filiam generum . . . . domo . . . . bis . . . .
hinc de . . . . quorum . . . . vastitatem . . . .

Ambr. 195 10. | Multum et graviter male[3] valui, mi Marce carissime. Dein casibus miserrimis adflictus, tum uxorem amisi, nepotem in Germania amisi, miserum me! Decimanum nostrum amisi. Ferreus si essem, plura scribere non possem isto in tempore.

Librum[4] misi tibi quem pro omnibus haberes.

Ad Verum Imp. ii. 9 (Naber, p. 137).

Domino meo Vero Augusto.

Fatigatum me valetudine diutina et praeter solitum gravi ac gravissimis etiam luctibus paene continuis adflictum, nam in paucissimis mensibus et uxorem carissimam et nepotem trimulum amisi—sic
Ambr. 428, following 429 his plerisque me malis perculsum,[5] recreatum | tamen aliquantum fateor, quod te meminisse nostri et quaedam nostra desiderasse cognovi. Misi igitur quae

[1] Six letters lost. [2] Five letters lost.
[3] So Cod. Brakman. [4] Query = *libellum*, a letter.
[5] Hauler, *Wien. Stud.* 24, Pt. 1, p. 232. I have preferred *sic* to his *sed*. Brakman, *Ita fessum* <*m*>*e malis permulsum recreatumque*.

have I ever been vexed by the ungrateful . . . . . .
. . . .
. . . .
. . . .
. . . .
. . . .
. . . .
. . . .
. . . .
. . . .

10. I have suffered from constant and serious ill-health, my dearest Marcus. Then afflicted by the most distressing calamities I have further lost my wife, I have lost my grandson in Germany—woe is me!—I have lost my Decimanus.[1] If I were of iron I could write no more just now.

I have sent you a book which you can take as representing all my thoughts.

Fronto to Lucius Verus

To my Lord Verus Augustus. 165 A.D.

Worn out as I am with long-continued and more than usually distressing ill-health, and afflicted besides with the most distressing and almost uninterrupted sorrows, for in a very few months I have lost both the dearest of wives and a three-year-old grandson[2]—though thus prostrated by these accumulated evils, I confess that I was nevertheless not a little cheered to learn that you had not forgotten me and wished for something of mine. I therefore send

[1] Some think this is the grandson's name.
[2] See the preceding letters *De Nepote*.

Dominus meus frater tuus litteris tuis admonitus mittenda censuit. Adiunxi praeterea orationem pro Demostrato, quam quom fratri tuo primum optuli, didici ex eo Asclepiodotum, qui oratione ista compelletur, a te non improbari. Quod ego ubi comperi, cupivi[1] equidem abolere orationem: sed iam pervaserat in manus plurium quam ut aboleri posset. Quid ig<itur f>ieri, quid, inquam, op<orte>t?[2] Nisi Asclepiodotum, quom a te probetur, mihi quoque fieri amicissimum, tam hercule quam est Herodes summus nunc meus, quamquam extet oratio.

Egit praeterea mecum frater tuus impense, quod ego multo impensius adgredi cupio, et ubi primum commentarium miseris, adgrediar ex summis voluntatis opibus: nam de facultate tute videbis, qui me idoneum censuisti.

Ad Verum Imp. ii. 10 (Naber, p. 138).

MAGISTRO meo.

Certum esse te, mi magister carissime, etiamsi reticeam, nihil dubito quantae mihi acerbitati[3] sit tua omnis vel minima tristitia. Enim|vero quom et
Ambr. 427 uxorem per tot annos caram et nepotem dulcissimum paene simul amiseris, miser<icordiam[4] . . . . maximam pernostique graviora mala quam ut> magistrum doctis dictis consolari audeam, sed patris est pectus

[1] So Hauler for Naber's *curari*.

[2] So Brakman; but Hauler reads *Quid igitur? quid igitur, inquam, probabis?*

[3] Heindorf for Cod. *acerbitatis*.

[4] Six lines are lost. For this passage see Hauler, *Wochensch.* 41, Oct. 11, 1918.

what my Lord your brother, acting upon your letter, has decided should be sent. I have added besides the speech for Demostratus, but on submitting this to your brother I learnt from him that Asclepiodotus, though he is taken to task in that speech, is not thought ill of by you. As soon as I was aware of this I was myself anxious to suppress the speech, but it had already been circulated too widely to be called in. What then? What then, I say, is best so be done, except that Asclepiodotus, since he has earned your approbation, should become to me also a very dear friend, just as by heaven Herodes and I are now on the best of terms, in spite of the speech being published.

Besides your brother earnestly discussed with me what I am still more earnestly anxious to take in hand and, as soon as you send me your memoranda,[1] I will take the task in hand with the best will in the world: for as to my qualifications, you who have judged me capable of it must see to that yourself.

Lucius Verus to Fronto

To my Master. 165 A.D.

You are aware I am sure, my dearest master, even if I keep silence, how keenly I feel every trouble of yours however slight. But, indeed, since you have lost simultaneously both a wife beloved through so many years, and a most sweet grandson, ... and you have known greater woes than I can dare to console my master for with well-turned words, but it is a father's part to pour forth a

[1] Notes on the conduct of the war mentioned above, *Ad Verum*, ii. 3. See above, p. 194.

amoris pietatisque plenum effundere[1] . . . . delibera . . . . Nunc ad reliqua litterarum tuarum convertar. Delectatus <sum> . . . . veri . . . . Quid <or>as, mi magister? . . . . nisi qui . . . . a me munus aut . . . . defendisset, qua si deficis . . . . quid aliud ego doctior[2] quicquam aut expeto aut somnio . . . .

Ad Verum Imp. ii. 4 (Naber, p. 132).

Ambr. 435, col. 2 | Domino meo Vero Augusto.

Quamquam me diu[3] cum ista valetudine vivere iam pridem pigeat taedeatque, tamen ubi te tanta gloria per virtutem parta reducem videro, neque incassum vixero neque invitus quantum vitae dabitur vivam. Vale, Domine desiderantissime. Socrum[4] et liberos vestros saluta.

Ad Verum Imp. ii. 5 (Naber, p 132).

Magistro meo.

Quidni ego gaudium tuum mihi repraesentaverim, mi magister carissime? Equidem videre te[5] et arte complecti et multum exosculari videor mihi toto . . . .

1 Hauler, *Wien Stud.* 24, Pt. 2, p. 293 (1918).
2 Query *doctius.*
3 Heindorf *diutius*, Naber *medius fidius.*
4 Possibly *uxorem* should be read.
5 Heindorf for Cod. *me.*

heart full of love and affection . . . .
Now I will turn to the rest of your letter. I was delighted . . . . What do you ask, my master? . . . . what else at all do I more learned either ask or dream of . . . .

Fronto to Lucius Verus

To my Lord Verus Augustus. 166 A.D.

Although for a long while past with this ill-health of mine it has been pain and grief for me to live on, yet when I see you return with such great glory gained by your valour, I shall not have lived in vain, nor shall I be loth to live, whatever span of life remains for me. Farewell, my Lord, whom I miss so much. Greet your mother-in-law[1] and your children.

Lucius Verus to Fronto

To my Master. 166 A.D.

Why should I not picture to myself your joy, my master? Verily I seem to myself to see you hugging me tightly and kissing me many times affectionately . . . .

[1] *Socrum* cannot = *socerum* and mean Marcus. Faustina must therefore have been with Verus and her daughter Lucilla, but whether in Asia or in Italy is not clear. As Lucius married Lucilla in 164, he is not likely to have had more than one child yet, and in any case the children would have been too young to have a message sent them. Therefore Faustina's other children must be included in *liberos*, as *vestros* also seems to shew.

Ad Verum Imp. ii. 8 (Naber, p. 136).

VERO AUGUSTO Domino meo.

Ambr. 430 . . . . | desideretur is honor, quo pariter quisque expetit si quid honoris aliis impertitum videat. Probasti me laudastique consilium, neque tamen triduo amplius vel quatriduo id a te optinere potuisti, ut mihi verbo *salutem*† responderes; sed ita excogitasti: primum me intromitti in cubiculum iubebas, ita sine cuiusquam invidia osculum dabas, credo ita cum animo tuo reputans, mihi cui curam cultumque tradidisses oris atque orationis tuae, ius quoque osculi habendum, omnesque eloquentiae magistros sui lege[1] fructum capere solitos[2] in vocis aditu locatum. Morem denique saviandi arbitror honori eloquentiae datum. Nam cur os potius salutantes ori admovemus quam oculos oculis aut frontes frontibus aut, quibus plurimum valemus, manus manibus, nisi quod honorem orationi impertimus? Muta denique animalia oratione carentia osculis carent. Hunc ego honorem mihi a te habitum taxo[3] maximo et gravissimo pondere. Plurima praeterea tua erga me summo cum honore et dicta et facta sensi. Quotiens

[1] Niebuhr *laboris*.
[2] For Mai's *saltem*. Novák prefers *savium*.
[3] Brakman for Cod *axo* (query *faxo*); but we should rather expect the genitive after it. But Klussmann *cp. Ad M. Caes.* iii. 20 (i. p. 172), and reads *habitum maximo gravius amo pondere*.

---

[1] The loss of the opening words makes it difficult to divine the meaning of the first two sentences. There had

Fronto to Lucius Verus

166 A.D.

To my Lord Verus Augustus.

. . . .[1] the honour would be missed, whereby equally everyone hankers after any honour bestowed on others. You gave me your approval and applauded my advice, and yet for more than three or four days you could not prevail on yourself to answer me with the word *greeting*†; but you thought out this plan: first you bid me be admitted into your chamber: so you were able to give me a kiss without exciting anyone's jealousy, with this thought I suppose in your mind, that the privilege also of a kiss should belong to me, to whom you had entrusted the care and cultivation of your voice and speech, and that all masters of eloquence by innate right are wont to reap the reward lodged in the portals of the voice. In fine, I think that the custom of kissing was intended as an honour to eloquence. For why in greeting do we touch lips with lips rather than eyes with eyes or foreheads with foreheads or hands[2] with hands—and yet these are more indispensable than anything else—if it be not as rendering an honour to speech? In fact, dumb animals being without speech are without kisses also. This privilege kept for me by you outweighs everything in my estimation. Many a time besides have I been sensible of the special honour which you have shewn me in word and deed.

apparently been some jealousy excited among the entourage of Verus at the favour shewn to Fronto. The latter seems to have suggested some plan for obviating this, which Verus had not fallen in with, but followed another course.

[2] Savages rub foreheads and noses. Shaking hands could not have been unknown, as clasped right hands were a common symbol of amity and unity.

Ambr. 429 tu manibus | tuis sustinuisti, adlevasti aegre adsurgentem aut difficile progredientem per valetudinem corporis paene portasti! Quam hilari voltu semper et placato tu[1] nos adfatus es! Quam libenter conseruisti sermonem, quam diu produxisti, quam invitus terminasti! Quae ego pro maximis duco. Sicut in extis inspicienti diffissa plerumque minima et tenuissima maximas significant prosperitates deque[2] formicarum et apicularum ostentis res maximae portenduntur, item vel minimis et levissimis ab uno et vero Principe habitis officii et bonae volentiae signis significari arbitror ea quae amplissima inter homines et exoptatissima sunt, amor honorque. Igitur quaecumque a Domino meo tuo fratre petenda fuerunt, per te petita et impetrata omnia malui.

Ad Amicos, i. 9 (Naber, p. 180).

Ambr. 320, col. 2 *ad med.* | Fronto Caelio Optato salutem.

Sardius Saturninus artissima mihi familiaritate coniunctus est per filios suos doctissimos iuvenes, quos in contubernio mecum adsiduos habeo. Magno opere eum tibi, frater, commendo et peto, si quid negotii eum ad te adduxerit,[3] carissimum mihi virum omni honore dignum iudices et ope tua protegas.

[1] Naber for Cod *placatissimo*.
[2] See Hauler, *Wien. Stud.* 25, pt. 1, p. 331 and 24, pt. 1, p. 232, for this passage. The words are also found in the margin, but with *ut* for *deque* and *benivolentiae* for *bonae vol.*
[3] For Cod. *eduxerit*.

How often have you supported me with your hands, lifted me up when scarcely able to rise, and well-nigh carried me when hardly able to walk from bodily weakness![1] With what a cheerful and friendly countenance have you always accosted me! How readily engaged in conversation, how long continued it, how reluctantly concluded it! All which I value above measure. Just as in the inspection of entrails the smallest and most insignificant parts when laid open generally imply the greatest good-fortune, and by omens from ants and bees the greatest events are foretold, so by even the least and most trivial signs of deference and good-will, vouchsafed by the one and very Emperor, are signified, as I think, those things that are the most estimable and the most coveted among men, love and honour. Therefore all the favours I have had to ask from my Lord your brother I have preferred to ask and obtain through you.

? 166 A.D.

FRONTO to Caelius Optatus,[2] greeting.

There is a bond of the closest intimacy between Sardius Saturninus and myself through his sons, young men of the highest culture, whom I have constantly under my roof. I recommend him to you most cordially, my brother, and ask that, if any business bring him to you, you should judge as worthy of all respect a man very dear to me, and should befriend him with all your power.

[1] Fronto suffered from rheumatism, but not, it appears, as his contemporary Polemo, from arthritis.

[2] Was legatus of Numidia in 166; this letter may be to him in his province.

Ad Amicos, i. 10 (Naber, p. 180).

Fronto Petronio Mamertino[1] salutem.

Sardius Saturninus filium habet Sardium Lupum, Ambr. 319 doctum et facundum | virum, de mea domo meoque contubernio in forum deductum, ad omnes bonas artes a me institutum, frequentissimum auditorem tuumque maximum laudatorem[2] <nec> minus . . . . habuit . . . . egregias . . . . gravissimum . . . . mihi . . . . cum Sardio Saturnino, qui . . . . nostrae numeres ac diligas.

Ad Amicos, i. 20 (Naber, p. 187).

Ambr. 281, col. 1 *ad med.* | Fronto Sardio Saturnino salutem.

Gravissimum casum tuum recenti malo consolari nequivi periculosa valetudine ipse et in hoc tempus conflictatus, quom quidem mihi languore fesso plurium aegritudinum venit nuntius amissi iuvenis nostri, quem tibi optimum filium fors iniqua abstulit, mihi iucundissimum contubernalem. Quam ob rem, quamquam recuperata sit commoda valetudo, tristitia tamen inhaeret animo meo magisque in dies augetur maerore Lupi nostri fratrem optimum misere desiderantis. Quom[3] praesentem ac loquentem[4] vix consolarer,[5] sentio quam difficile <sit> te absentem

[1] The Cons. Suff. in 150 was M. Petr. Mamertinus, the father, no doubt, of the Petr. Mamertinus who married a daughter of Marcus; see Capit. *Vit. Comm.* vii. 5.

[2] There are seventeen lines from here to the end of the letter.

? 166 A.D.

FRONTO to Petronius Mamertinus, greeting.

Sardius Saturninus has a son Sardius Lupus, a learned and eloquent man, introduced to the Forum from my hearth and home, instructed by me in all the noble arts, a most assiduous hearer and a very great admirer of yours, nor the less . . . . with Sardius Saturninus, ... you should count and love (as a member of) our (family).

? 166 A.D.

FRONTO to Sardius Saturninus, greeting.

I have been unable to condole with you, while the wound was still fresh, in your most terrible affliction, being myself prostrated even up till now with a dangerous illness, at which very time, when I am worn out with the depression caused by many troubles, there has come the news of the loss of our young friend whom an unjust fate has torn away, from you the best of sons, from me the most delightful of housemates. Wherefore, though I am much better in health, yet sorrow cleaves to my heart and is intensified by the anguish of our Lupus, who feels dreadfully the loss of the best of brothers. Since it would not be easy to console you, even if you were present and talking with me, I feel how

[3] Heindorf <*Quem*> *quom*.
[4] Query *adloquens te*.
[5] For Mai's *consoler*.

per litteras consolari. Neque postulo ut maerere desinas—id enim frustra postulabo—sed ut moder<atius maereas>[1] . . . .[2]

Ad Amicos, i. 24 (Naber, p. 188).

Iunio Maximo Fronto salutem.

Ambr. 278, after two pages lost Per Ulpium nostrum[3] . . . . ho|nestatis gravitatisque tuae praedicatorem, quem cupio ad me celeriter remittas. Neque enim cum alio ullo tanta mihi familiaritas est aut tantus usus studiorum bonarumque artium communicandi. Multo etiam mihi iucundior erit, quom sermones de te mutuo recolemus ac recensebimus.

Ad Amicos, i. 25 (Naber, p. 188).

Fronto Squillae Gallicano[4] salutem.

Tibi, domine frater, commodius evenit qui pro filio nostro praesens trepidaveris, quam mihi, qui trepidaverim absens. Nam tua trepidatio pro eventu actionis facile sedata est; ego quoad mihi ab omnibus contubernalibus nuntiatum est, quo successu noster orator egisset, trepidare non destiti. Et tu quidem ad singulos orationis successus, prout quaeque

[1] Alan.

[2] Two pages are missing between this and what we have of the next letter. These contained three letters, probably like this one, letters of consolation, for the margin has *consolatoriae*. See Index (Naber, p. 172; Ambr. 337): (1) Iunio Maximo; *Humani casus homini*. . . . (2) Praecilio Pompeiano: *Labris eius labra fori*. . . . (3) Sardio Saturnino: *Hortatus sum constanter*. . . .

[3] From the Index (Naber, p. 172; Ambr. 337).

[4] Consul in 150.

difficult it is to console you when absent by letter. And I do not ask you to cease grieving—for it would be useless to ask that—but to grieve with some moderation . . . .

? 166 A.D.

FRONTO to Junius Maximus, greeting.

By our friend Ulpius[1] . . . . (this) eulogizer of your probity and dignity, whom I desire you to send back to me speedily. For there is no one with whom I am on such intimate terms, or with whom I am wont so much to share my pursuits and love of the noble arts. He will be still more delightful to me when we exchange our mutual reminiscences and views of you.

? 166 A.D.

FRONTO to Squilla Gallicanus, greeting.

Yours has been a happier lot,[2] my lord brother, for you have felt nervous for your son on the spot, than mine, who have had to endure my nervousness at home. For your nervousness was easily allayed with the completion of the pleading, while I did not cease to be nervous until all my pupil housemates had brought me news of the success with which our orator had conducted the case. And you, indeed, at each separate triumph of the speech, as each

[1] Possibly the famous jurist Ulpius Marcellus, who was one of the *Consilium* of Marcus.

[2] Fronto writes to his friend Gallicanus on the success of his son at the bar. This son was evidently one of his pupils who lived in his house (*contubernales*). The word *dominus* had come to be used as a complimentary title with *filius* and *frater*.

sententia laudem meruerat,[1] gaudio fruebare; at ego domi sedens perpetua sollicitudine angebar, ut qui periculum actoris recordarer, laudibus actionis non interessem. Tum praeterea multiplices tu fructus abstulisti: non enim audisti tantum sed et vidisti agentem; nec eloquentia sola sed etiam vultu eius et gestu laetatus es. Ego tametsi quid dixerit scio,
Ambr. 277 tamen ignoro quemadmodum | dixerit. Postremo[2] . . . . cui Callistus[3] lacrimas . . . . patrem . . . . adeptus es . . . . quia . . . . gaudeo . . . . et . . . . hodie . . . . esse si hodie . . . . mens . . . . in forum descendit natalibus nobilis, de foro rediit eloquentia quam genere nobilior[4] . . . .

[1] Heindorf for Cod. *meruerit.*
[2] From here to the end of the letter are twenty-six lines.
[3] This word is not certain.
[4] From the margin of the Codex. After head of the letter the margin has *mire scripta epistola.*

sentence evoked applause, were filled with joy, while I, sitting at home, was tortured with continuous anxiety, conscious as I was of the difficulties before the pleader, yet unable to share in the praises of his pleading. Then you carried away manifold advantages besides, for you not only heard, but also saw the performer, and were delighted not by his eloquence only, but by his look and gesture. For me, though I know what he said, yet I do not know how he said it . . . .

. . . .

He went down to the Forum noble by birth, he came back from it more noble by eloquence than by lineage . . . .

OTHER MISCELLANEOUS REMAINS OF FRONTO

OTHER MISCELLANEOUS REMAINS OF FRONTO

Ex Dione Cassio, lxix. 18

Κορνήλιος Φρόντων ὁ τὰ πρῶτα τῶν τότε Ῥωμαίων ἐν δίκαις φερόμενος, ἑσπέρας ποτὲ βαθείας ἀπὸ δείπνου οἴκαδε ἐπανιὼν καὶ μαθὼν παρά τινος, ᾧ συνηγορήσειν ὑπέσχητο, δικάζειν αὐτόν, ἔν τε τῇ στολῇ τῇ δειπνίτιδι, ὥσπερ εἶχεν, ἐς τὸ δικαστήριον αὐτοῦ εἰσῆλθε καὶ ἠσπάσατο, οὔτι γε τῷ ἑωθινῷ προσρήματι, τῷ "χαῖρε," ἀλλὰ τῷ ἑσπερινῷ τῷ "ὑγίαινε" χρησάμενος.

Ex Eumenii *Panegyrico Constantii,* 14

Fronto, Romanae eloquentiae non secundum sed alterum decus, quom belli in Britannia confecti laudem Antonino principi daret, quamvis ille in ipso Urbis Palatio residens gerendi eius mandasset auspicium, veluti longae navis gubernaculis praesidentem totius velificationis et cursus gloriam meruisse testatus est.

---

[1] The point in this story, such as it is, seems to be that the court was still sitting in the early morning hours when Fronto came in from his banquet. It was a new day to the court, but the end of Fronto's day. Hence his use of the evening salutation. For the difference between χαῖρε, "Good

OTHER MISCELLANEOUS REMAINS OF FRONTO

FRONTO'S SALUTATION TO HADRIAN[1]

? *About* 136 A.D.

CORNELIUS FRONTO, who held the first place at the bar among the Romans of that day, was returning home on one occasion very late in the evening from a banquet, and learning from one for whom he had promised to plead that Hadrian was sitting in court, he went in as he was in his banqueting dress to the court and saluted him, not with the morning salutation *χαῖρε* but with the evening one *ὑγίαινε*.

FROM THE SPEECH ON THE WAR IN BRITAIN

140–1 A.D.

FRONTO, not the second but the alternative glory of Roman eloquence, when he was giving the emperor Antoninus[2] praise for the successful completion of the war in Britain,[3] declared that although he had committed the conduct of the campaign to others, while sitting at home himself in the Palace at Rome, yet like the helmsman at the tiller of a ship of war, the glory of the whole navigation and voyage belonged to him.

cheer" (our "Good morning," or "How do you do?"), and *ὑγίαινε*, "Vale" (our "Good night," or "Good-bye"), see Lucian, *Pro Lapsu in Salutando*, i., where a mistake in the use of these expressions is illustrated at length.

[2] Pius. [3] 140 A.D.

OTHER MISCELLANEOUS

Ex Artemidori *De Somniis*, iv. 24

Ὡς καὶ Φρόντων ὁ ἀρθριτικὸς θεραπείαν αἰτήσας ἔδοξεν ἐν τοῖς προαστείοις περιπατεῖν καὶ πυρπολήσει χρησάμενος παρηγορήθη ἱκανῶς· ὡς ἴσον εἶναι τὸ χρῆμα θεραπείᾳ.

Ex Auli Gellii *Noctibus Atticis*, xix. 8

An arena caelum triticum *pluralia inveniantur : atque inibi de* quadrigis inimicitiis *nonnullis praeterea vocabulis, an singulari numero comperiantur.*

1. Adulescentulus Romae priusquam Athenas concederem, quando erat a magistris auditionibusque obeundis otium, ad Frontonem Cornelium visendi gratia pergebam, sermonibusque eius purissimis bonarumque doctrinarum plenis fruebar. Nec umquam factum est, quoties eum vidimus loquentemque audivimus, quin rediremus cultiores doctioresque : veluti fuit illa quodam die sermocinatio illius, levi quidem de re, sed a Latinae tamen linguae studio non abhorrens.

2. Nam quom quispiam familiaris eius, bene eruditus homo, et tum poeta illustris, liberatum se esse aquae intercutis morbo diceret, quod arenis calentibus esset usus, tum illudens Fronto :

REMAINS OF FRONTO

FRONTO'S DREAM-CURE

? 140 A.D.

FRONTO, who suffered from rheumatism, having prayed for a cure, dreamt that he was walking in the suburbs of the city, and was not a little comforted by a close application of fire: so much was this so that the result was little short of a cure.

THE PLURAL OF *arena*, *caelum*, ETC.

About 137 A.D.

Whether arena, caelum, triticum *are found in the plural, and incidentally of* quadrigae, inimicitiae, *and some other words, whether they are met with in the singular number.*

1. WHEN I was a young man at Rome, before I migrated to Athens, and had a respite from attendance on masters and at lectures, I used to visit Cornelius Fronto for the pleasure of seeing him, and derived great advantage from his conversation, which was in the purest language and full of excellent information. And it was invariably the case that, as often as we saw him and heard his talk, we came away with our taste improved and our minds informed: as, for instance, was the case with that discussion by him on one occasion of a question trivial in itself indeed yet not unconnected with the study of the Latin language.

2. For when a certain close acquaintance of his, a man of learning and a distinguished poet of the time, told us that he had been cured of a dropsy by the application of heated "sands," Fronto, bantering him, said:

"Morbo quidem" inquit "cares sed verbi vitio non cares. Gaius enim Caesar ille perpetuus dictator, Cn. Pompeii socer, a quo familia et appellatio Caesarum deinceps propagata est, vir ingenii praecellentis, sermonis praeter alios suae aetatis castissimi, in libris quos ad M. Ciceronem *De Analogia* conscripsit, *arenas* vitiose dici existimat: quod arena numquam multitudinis numero appellanda sit, sicuti neque *caelum* neque *triticum*. Contra autem *quadrigas*, etiam si currus unus equorum quattuor iunctorum agmen unum sit, plurativo semper numero dicendas putat, sicut *arma* et *moenia* et *comitia* et *inimicitiae*—ni quid contra ea dicis, poetarum pulcherrime, quo et te purges et non esse id vitium demonstres."

3. "De *caelo*" inquit ille "et *tritico* non infitias eo, quin singulo semper numero dicenda sint, neque de *armis* et *moenibus* et *comitiis*, quin figura multitudinis perpetua censeantur: videbimus autem post de *inimicitiis* et *quadrigis*. Ac fortasse an de *quadrigis* veterum auctoritati concessero; *inimicitiam* tamen, sicut inscientiam et impotentiam et iniuriam, quae ratio est quam ob rem C. Caesar vel dictam esse a veteribus vel dicendam a nobis non putat? quando Plautus, linguae Latinae decus, *deliciam* quoque ἑνικῶς dixerit pro *deliciis*:

Mea inquit *voluptas, mea delicia.*

---

[1] *De Bello Parthico, ad fin.*

[2] Verg. *Ecl.* v. 36, *Georg.* i. 317, uses *hordeum* (barley) in

"You are quit indeed of the disease, but of defect in diction you are not quit. For Gaius Caesar, the father-in-law of Gnaeus Pompeius, he who was dictator for life, from whom the family and designation of the Caesars are derived and still continue, a man of pre-eminent genius and distinguished beyond all his contemporaries for purity of style, in those books which he wrote to Cicero *On Analogy*,[1] holds that *arenae* is a faulty locution, in that *arena* is never used in the plural any more than *caelum* or *triticum*;[2] but his opinion is that *quadrigae*, on the other hand, although a single chariot is a single team of horses yoked together, should always be spoken of in the plural number, just as *arma* and *moenia* and *comitia* and *inimicitiae*: unless, my most brilliant of poets, you have anything to say to the contrary that shall clear you and prove that you were not in fault."

3. "As to *caelum*," said the other, "and *triticum*, I do not deny that they should always be used in the singular number; nor as to *arma* and *moenia* and *comitia* that they should be regarded as invariably plural words: about *inimicitiae* and *quadrigae*, however, we will consider later; and possibly as to the latter I shall bow to the authority of the ancients. But what grounds has C. Caesar for supposing that *inimicitia* was not used by the ancients and cannot be used by us, just as much as *scientia* and *impotentia* and *iniuria*? since Plautus, the glory of the Latin tongue, has used *delicia* also in the singular number for *deliciae*:

My darling, says he, *my delight*.[3]

the plural, and is taken to task by Bavius, a rival poet, who says he might as well say *tritica* (wheats).

[3] Plautus, *Poen*. I. ii. 152.

Inimicitiam autem Q. Ennius in illo memoratissimo libro dixit:

> *Eo* inquit *ingenio natus sum;*
> *Amicitiam et inimicitiam in fronte promptam gero.*

Sed enim *arenas* parum Latine dici quis, oro te, alius aut scripsit aut dixit? Ac propterea peto ut, si C. Caesaris liber prae manibus est, promi iubeas, ut quam confidenter hoc dicat aestimari a te possit."

4. Tunc prolato libro *De Analogia* primo, verba haec ex eo pauca memoriae mandavi. Nam quom supra dixisset neque *caelum triticumve* neque *arenam* multitudinis significationem pati: *Num tu* inquit *harum rerum natura accidere arbitraris, quod unam terram et plures terras, et urbem et urbes, et imperium et imperia dicamus, neque quadrigas in unam nominis figuram redigere, neque arenam in multitudinis appellationem convertere possimus?*

5. His deinde verbis lectis sibi, Fronto ad illum poetam:

"Videturne tibi" inquit "C. Caesarem de statu verbi contra te satis aperte satisque constanter pronuntiasse?"

Tum permotus auctoritate libri poeta: "Si a Caesare" inquit "ius provocandi foret, ego nunc ab hoc Caesaris libro provocarem. Sed quoniam ipse rationem sententiae suae reddere supersedit, nos te nunc rogamus ut dicas, quam esse causam vitii putes et in *quadriga* dicenda et in *arenis.*"

Inimicitia Q. Ennius has, in fact, used in that constantly-quoted book of his:

> *With such a character did Nature me endow,*
> *Friendship and enmity I bear upon my brow.*[1]

But indeed, I beseech you, who else has either written or said that *arenae* is bad Latin? And therefore I beg that, if Caesar's book be in your possession, you should bid it be brought, that you may judge how positively he says this."

4. On the first book *On Analogy* being produced, I committed to memory these few words from it. For after remarking that neither *caelum* nor *triticum* nor *arena* admits of a plural meaning, he[2] goes on, *Do you think that it results from the nature of these things, that we speak of one land and many lands, and of a city and cities, and of an empire and empires, but cannot reduce "quadrigae" to a noun of singular number nor convert "arena" into a term signifying plurality?*

5. After reading these words Fronto said to the poet:

"Are you satisfied that C. Caesar has decided against you clearly and firmly enough as to the status of the word?"

Then the poet, impressed by the authoritative nature of the book, said: "If there were the right of appeal from Caesar, I would now appeal from this book of Caesar's. But since he has himself omitted to give any reason for his verdict, I ask you now to tell us what fault you think there is in saying either *quadriga* or *arenae.*"

[1] Achilles is speaking. Said also of Essex by Cuffe.
[2] Caesar.

6. Tum Fronto ita respondit:

"*Quadrigae* semper, etsi multiiugae non sunt, multitudinis tamen tenentur numero, quoniam quattuor simul equi iuncti quadrigae, quasi quadriiugae, vocantur. Neque debet prorsus appellatio equorum plurium includi in singularis numeri unitatem. Eandem quoque de *arena* rationem habendam, sed in specie dispari, nam quom *arena* singulari numero dicta multitudinem tamen et copiam significet minimarum ex quibus constat partium, indocte et inscite *arenae* dici videntur, tamquam id vocabulum indigeat numeri amplitudine, quom ei singulariter dici[1] ingenita sit naturalis sui multitudo. Sed haec ego" inquit "dixi non ut huius sententiae legisque fundus subscriptorque fierem, sed ut ne Caesaris, viri docti, opinionem ἀπαραμύθητον destituerem.

7. "Nam quom *caelum* semper ἑνικῶς dicatur, *mare* et *terra* non semper, et *pulvis* et *ventus* et *fumus* non semper, cur *inducias* et *caerimonias* scriptores veteres nonnumquam singulari numero appellaverunt, *ferias* et *nundinas* et *inferias* et *exsequias* numquam? Cur *mel* et *vinum* et id genus cetera multitudinis numerum capiunt, *lac* non capiat? Quaeri, inquam, ista omnia et enucleari et excudi ab hominibus negotiosis in civitate tam occupata non queunt. Quin his

[1] Read *dicto* with Madvig, or after *dici* add <*proprium cui*>.

---

[1] Fronto himself used *arena* some few years later in 143 A.D.; see i. p. 160. It is often used by Ovid, and also by Vergil, Horace, Seneca, etc.

6. Then Fronto replied as follows:

"*Quadrigae*, even though only one horse is yoked, always keeps the plural number, since four horses yoked together are called *quadrigae*, as if it were *quadriiugae*, and certainly that which denotes several horses should not be compressed into the oneness of the singular number. The same reasoning applies also to *arena*, but from a different point of view, for since *arena*, though used in the singular number, yet signifies a plurality and abundance of tiny particles of which it is composed, *arenae* would seem to be used ignorantly and improperly, as though that term required an enlargement of number, though the conception of multitude essential to it is naturally expressed by the singular number. But I have said this," he added, "not as the ratifier and endorser of this verdict and rule,[1] but that I might not leave the opinion of Caesar, a learned man, without anyone to stand up for it.

7. "For while *caelum* is always spoken of in the singular, *mare* and *terra* not always, and *pulvis* and *ventus* and *fumus* not always, why have the old writers occasionally used *induciae* (a truce) and *caerimoniae* in the singular, but never *feriae* (holidays) and *nundinae* (market-day) and *inferiae* (sacrifice to the dead) and *exsequiae* (obsequies)?[2] Why do *mel* and *vinum* and all other words of that kind admit of a plural, and *lac* not admit of one? All these things, I say, cannot be investigated and unravelled and hammered out by citizens so fully occupied in so busy a state. Nay, I see that I have kept

[2] So *funerals* in Old English. We use *obsequies*, though Shakespeare has *obsequy*.

quoque ipsis, quae iam dixi, demoratus vos esse video, alicui opinor negotio destinatos. Ite ergo nunc et, quando forte erit otium, quaerite an *quadrigam* et *arenas* dixerit e cohorte illa dumtaxat antiquiore vel oratorum aliquis vel poetarum, id est classicus adsiduusque aliquis scriptor, non proletarius."

8. Haec quidem Fronto requirere nos iussit vocabula, non ea re opinor quod scripta esse in ullis veterum libris existimaret, sed ut nobis studium lectitandi in quaerendis rarioribus verbis exerceret.

Quod unum ergo rarissimum videbatur invenimus, *quadrigam* numero singulari dictam, in libro *Satirarum* M. Varronis qui inscriptus est *Exdemetricus*. *Arenas* autem πληθυντικῶς dictas minore studio quaerimus, quia praeter C. Caesarem, quod equidem meminerim, nemo id doctorum hominum dedit.[1]

Ex Auli Gellii *Noctibus Atticis*, ii. 26

Sermones M. Frontonis et Favorini philosophi de generibus colorum vocabulisque eorum Graecis et Latinis; atque inibi color spadix *cuiusmodi sit.*

1. Favorinus philosophus quom ad Frontonem consularem pedibus aegrum visum iret, voluit me quoque ad eum secum ire. Ac deinde, quom ibi apud

[1] There is some confusion here. Caesar ruled *arenae* out. Pearce suggests <*vitio*> *dedit* or *vetuit*.

you over time even by so much as I have already said, bound as you are I suppose on some business. Go then now, and when you chance to have the time, search whether some orator or poet, belonging at least to the more ancient school, that is, some writer of classic rank and of substance, and not of the common sort, have not used *quadriga* and *arenae.*"

8. Fronto bade us indeed look out for these words, not, I take it, because he thought they were to be found in any writings of the ancients, but that he might through the search after uncommon words practise us in the habit of reading.

The form, then, which seemed the most uncommon of all we did find, *quadriga* spoken of in the singular, in the book of *Satires* by M. Varro entitled *Exdemetricus.* But for *arenae* in the plural we looked with less care, because besides Caesar, as far as I remember, no man of learning has banned it.

Names for the Colours in Latin and Greek

After 143 A.D.

Conversation of M. Fronto and Favorinus the philosopher on the different kinds of colours and the terms for them in Greek and Latin; and incidentally what sort of colour is spadix.

1. When Favorinus the philosopher was on his way to visit Fronto, formerly consul, who had gout, he wished me also to accompany him thither. And then, when there, at Fronto's house, many

Frontonem plerisque viris doctis praesentibus sermones de coloribus vocabulisque eorum agitarentur, quod multiplex colorum facies, appellationes autem incertae et exiguae forent, "plura sunt," inquit Favorinus, "in sensibus oculorum quam in verbis vocibusque colorum discrimina. Nam ut alias eorum concinnitates omittamus, simplices isti rufus et viridis colores singula quidem vocabula, multas autem species differentes habent. Atque eam vocum inopiam in lingua magis Latina video quam in Graeca. Quippe qui rufus color a rubore quidem appellatus est: sed quom aliter rubeat ignis, aliter sanguis, aliter ostrum, aliter crocum,[1] has singulas rufi varietates Latina oratio singulis propriisque vocabulis non demonstrat, omniaque ista significat una ruboris appellatione, quom tamen ex ipsis rebus vocabula colorum mutuetur; et igneum aliquid dicit et flammeum et sanguineum et croceum et ostrinum et aureum. Russus enim color et ruber nihil a vocabulo rufi differunt, neque proprietates eius omnes declarant, ξανθός autem et ἐρυθρός et πυρρός et φοῖνιξ habere quasdam distantias coloris rufi videntur, vel augentes eum vel remittentes vel mixta quadam specie temperantes."

[1] *<aliter aurum>* seems to have fallen out; see *aureum* below.

learned men being present, a discussion took place about colours and their designations, since there were many varieties of colours, but their denominations few and ambiguous, Favorinus remarked that "more varieties of colour are distinguished by the sense of sight than differentiated by words and terms of speech. For, to omit their other nice blendings, the simple colours *red* and *green* have indeed separate names but include many different varieties and the dearth of terms for these I find to be greater in Latin than in Greek. For instance, the colour *rufus* is indeed called so from *rubor* (redness), but while there is one redness of fire, another of blood, another of the shell-fish dye, another of saffron, (another of gold), yet our Latin speech does not discriminate between these separate varieties of red by separate and distinctive terms, but designates them all by the single term redness, though at the same time it borrows names for the colours from the objects themselves, and calls a thing fiery-red and flame-red and blood-red and purple-red and saffron-red and gold-red,[1] for the colours *russus* and *ruber* do not differ at all from the colour called *rufus*, nor do they express its peculiar shades; but ξανθός (*chestnut*) and ἐρυθρός (*wine-red*) and πυρρός (*flame-red*)[2] and φοῖνιξ (*purple-red*)[3] seem to distinguish certain differences in the colour red, either darkening it or making it lighter or giving it an intermediate shade."

[1] In our old ballads the "red gold" often occurs.

[2] Plato (*Tim.* lxviii. 3) says it is a mixture of chestnut and gray.

[3] From the Phoenician discoverers, or perhaps *date-red* from the palm-tree. See below.

2. Tum Fronto ad Favorinum:

"Non infitias," inquit, "imus quin lingua Graeca, quam tu videre legisse, prolixior fusiorque sit quam nostra: sed in his tamen coloribus, quibus modo dixisti, designandis non perinde inopes sumus, ut tibi videmur. Non enim haec sunt sola vocabula rufum colorem demonstrantia, quae tu modo dixisti, *rufus* et *ruber*; sed alia quoque habemus plura quam quae dicta abs te Graeca sunt: *fulvus* enim et *flavus* et *rubidus* et *rutilus* et *luteus* et *spadix* appellationes sunt rufi coloris, aut acuentes eum quasi incendentes aut cum colore viridi miscentes aut nigro infuscantes aut virenti sensim albo illuminantes.

3. "Nam phoeniceus, quem tu Graece φοίνικα dixisti, noster est, et rutilus et spadix phoenicei συνώνυμος, qui factus Graece noster est, exuberantiam splendoremque significat ruboris; quales sunt fructus palmae arboris non admodum sole incocti, unde spadicis et phoenicei nomen est. *Spadica* enim Dorici vocant avulsum e palma termitem cum fructu.

4. "*Fulvus* autem videtur, de rufo atque viridi mixtus, in aliis plus viridis, in aliis plus rufi habere: sicut poeta, verborum diligentissimus, *fulvam aquilam* dicit et *iaspidem, fulvos galeros* et *fulvum aurum* et

2. Then Fronto said to Favorinus:

"We do not go as far as to deny that the Greek language, in which you seem to be well-read, is more comprehensive and copious than our own: still in designating those colours which you have just mentioned, we are not so poorly off as you seem to suppose. For, in fact, those words which you lately mentioned, *rufus* and *ruber,* are not our only ones to denote the colour *red*; but we have others besides and more than the Greek ones mentioned by you. For *fulvus* and *flavus* and *rubidus* and *phoeniceus* and *rutilus* and *luteus* and *spadix*[1] are designations of the colour red, either intensifying it, as if firing it, or blending it with green, or deepening it with black, or softly brightening it with greenish white.

3. "For *phoeniceus,* which you mentioned in its Greek form φοῖνιξ, is a word of our own, and *rutilus,* and *spadix,* which is synonymous with *phoeniceus*—a word that, though Greek by origin, is naturalized with us—signifies the richness and brilliance of red, such as it appears in the fruit of the palm-tree when not very much burnt by the sun; and hence come the words *spadix* and *phoeniceus.* For the Dorians call a branch with fruit broken off from the palm-tree a *spadix.*

4. "*Fulvus,* however, seems to be a blend of red and green, in which sometimes the one colour, sometimes the other, predominates: as a poet, the most careful in his choice of words, calls an eagle *fulvus,* and jasper and wolfskin caps and gold, and sand

[1] These words represent the shades of red: tawny, auburn, brick-red, purple-red, golden-red, orange-red, date-red.

arenam fulvam et *fulvum leonem;* sicque Q. Ennius in Annalibus *aere fulvo* dixit. *Flavus* contra videtur ex viridi et rufo et albo concretus: sic *flaventes comae* et, quod mirari quosdam video, *frondes olearum* a Vergilio dicuntur *flavae.* Sic multo ante Pacuvius *aquam flavam* dixit et *flavum pulverem;* cuius versus, quoniam sunt iucundissimi, libens commemini:

Cedo tamen pedem,[1] *lymphis flavis flavum ut pulverem*
Manibus isdem, quibus Ulixi saepe permulsi, abluam,
Lassitudinemque minuam manuum mollitudine.

Rubidus autem est rufus atrior[2] et nigrore multo mixtus. *Luteus* contra rufus color est dilucidior: unde eius quoque nomen esse factum videtur. Non ergo," inquit, "mi Favorine, species rufi coloris plures apud Graecos quam apud nos nominantur. Sed ne viridis quidem color pluribus ab illis, quam a nobis, vocabulis dicitur. Neque non potuit Vergilius, colorem equi significare viridem volens, caeruleum magis dicere equum quam glaucum: sed maluit verbo uti notiore Graeco quam inusitato Latino. Nostris autem Latinis veteribus *caesia* dicta est, quae a Graecis γλαυκῶπις, ut Nigridius ait, de colore caeli quasi caelia."

5. Postquam haec Fronto dixit, tum Favorinus scientiam rerum uberem verborumque eius elegan-

[1] Some editors read *cedo tuum pedem mi.* [2] MSS. *atrore.*

[1] See Verg. *Aen.* xi. 751; iv. 261; vii. 688; vii. 279; xii. 741; iv. 159 (*cp.* Lucr. v. 902); but he also says *flavum aurum* (i. 592). Servius on the passage vii. 688 mentions Fronto as speaking of *galerum.*

[2] Verg. *Aen.* iv. 590; *cp.* Hor. *Od.* I. v. 4.

[3] From the *Niptra.*

and the lion all *fulvus*;[1] and so Quintus in his *Annals* used it of bronze. *Flavus*, on the other hand, seems to be a combination of green and red and white; thus tresses are called *flaventes*,[2] and, what I find surprising to some, Vergil speaks of the leaves of olives as *flavae*: and so, long before, Pacuvius[3] talked of water[4] and dust being *flavus*; and as his lines are most delightful, I willingly recall them:

Reach me thy foot, that these same hands that bathed
Ulysses oft,
May with the yellow waters cleanse the yellow dust,
And with the hand's soft stroking soothe thy weariness.

Rubidus, however, is a darker red with a large proportion of black. *Luteus*, on the other hand, is a more transparent red, from which its name also seems to be derived.[5] So you see, my Favorinus, that more shades of red have not distinctive names among the Greeks than among us. Nor have they more terms than we have for expressing the colour green either. Vergil, having occasion to describe a horse as green, could have used the word *caeruleus* rather than *glaucus*, but preferred to use a better known Greek word than an unusual Latin one.[6] Our ancient Latin writers called that *caesia*, which in Greek is γλαυκῶπις, as Nigidius[7] says, from the colour of the sky, as if *caelia*."

5. When Fronto had said this, Favorinus, complimenting him warmly on his abundant knowledge of

[4] Vergil calls the Tiber *flavus* (*Aen.* vii. 31) and Horace.

[5] The word seems to be taken from a weed *lutum*, which was rather yellow than red. It is used of the dawn by Verg. *Aen.* vii. 26.

[6] *i.e. caeruleus* in the sense of green, for which see Propertius, IV. ii. 43; Ovid, *Met.* xi. 158.

[7] A Pythagorean philosopher and grammarian of Cicero's time.

tiam exosculatus: "Absque te" inquit "uno forsitan lingua profecto Graeca longe anteisset: sed tu, mi Fronto, quod in versu Homerico est, id facis:

καί νύ κεν ἢ παρέλασσας ἢ ἀμφήριστον ἔθηκας.

Sed quom omnia libens audivi, quae peritissime dixisti, tum maxime, quod varietatem flavi coloris enarrasti, fecistique, ut intelligerem verba illa ex annali quarto decimo Ennii amoenissima quae minime intelligebam:

Verrunt extemplo placide[1] *mare marmore flavo:*
Caeruleum spumat mare conferta rate pulsum.

Non enim videbatur, caeruleum mare cum marmore flavo convenire. Sed quom sit, ita ut dixisti, flavus color viridi et albo mixtus, pulcherrime prorsus spumas virentis maris *flavo marmore* appellavit."

Ex Auli Gellii *Noctibus Atticis,* xiii. 28

Quod Quadrigarius cum multis mortalibus *dixit, an quid et quantum differret si dixisset* cum multis hominibus.

Verba sunt Claudii Quadrigarii ex *Annalium* eius tertio decimo:

Concione dimissa Metellus in Capitolium venit cum multis mortalibus: inde quom domum proficisceretur tota civitas eum reduxit.

[1] Editors read *placidum*

facts and his felicity of expression, remarked, "But for you alone perhaps the Greek language would have come in first by a long way. But you, my Fronto, exemplify Homer's verse:

Now had you passed me by in the race or made it a dead heat.[1]

But while I listened with delight to all that you have so learnedly said, yet I was especially pleased with your analysis of the varieties of the colour *flavus*, and at your enabling me to understand those most charming lines from the fourteenth book of the *Annals* of Ennius, which I never understood:

They sweep forthwith the tranquil water's yellow flow;
Churned by the close-packt fleet the dark-blue ocean foams.

For the 'dark-blue' sea did not seem to correspond with the 'yellow' flow. But since you have told us that the colour *flavus* is a blend of green and white, the foam of the green sea was assuredly most beautifully expressed by *flavo marmore*."

"Many Men" and "Many Mortals"

After 143 A.D.

Inasmuch as Quadrigarius[2] *uses the expression "with many mortals," what and how much difference it would make if he had said "with many men."*

The words from the thirteenth book of the *Annals* of Claudius Quadrigarius are:

The assembly being dismissed, Metellus came into the Capitol with many mortals: on his return home from there he was escorted by the whole city.

[1] Hom. *Il.* xxiii. 382.

[2] A historian at the beginning of the first century B.C. who wrote a history of Rome from its capture by the Gauls.

Quom is liber eaque verba M. Frontoni, nobis ei ac plerisque aliis adsistentibus, legerentur, et cuidam haud sane viro indocto videretur *multis mortalibus* pro hominibus multis inepte frigideque in historia nimisque id poetice dixisse, tum Fronto illi, cui hoc videbatur:

"Ain' tu" inquit "aliarum homo rerum iudicii elegantissimi *mortalibus multis* ineptum tibi videri et frigidum? Nil autem arbitrare causae fuisse quod vir modestus et puri et prope cotidiani sermonis *mortalibus* maluit quam *hominibus* dicere? Eandemque credis futuram fuisse multitudinis demonstrationem, si *cum multis hominibus* ac non *cum multis mortalibus* diceret? Ego quidem sic existimo, nisi si me scriptoris istius omnisque antiquae orationis amor atque veneratio caeco esse iudicio facit, longe lateque esse amplius prolixius fusiusque in significanda totius prope civitatis multitudine *mortales* quam *homines* dixisse. Namque multorum hominum appellatio intra modicum quoque numerum cohiberi atque includi potest, multi autem mortales nescio quo pacto et quodam sensu enarrabili omne fere genus quod in civitate est et ordinum et aetatum et sexus comprehendunt. Quod scilicet Quadrigarius, ita ut res erat, ingentem et promiscam multitudinem volens ostendere, cum multis mortalibus Metellum in Capitolium venisse dixit, ἐμφατικώτερον quam si cum multis hominibus dixisset."

When that book and those words were read to Fronto, while I and many more were sitting with him, it was the opinion of a person present, and one by no means unlearned, that it was absurd and frigid in a historical work to say "with many mortals" instead of "with many men," and savoured too much of poetry: then said Fronto to him who had expressed this view:

"Do you, a man of the correctest taste in other things, affirm that you think 'many mortals' an absurd and frigid expression? And do you suppose that a man so discreet and master of so pure and current a style had no motive for preferring 'mortals' to 'men'? And do you believe that it would have given the same convincing picture of a multitude of men if he had substituted *multis hominibus* for *multis mortalibus*? For my part, unless my love and reverence for that writer and for all the language of our old authors blinds my judgment, I hold that, in so describing the concourse of nearly a whole city, 'mortals' is an expression far and away more ample, more comprehensive, and more copious than simply 'men.' For the phrase *multi homines* can be contracted and compressed to mean quite a moderate number, while *multi mortales* in some mysterious way and by some subtle nuance includes almost the whole body of citizens of every class and age and sex. And surely Quadrigarius, wishing to describe what was actually the fact, the presence of a huge and mixed multitude, said that Metellus went into the Capitol 'with many mortals' more emphatically than if he had said 'with many men.'"

Ea nos omnia quae Fronto dixit quom ita, ut par erat, non adprobantes tantum sed admirantes quoque audiremus,

"Videte tamen" inquit "ne existimetis semper atque omni loco mortales multos pro multis mortalibus esse dicendum, ne plane fiat Graecum illud de Varronis *Satira* proverbium τὸ ἐπὶ τῇ φακῇ μύρον."

Hoc iudicium Frontonis, etiam in parvis minutisque vocabulis, non praetermittendum putavi, ne nos forte fugeret lateretque subtilior huiuscemodi verborum consideratio.

Ex Auli Gellii *Noctibus Atticis*, xix. 10

Verba haec praeter propter *in usu volgari prodita etiam Ennii fuisse.*

1. Memini me quondam et Celsinum Iulium Numidam ad Frontonem Cornelium, pedes tunc graviter aegrum, ire visere. Atque ibi qui introducti sumus offendimus eum cubantem in scimpodio Graeciensi, circum undique sedentibus multis doctrina aut genere aut fortuna nobilibus viris. Adsistebant fabri aedium complures balneis novis moliendis adhibiti; ostendebantque depictas in membranulis varias species balnearum. Ex quibus quom elegisset unam formam

When we were thus listening to all this that Fronto said, as was natural, not only with approbation but with admiration, he added:

"Take care, however, not to think that *multi mortales* should be used always and on every occasion for *multi homines*, that the Greek proverb from Varro's *Satire*, *myrrh-oil on a dish of lentils*, may not be actually exemplified."[1]

This criticism of Fronto's, though concerned with trifling and unimportant locutions, I thought worthy to be recorded, that we should not fail, perchance, through neglect or inadvertence to apply a nice discrimination to words of this kind.

On *praeter propter*

That the expression praeter propter, *which has come to be a vulgarism, is found in Ennius.*

After 143 A.D.

1. I remember that Julius Celsinus Numida and I once went to call on Cornelius Fronto who was at the time suffering from gout. When we were admitted, we found him lying on a pallet-bed of Grecian pattern with many persons eminent for learning, birth or fortune sitting round him. Several architects, called in for the construction of a new bath, were in attendance, and they were exhibiting various sketches of baths drawn upon little scrolls of parchment. When he had chosen one

[1] A proverb for "wasting a good thing"; see also Cic. *Ad Att.* i. 19.

speciemque veri,[1] interrogavit quantus esset pecuniae conspectus ad id totum opus absolvendum? Quom architectus dixisset necessario videri esse sestertia ferme trecenta, unus ex amicis Frontonis "et praeter propter" inquit "alia quinquaginta."

2. Tum Fronto dilatis sermonibus, quos habere de balnearum sumptu instituerat, aspiciens ad eum amicum, qui dixerat "quinquaginta esse alia opus *praeter propter*," "Quid hoc verbi esset *praeter propter*?" interrogavit.

Atque ille amicus "non meum" inquit "hoc verbum est sed multorum hominum quos loquentes id audias. Quid autem id verbum significet non ex me sed ex grammatico quaerendum est," ac simul digito demonstrat grammaticum, haud incelebri nomine Romae docentem, sedentem.

3. Tum grammaticus usitati pervolgatique verbi obscuritate motus, "quaerimus" inquit "quod honore quaestionis minime dignum est. Nam nescio quid hoc praenimis plebeium est et in opificum sermonibus quam in hominum doctorum notius."

At enim Fronto iam voce atque voltu intentiore:

"Itane" inquit "magister, dehonestum tibi deculpatumque hoc verbum videtur, quo et M. Cato et M. Varro et pleraque aetas superior ut necessario et Latino usi sunt?"

4. Atque ibi Iulius Celsinus admonuit in tragoedia quoque Q. Ennii, quae *Iphigenia* inscripta est, id

[1] MS. *veris*. Lipsius and J. W. E. Pearce suggest *speciosi operis*.

of these plans, and a sketch of the actual thing, he asked what was the estimate for completing the whole work; and on the architect saying that about 300,000 sesterces[1] would seem to be required, one of Fronto's friends said "and another 50,000[2] there or thereabout."

2. Then Fronto postponing the discussion which he had begun, as to the cost of the bath, turned to the friend, who had said that another 50,000 there or thereabout was required, and asked him what he meant by the expression *praeter propter*.

And the friend answered, "It is not my word; you can hear numbers of people using it. But as to its meaning, you must not ask me but the grammarian yonder," indicating at the same time a person who was present of no small note as a teacher of grammar at Rome.

3. Then the grammarian, influenced by the meanness of a word in very common use, said, "The question is quite unworthy of our discussion. For the word is somehow too vulgar and more often to be met with in the conversation of mechanics than of educated men."

But Fronto at this point shewing more earnestness in his tone and looks said:

"And so this word appears to you, master, improper and faulty, which M. Cato and M. Varro and many generations of our predecessors used as indispensable and good Latin?"

4. Here Julius Celsinus reminded us that the very word which we were enquiring about occurred also in the tragedy of Ennius called *Iphigenia*, and

[1] About £3,000. [2] About £500.

ipsum de quo quaereretur scriptum esse, et a grammaticis contaminari magis solitum quam enarrari. Quocirca statim proferri *Iphigeniam* Q. Ennii iubet. In eius tragoediae choro inscriptos esse hos versus legimus:

Otio qui nescit uti, plus negotii
Habet quam quom est negotium in negotio.[1]
Nam cui quod agat institutum est, nullo negotio
In agit, id studet, ibi mentem atque animum delectat suum.
Otioso in otio animus nescit quid velit.
Hoc idem est; neque[2] *domi nunc nos nec militiae sumus;*
Imus huc, hinc illuc; quom illuc ventum'st ire illinc lubet;
Incerte errat animus, praeter propter vitam vivitur.

5. Hoc ubi lectum est, tum deinde Fronto ad grammaticum iam labantem:

"Audistine," inquit, "magister optime, Ennium tuum dixisse *praeter propter*, et cum sententia quidem tali, quali severissimae philosophorum esse obiurgationes solent? Petimus igitur dicas, quoniam de Enniano iam verbo quaeritur, qui sit notus huiusce versus sensus:

Incerte errat animus, praeter propter vitam vivitur."

Et grammaticus sudans multum ac rubens multum, quom id plerique prolixius riderent, exsurgit, et abiens "Tibi," inquit, "Fronto, postea uni dicam, ne inscitiores audiant et discant."

Atque ita omnes relicta ibi quaestione verbi consurreximus.

[1] Merry reads *negotiosod utitur negotio.*
[2] Merry reads *idem <hic> est neque.*

that the meaning was as a rule rather tangled than unravelled by the grammarians. So he desired the *Iphigenia* of Q. Ennius to be brought forthwith; and in a chorus of that tragedy we read these lines:

He who can use not ease more labour has
Than when his labour in his labour lies.
For he who does what he has planned makes it
No labour; heart and mind delight therein:
In idle ease the heart knows not its wish.
So we: at home we are not nor abroad;
This way we go, then that; no sooner come,
We wish to go elsewhere; we vacillate,
And live but there or thereabout our life.

5. When this passage had been read, Fronto turning to the grammarian, who was now feeling uncomfortable, said:

"Do you hear, excellent master, that your friend Ennius has used *praeter propter,* and in a sentiment as dignified as the severest scolding by philosophers could be? We beg you, therefore, since we are enquiring about a word used by Ennius, to tell us what is held to be the meaning of this verse:

Incerte errat animus, praeter propter vitam vivitur."

And the grammarian, sweating profusely and blushing profusely, as most of us were laughing heartily at his dilemma, got up and, as he went out, said, "I will give you an answer some time when you are alone, as I do not wish the more ignorant listeners to hear and profit by what I say."

After this we all rose up, leaving the discussion of the word there.

Ex Auli Gellii *Noctibus Atticis*, xix. 13

Quos pumiliones *dicimus Graece νάνους appellari.*

1. Stabant forte una in vestibulo Palatii fabulantes Fronto Cornelius et Festus Postumius et Apollinaris Sulpicius; atque ego adsistens cum quibusdam aliis sermones eorum, quos de litterarum disciplinis habebant, curiosius captabam.

2. Tum Fronto Apollinari:

"Fac me" inquit "oro, magister, ut sim certus, an recte supersederim *nanos* dicere parva nimis statura homines maluerimque eos *pumiliones* appellare, quoniam hoc scriptum esse in libris veterum memineram: *nanos* autem sordidum esse verbum et barbarum credebam."

3. "Est quidem hoc" inquit Apollinaris "in consuetudine imperiti volgi frequens, sed barbarum non est, censeturque linguae Graecae origine; νάνους enim Graeci vocaverunt brevi atque humili corpore homines, paulum supra terram extantes, idque ita dixerunt adhibita quadam ratione etymologiae, cum sententia vocabuli competente; et si memoria" inquit "mihi non labat, scriptum hoc est in comoedia Aristophanis, cui nomen est Ἀκλαής.[1] Fuissetque autem verbum hoc ab te civitate donatum aut in Latinam coloniam deductum, si tu eo uti dignatus fores, essetque id impendio probabilius, quam quae a

[1] MS. Ἀκαλές or Ἀκλανές. Brunck thinks the word should be Κώκαλος (Dindorf, *Fragm.* 134).

On the word for *Dwarf*

That those whom we call pumiliones *are named νάνοι in Greek.*

After 143 A.D.

1. It chanced that Cornelius Fronto and Postumius Festus and Sulpicius Apollinaris were standing together in the porch of the Palace talking. I was standing by at the same time with some others and eagerly listening to their conversation on the niceties of language.

2. Then said Fronto to Apollinaris:

"Certify me, I beseech you, master, whether I was right in giving up speaking of men of very small stature as *nani* and preferring to call them *pumiliones,* since I remembered to have seen the word in the old writers:[1] but *nani* I believed to be a mean and barbarous word."

3. "This word," said Apollinaris in reply, "is in fact commonly used by the uneducated vulgar, but it is not barbarous, and is classified as Greek by origin; for the Greeks styled *νάνοι* men of short and low stature, such as stood but little above the ground; and they used it in this way from some reference to its etymology, which tallies with the meaning of the word. And if my memory," he added, "is not at fault, it is found in the comedy of Aristophanes which is called Ἀκλαής. But this word would at once have been granted the franchise or been naturalized as a Latin colonist, if you had deigned to use it, and would be ever so much more worthy of approval than

[1] Lucr. iv. 1162, *parvula pumilio.*

Laberio ignobilia nimis et sordentia in usum linguae Latinae intromissa sunt."

4. Tum Festus Postumius grammatico cuipiam Latino, Frontoni familiari, "Docuit" inquit "nos Apollinaris *nanos* verbum Graecum esse; tu nos doce, in quo de mulis aut equuleis humilioribus volgo dicitur, anne Latinum sit, et apud quem scriptum reperiatur?"

5. Atqui ille grammaticus, homo sane perquam in noscendis veteribus scriptis exercitus, "Si piaculum" inquit "non committitur, praesente Apollinari, quid de voce ulla Graeca Latinave sentiam dicere, audeo tibi, Feste, quaerenti respondere, esse hoc verbum Latinum, scriptumque inveniri in poematis Helvii Cinnae, non ignobilis neque indocti poetae"; versusque eius ipsos dixit quos, quoniam memoriae mihi forte aderant, adscripsi:

At nunc me Cenumana per salicta
Binis rheda rapit citata nanis.

Gratiarum Actio in Senatu pro Carthaginiensibus[1]

. . . .

. . . .

Sicut Rhodum condidisti. Ceteros omnium popu-

[1] Found by Mai in a palimpsest (*Cod. Palat.* xxiv. ff. 53 and 46). Only the last 400 or so letters from the end of the speech are consecutively decipherable out of about 2,600. The scattered words legible from the rest of the speech contained a reference to the Carthaginian sea-power and

the much too mean and vulgar expressions brought by Laberius into use in Latin."

4. Then Postumius Festus, turning to a Latin grammarian, a friend of Fronto's, said, "Apollinaris has told us that *nani* is a Greek word. Will you inform us whether, as commonly used of mules and small horses, it is a Latin word, and in what author it is found?"

5. And the grammarian, a man without a doubt exceptionally versed in the writings of the ancients, said, "If I am not guilty of criminal presumption in saying, with Apollinaris present, what I think of any Greek or Latin word, I venture, Festus, in answer to your question to say that this word is Latin and is found written in the poems of Helvius Cinna,[1] no mean or unlearned poet," and he recited his actual verses, which, as they happened to stick in my memory, I have added:

Now swiftly past Cisalpine willow-thickets
My phaëton and pair of jennets whirled me.

Speech of Thanks in the Senate on behalf of the Carthaginians. Address to Antoninus Pius

About 153 A.D.

. . . .

. . . .

Just as you rebuilt Rhodes. Whatever Gods there

[1] The poet slain by mistake for the conspirator Cinna at the murder of Caesar.

---

empire, to *seditiones orbi*, to a shrine, and possibly, as Mai thinks, to the elder Faustina. The dots in the last lines represent the actual letters lost.

lorum atque omnium urbium deos precor quaesoque ut salutem tuam, qua imperium populi Romani nostraque salus et provinciarum et omnium gentium ac nationum libertas dignitas securitas nititur, in longa tempora protegant et diuturnius te salvom sistant, atque urbes ita ut incolumes sint in . . imum . . restituas . . atque praecipuas virtutes conservent <ut> Latini nominis . . ornamentum . . causa tem . . . . nostrarum variarum fortunarum subsidium.

Ex *Octavio* Minucii Felicis, ix. 8

Et de convivio notum est: passim omnes loquuntur: id etiam Cirtensis nostri[1] testatur oratio:—

"Ad epulas solemni die coeunt cum omnibus liberis sororibus matribus sexus omnis homines et omnis aetatis. Illic post multas epulas, ubi convivium caluit[2] et incestae libidinis, ebrietatis[3] fervor exarsit, canis qui candelabro nexus est, iactu offulae ultra spatium lineae, qua vinctus est, ad impetum et saltum provocatur: sic everso et extincto conscio lumine impudentibus tenebris nexus infandae cupiditatis involvunt per incertum sortis, et si non

[1] cp. Min. Fel. xxxi. 1. *Sic de isto (convivio) et tuus Fronto non ut adfirmator testimonium fecit sed convicium ut orator aspersit.*
[2] Or *incaluit.* Naber reads *coaluit.*
[3] Hildebrand would read *ebriolatis.*

[1] Nothing more is known of this speech or the attitude of Fronto towards the Christians Some of these were put to death under Lollius Urbicus, the *praef. urbi* at Rome in 152, and again under Rusticus in 163. Had Fronto gone to Asia

be of all peoples and of all cities I pray and beseech to guard for long years to come your health, on which is based the empire of the Roman People and our safety and the liberty, dignity, and security of the provinces and of all races and nations, and to keep you safe far into the future, and the cities so that they be unharmed . . . . may you restore . . . . and may they keep their conspicuous virtues (to be) . . . . an ornament of the Latin name . . . . the mainstay of our changing fortunes.

The "Incestuous Banquets" of the Christians

And about their banquet the facts are known: they are common talk everywhere: the speech[1] of our fellow citizen from Cirta also bears witness to them:—

"On a regular day they come together for a feast with all their children and sisters and mothers, persons of both sexes and of every age. Then after much feasting, when the banquet has waxed hot and the passion of impure lust and drunkenness has been kindled in the company, a dog which has been tied to the standing lamp is incited to jump and bound up by a little cake thrown to it beyond its tether. The tell-tale light being by this means cast down and extinguished, the guests under cover of the shameless darkness embrace one another in their unspeakable concupiscence, as chance brings

as proconsul in 154 (see i. p. 237), he would have had to deal with the incident of Polycarp's martyrdom. The accusation of Θυέστια δεῖπνα against the Christians was common: see Tert. *Apol.* vii.; Justin, *Apol.* i. 26, etc.

omnes opera, conscientia tamen pariter incesti, quoniam voto universorum adpetitur quidquid accidere potest in actu singulorum."[1]

Ex M. Antonini libro *Pro Rebus Suis*, i. 11

Παρὰ Φρόντωνος τὸ ἐπιστῆσαι, οἷα ἡ τυραννικὴ βασκανία καὶ ποικιλία καὶ ὑπόκρισις καὶ ὅτι ὡς ἐπίπαν οἱ καλούμενοι οὗτοι παρ' ἡμῖν Εὐπατρίδαι ἀστοργότεροί πως εἰσίν.

[1] The paragraph immediately preceding this in Min. Felix, giving an equally unveracious description of the "Thyestean banquets" attributed to the Christians, is similar in style to this extract, and probably came from the same source. Another quotation from Fronto's speech against the Christians may be possibly found in a sentence *Ex Isidori Originibus*, xv. 2, 46 (*De carcere a coercendo dicto*): *Ut pergraecari potius amoenis locis quam coerceri videretur.* The words certainly read like Fronto's.

them together, and, if not in fact yet in guilt, all are alike incestuous, since whatever can result by the act of individuals is potentially desired by the wish of all."

WHAT MARCUS LEARNT FROM FRONTO

About 176 A.D.

FROM Fronto:[1] to note the envy, the subtlety, and the dissimulation which are habitual to a tyrant; and that, as a general rule, those amongst us who rank as Patricians are somewhat wanting in natural affection.[2]

[1] He learnt other and even better things from him; see i. p. 17.

[2] See *Ad Verum*, ii. 7, and Just. *Instit.* ii. 18 fr.

MISCELLANEOUS LETTERS OF MARCUS AURELIUS

INTRODUCTION

Marcus as Letter-writer

Perhaps the more interesting part of the Fronto correspondence is that which contains the letters of Marcus and Pius. But we cannot fairly judge of their epistolary style from these alone. Philostratus says[1] that "in his opinion the best letter writers for style were . . . . of kings the deified Marcus in the letters he wrote himself, for the firmness (τὸ ἑδραῖον) of his character was reflected in his writing by his choice of language; and of orators Herodes the Athenian, though by his over-atticism and prolixity[2] he often oversteps the bounds proper to the epistolary style."

Marcus was a prolific letter-writer. According to Capitolinus[3] he defended himself against calumny by letters. To his friends he sometimes, as we see below, wrote three times in one day. On one occasion he tells us that he had dictated thirty letters,[4] but these were probably official correspondence. Nearly 200 of his imperial rescripts are extant, which though interesting would be out of place here. Many are in

[1] *Epistles*, p. 364, Kayser.

[2] We have only one letter of his, and it certainly is not prolix, for it consists of but one word, ἐμάνης, addressed to Avidius Cassius when he revolted.

[3] *Vit. Mar.* xxii. 6; xxix. 5; *cp.* xxiii. 7, 9.

[4] See i. p. 185.

the form of letters.[1] They contain characteristic sayings such as "No one has a right to let his own negligence prejudice others";[2] "Let those who have charge of our interests know that the cause of liberty is to be set before any pecuniary advantage to ourselves";[3] "It would not be consistent with humanity to delay the enfranchisement of a slave for the sake of pecuniary gain";[4] "It would seem beyond measure unfair that a husband should insist upon a chastity from his wife which he does not practise himself";[5] "Nothing must be done contrary to local custom."

In answer to Ulpius Eurycles,[6] *curator* of Ephesus, asking what should be done with old decayed statues of preceding emperors in the Ephesian senate house, we find the interesting pronouncement, "There must be no re-working of the material into likenesses of us. For as we are not in other respects solicitous of honours for ourselves, much less should we permit those of others to be transferred to us. As many of the statues as are in good preservation should be kept under their original names, but with respect to those that are too battered to be identified, perhaps their titles can be recovered from inscriptions on their bases or from records that may exist in the possession of the Council, so that our progenitors may rather receive a renewal of their honour than

[1] *e.g.* those which are addressed to "My dearest Piso," "My dearest Saxa," etc. *Digest*, xlviii. 18, 1, § 27; *ibid.* xxix. 5, 3, etc.

[2] *Digest*, ii. 15, 3.

[3] Just. *Inst.* iii. 11.

[4] *Digest*, xl. 5, 37.

[5] Augustine, *de Adult.* ii. 8.

[6] An inscription found at Ephesus dated 164 A.D. See *Oesterr. Archäol. Instit.* 1913, ii. 121. *Dittenb.* 508; *Enc. Eph.* II. 131.

its extinction through the melting down of their images."

There are, besides, two or three inscriptions and one papyrus, all much mutilated,[1] recording letters or rescripts of Marcus. one in 163 to Pontius Laelianus, consul of that year. It contains a rare word γλωσσόκομον, rejected by Phrynichus.[2]

Besides the above there are extant only two letters or parts of letters that are certainly genuine. Following these are two letters from Christian sources, the letter to Euxenianus Publio with respect to Abercius, bishop of Hieropolis, and the letter to the Senate purporting to give a report of the "Miraculous Victory" over the Quadi. The fact of the victory with the unexpected salvation of the Roman army is certain, but the heathen writers attribute it to the prayers of the emperor or the incantations of an Egyptian *magus*.

After these two letters come ten short epistles, or parts of such, which would be of considerable interest if their authenticity were established. Till comparatively lately they were accepted unquestioningly, and afforded material for charges against Marcus. They are all found in the *Scriptores Historiae Augustae*, a late compilation of the fourth Century, intended as a supplement to Suetonius's *Lives of the Caesars*, and attributed to various authors.

But in spite of Renan and Waddington and Naber and others, who have quoted them as evidence, they cannot be regarded as genuine. They contain several

[1] Boeckh, *Inscr. Graec.* i. 1319; Kaibel, *ibid.* iii. 39a; iv. 363; v. 446. *Aegypt. Urkunden.* i. 74; *Griech. Urkunden* (Fayum) i. 74.

[2] Kaibel, *Greek Insc.* iv. 1534, Phrynichus 98, AB 32.

later words, and their style is rhetorical and unworthy of the subjects treated. The puerile playing upon words, *Avidius* . . . *avidus*, etc. betrays their artificial character. Writing of Cassius, the general who conducted the Parthian war to a successful conclusion and afterwards in 175 rebelled against Marcus, the latter is represented as quoting γνῶμαι from Suetonius instead of giving his own opinions. Moreover facts mentioned in the letters are at variance with what is known from other sources. For instance, Marcus was not in or near Rome in 175, as required by the Faustina correspondence; nor was Pompeianus, his son-law, consul in 176; nor was Lucius ever spoken of as grandson of Pius, but always as his son and the brother of Marcus; nor could Fadilla in 175 be alluded to as *puella virgo*, for by that time she would have been twenty-five and almost certainly married.

It is also incredible that Avidius Cassius should have contemplated revolt, and so openly as to arouse definite suspicions in the mind of Verus, so long before the actual outbreak. We know from Fronto's letters[1] that Verus and Cassius were on excellent terms as late as 165, and Fronto's own letter[2] to him shews the estimation in which he was then held. When Cassius revolted, Marcus felt it deeply as the defection of a friend.[3] Equally rhetorical and fictitious is a letter said to be from Cassius to his son-in-law:[4] "Marcus is assuredly an excellent man, but while he covets a reputation for clemency, he lets those live whose lives he does not approve. Where is Lucius Cassius, whose name I bear in vain?

[1] *Ad Ver.* ii. 3. [2] *Ad Amicos*, i. 6.
[3] Dio, lxxi. 24.
[4] Vulcatius Gallicanus, *Vit. Avid. Cass.* 14.

Where the great Marcus Cato the Censor? Where all the discipline of our ancestors? Marcus Antoninus philosophizes and enquires about first principles and about the soul and about what is honourable and just, and has no thought for the State[1] . . . . . You have heard of the *praefectus praetorio*[2] of our philosopher, who was a beggarly pauper three days before he was appointed, but has suddenly become rich—whence, pray, if not from the vitals of the State and the property of the provincials?[3] Well, let them be rich, let them be opulent: they will serve to fill the public treasury." By a commonplace of the rhetorical schools Cassius in another passage is made to liken himself to Catiline and Marcus to the *dialogista* (Cicero).[4]

However there are some touches in the correspondence which are true to character, such as the words attributed to Lucius, "I do not hate the man," which are in keeping with his well-known *bonitas*, and the "Perish my children" of Marcus, which he might well have said. But he is not likely to have quoted Suetonius or Horace, to the latter of whom he took a dislike[5] in his younger days. The fabricator of the letters was perhaps Aemilius Parthenianus, a writer of the third or fourth century.

[1] Contrary to fact; see Herodian, i. 4, § 2, and Dio, quoted above.

[2] Bassaeus Rufus is meant. He was *praef. praet.* 168–177.

[3] But see Dio, lxxi. 3. 3.

[4] For the whole question of the authenticity of these letters see Czwalina, *De Epistularum quae a scriptoribus historiae Augustae proferuntur fide.*

[5] See i. p. 139.

MISCELLANEOUS LETTERS OF MARCUS AURELIUS

Boeckh, *Inscr. Graec.* 3176

Μάρκος Αὐρήλιος Καῖσαρ αὐτοκράτορος Καίσαρος Τίτου Αἰλίου Ἀδριανοῦ Ἀντωνείνου Σεβαστοῦ πατρὸς πατρίδος υἱός, δημαρχικῆς ἐξουσίας, ὕπατος τὸ β̄, συνόδῳ τῷ περὶ τὸν Βρισέα Διόνυσον χαίρειν·

Εὔνοια ὑμῶν ἣν ἐνεδείξασθε συνησθέντες μοι γεννηθέντος υἱοῦ, εἰ καὶ ἑτέρως τοῦτο ἀπέβη, οὐδὲν ἧττον φανερὰ ἐγένετο.

Τὸ ψήφισμα ἐπέγραψεν Τ. Ἀτείλιος Μάξιμος ὁ κράτιστος ἀνθύπατος καὶ φίλος ἡμῶν.

Ἐρρῶσθαι ὑμᾶς βούλομαι. Πρὸ ϛ Καλ. Ἀπρειλ. ἀπὸ Λωρίου.

Τὴν ἐπιγραφὴν ποιήσαντος Μ. Ἀντωνίου Ἀρτεμᾶ, δωρεὰν ταμιεύοντος Σουλπικίου Ρουφείνου.

Ex Philostrati *Vitis Sophistarum*, p. 242 (Kayser)

Μετὰ τὰ ἐν τῇ Παννωνίᾳ διῃτᾶτο μὲν ὁ Ἡρώδης ἐν τῇ Ἀττικῇ περὶ τοὺς φιλτάτους ἑαυτῷ δήμους Μαραθῶνα καὶ

---

[1] This inscription is on a stone, found at Smyrna, recording the minutes of a guild-meeting of the *mystae* (initiated), who met in the temple of Dionysus Briseus at Smyrna.

[2] Titus Aelius Antoninus, to whom there is an inscription in the *Exhedra* of Herodes at Olympia; see Dessau, ii. 8803.

MISCELLANEOUS LETTERS OF MARCUS AURELIUS

Marcus to the Guild of Dionysus Briseus at Smyrna [1]

March 28, 147 a.d.

Marcus Aurelius Caesar, son of the Emperor Caesar Titus Aelius Adrianus Augustus, Father of his country, invested with Tribunitian Power, Consul for the second time, to the Synod of the Guild of Dionysus Briseus, greeting:

Your good will which you shewed in congratulating me on the birth of a son,[2] even though the issue belied our hopes, was none the less manifest.

T. Atilius Maximus, the most honourable proconsul and our friend, inscribed the decree.

I wish you farewell: from Lorium, the 28th March.

The inscription was made by M. Antonius Artemas, Sulpicius Rufinus being honorary treasurer.

Marcus and Herodes Atticus

176 a.d.

After the events in Pannonia [3] Herodes lived in Attica in his favourite demes of Marathon and

There is a difficulty about the birth of this son, as Capit. *Vit. Marci*, vi. 6, says that Marcus received the *Trib. Pot.* on the birth of a *daughter*, and yet we know he received it in 147 The daughter was born in 146.

[3] For these see *Marcus Antoninus* in the Loeb series, pp. 366 ff.

Κηφισίαν, ἐξηρτημένης αὐτοῦ τῆς πανταχόθεν νεότητος, οἳ κατ' ἔρωτα τῶν ἐκείνου λόγων ἐφοίτων Ἀθήναζε.

Πεῖραν δὲ ποιούμενος, μὴ χαλεπὸς αὐτῷ εἴη διὰ τὰ ἐν τῷ δικαστηρίῳ, πέμπει πρὸς αὐτὸν ἐπιστολὴν οὐκ ἀπολογίαν ἔχουσαν ἀλλ' ἔγκλημα, "θαυμάζειν" γάρ, ἔφη, "τοῦ χάριν οὐκέτι αὐτῷ ἐπιστέλλοι καίτοι τὸν πρὸ τοῦ χρόνον θαμὰ οὕτω γράφων, ὡς καὶ τρεῖς γραμματοφόρους ἀφικέσθαι ποτὲ παρ' αὐτὸν ἐν ἡμέρᾳ μιᾷ κατὰ πόδας ἀλλήλων."

Καὶ ὁ αὐτοκράτωρ διὰ πλειόνων μὲν καὶ ὑπὲρ πλειόνων, θαυμάσιον δὲ ἦθος ἐγκαταμίξας τοῖς γράμμασιν, ἐπέστειλε πρὸς τὸν Ἡρώδην, ὧν ἐγὼ τὰ ξυντείνοντα ἐς τὸν παρόντα μοι λόγον ἐξελὼν τῆς ἐπιστολῆς δηλώσω. τὸ μὲν δὴ προοίμιον τῶν ἐπεσταλμένων "Χαῖρέ μοι, φίλε Ἡρώδη." διαλεχθεὶς δὲ ὑπὲρ τῶν τοῦ πολέμου χειμαδίων, ἐν οἷς ἦν τότε, καὶ τὴν γυναῖκα ὀλοφυράμενος ἄρτι αὐτῷ τεθνεῶσαν, εἰπών τέ τι καὶ περὶ τῆς τοῦ σώματος ἀσθενείας ἐφεξῆς γράφει· "Σοὶ δὲ ὑγιαίνειν τε εὔχομαι καὶ περὶ ἐμοῦ ὡς εὔνου σοι διανοεῖσθαι, μηδὲ ἡγεῖσθαι ἀδικεῖσθαι, εἰ καταφωράσας τινας τῶν σῶν πλημμελοῦντας κολάσει ἐπ' αὐτοὺς ἐχρησάμην ὡς οἷόν τε ἐπιεικεῖ. διὰ μὲν δὴ ταῦτα μὴ ὀργίζου, εἰ δέ τι λελύπηκά σε ἢ λυπῶ, ἀπαίτησον παρ' ἐμοῦ δίκας ἐν τῷ ἱερῷ τῆς ἐν ἄστει Ἀθηνᾶς ἐν μυστηρίοις.

---

[1] See Aul. Gellius. i. 2; xviii. 10.

Cephisia,[1] attended by young men from every quarter, who travelled to Athens from a desire to hear his oratory.

Wishing to make trial whether Marcus was angry with him owing to what had occurred at the trial,[2] he sent him a letter not containing excuses but a complaint, for he said that "he wondered for what reason Marcus no longer wrote to him, though in times past he wrote so often that on one occasion three letter-carriers reached him on a single day, one treading on the heels of another."

And the Emperor at greater length and on greater subjects, and putting a wonderful amount of character into the letter, sent an answer to Herodes, from which I will extract what bears upon my present subject and quote it. The letter opened with the words "Hail, my dear Herodes"; and after speaking of his winter quarters after the war, in which he was at the time, and lamenting the wife whom he had lately lost,[3] and saying something also about his bodily weakness, he went on as follows: "But for you I pray that you may have good health, and may think of me as your well-wisher and not consider yourself wronged because, detecting some of your household in wrong-doings, I punished them in the mildest way possible. Be not angry with me on this account, but, if I have done you, or am doing you, any injury, ask satisfaction of me in the temple of Athena-in-the-City[4] during the Mysteries. For I

[2] See reference in note 3, p. 295.

[3] At Halalae in Asia Minor, during the winter of 175–6.

[4] At Athens.

ηὐξάμην γάρ, ὅποτε ὁ πόλεμος μάλιστα ἐφλέγμαινε, καὶ μυηθῆναι, εἴη δὲ καὶ σοῦ μυσταγωγοῦντος."

Τοιάδε ἡ ἀπολογία τοῦ Μάρκου καὶ οὕτω φιλάνθρωπος καὶ ἐρρωμένη.

Μάρκος πρὸς τὸν Εὐξενιανὸν Ποπλίωνα.—(Migne's *Patrol. Graec.* cxv. p. 1211)

Ἀντωνῖνος Αὐτοκράτωρ Σεβαστὸς Εὐξενιανῷ Ποπλίωνι χαίρειν·

Ἐγὼ εἰς πεῖραν τῆς σῆς ἀγχινοίας ἔργοις αὐτοῖς καταστάς, καὶ μάλιστα οἷς ἔναγχος προστάξει τοῦ ἡμετέρου κράτους διεπράξω κατὰ τὴν Σμύρναν, ἐπικουφίσας Σμυρναίοις τὴν ἐκ τοῦ κλόνου τῆς γῆς ἐπιγενομένην αὐτοῖς συμφοράν, ἥσθην τε, ὥσπερ εἰκός, καὶ σὲ τῆς τῶν πραγμάτων ἐπιμελείας ἐπῄνεσα· ἔμαθον γὰρ ἅπαντα μετὰ ἀκριβείας, ὥσπερ ἂν εἰ παρών. ἥ τε γὰρ παρὰ σοῦ πεμφθεῖσα ἀναφορά, ὅ τε ἀποδιδοὺς ταύτην, καὶ Καικίλιος ὁ ἐπίτροπος ἡμῶν ἅπαντά μοι σαφῶς διηγήσατο. ἐπὶ δὲ τοῦ παρόντος γνωσθὲν τῷ ἡμετέρῳ κράτει Ἀβέρκιόν τινα τῆς Ἱεραπολιτῶν[1] ἐπίσκοπον παρὰ σοὶ διατρίβειν, ἄνδρα

[1] sc. πόλεως.

---

[1] With Cassius, or more likely perhaps the Marcomannic war He may be referring to the so-called "miraculous victory" in 174.

[2] The great earthquake, when Marcus practically rebuilt the city, was probably in 178 A.D. See Aristides, Μονῳδία ἐπὶ Σμύρνῃ and Παλινῳδία ἐπὶ Σ.

[3] The *Acta* of Abercius (Migne's *Patrol Graec.* cxv. p. 1211) state that the bishop reached Rome while Marcus was away

vowed, when the war[1] was at its hottest, that I would be initiated, and I hope you will be my sponsor on the occasion."

Such was Marcus's plea for himself, at once so kindly and so manly.

Marcus to Euxenianus Publio

? 163–164 A.D.

The Emperor Antoninus Augustus to Euxenianus Publio, greeting:

Having had experience of your sagacity in your works themselves, and especially in those which you carried out by order of our authority in respect to Smyrna in alleviating the calamity that befell the Smyrniotes owing to the earthquake[2] there, I have been pleased, as was natural, and praise you for your diligence in carrying out these duties. For I have been apprized of everything exactly as if I had been present. For everything has been clearly recounted to me by the report sent from you, and by him who presented it, and by Caecilius the procurator. But with respect to the present matter, it has come to the knowledge of our power that a certain Abercius,[3] bishop of Hieropolis, is living in your jurisdiction, a

fighting the barbarians. He was taken to the *Praefectus* Cornelianus and to Faustina, and cured Lucilla, who was then sixteen (which would be in 162/3 A.D.), by casting out a devil from her. As a reward he asked for a bath to be made for the hot-springs at Hieropolis, and that 3,000 bushels of corn should be given yearly to that his native city. The epitaph of the bishop has been recovered, and states that he visited Rome and saw *βασιλῆα[ν] καὶ βασίλισσαν*. He is said to have cured Publio's mother of blindness.

εὐσεβῆ οὕτω τὰ τῶν Χριστιανῶν, ὡς δαιμονῶντάς τε ἰᾶσθαι καὶ νόσους ἄλλας εὐκολώτατα θεραπεύειν, τοῦτον κατὰ τὸ ἀναγκαῖον ἡμεῖς χρήζοντες, Οὐαλέριον καὶ Βασσιανὸν μαγιστριανοὺς τῶν θείων ἡμῶν ὀφφικίων ἐπέμψαμεν τὸν ἄνδρα μετ' αἰδοῦς καὶ τιμῆς ἁπάσης ὡς ἡμᾶς ἀγαγεῖν. κελεύομεν οὖν τῇ σῇ στερρότητι πεῖσαι τὸν ἄνδρα σὺν προθυμίᾳ πάσῃ πρὸς ἡμᾶς ἀφικέσθαι, εὖ εἰδότι ὡς οὐ μέτριός σοι κείσεται παρ' ἡμῖν καὶ ὑπὲρ τούτου ὁ ἔπαινος. ἔρρωσο.

Μάρκου Βασιλέως ἐπιστολὴ πρὸς τὴν σύγκλητον, ἐν ᾗ μαρτυρεῖ Χριστιανοὺς αἰτίους γεγενῆσθαι τῆς νίκης αὐτῶν.

1. Αὐτοκράτωρ Καῖσαρ Μάρκος Αὐρήλιος Ἀντωνῖνος Γερμανικὸς Παρθικὸς Σαρματικὸς δήμῳ Ῥωμαίων καὶ τῇ ἱερᾷ συγκλήτῳ χαίρειν·

Φανερὰ ὑμῖν ἐποίησα τὰ τοῦ ἐμοῦ σκοποῦ μεγέθη, ὁποῖα ἐν τῇ Γερμανίᾳ ἐκ περιστάσεως διὰ περιβολῆς ἐπακολουθήματα ἐποίησα ἐν τῇ μεθορίᾳ καμὼν καὶ παθών,[1] ἐν

[1] Sylburg has suggested that these words should be Κουάδων καὶ Σαρματῶν. The MSS. have σπαθών.

---

[1] Marcus in his *Thoughts* professes disbelief in exorcism (i. 6). This is only one proof out of many that this letter is a Christian forgery. Christian tradition was strongly in favour of Marcus. Baronius early in the seventeenth century had in his possession a letter purporting to be from Abercius to M. Aurelius, which he intended to publish, but lost.

[2] Found at the end of Justin's second *Apology*.

[3] This title does not seem to have been assumed till 175. The "miraculous victory" took place, as generally held, in 174.

man of such sanctity among the Christians as both to cure those who are possessed by demons[1] and easily heal all other diseases. Having imperative need of him we have sent Valerius and Bassianus representatives of our officials for sacred things, to bring the man to us with all reverence and honour. Accordingly we bid you with your usual firmness to persuade him to come to us with all speed, and you know that this, too, will gain for you no little praise from us. Farewell.

THE LETTER[2] OF THE EMPEROR MARCUS TO THE SENATE IN WHICH HE TESTIFIES THAT THE CHRISTIANS WERE THE CAUSE OF THE VICTORY OF THE ROMANS

? 174 A.D.

1. THE Emperor Caesar Marcus Aurelius Antoninus Germanicus Parthicus Sarmaticus[3] to the People of the Romans and the Sacred Senate, greeting:

I made known[4] to you the greatness of my enterprize, and what things I did in Germany after the critical occasion of my being hemmed in on the frontier, in dire distress and suffering, when I was

[4] Though this letter is certainly spurious, yet there must have been a report to the senate by Marcus on the remarkable victory gained over the Quadi, of which both Christian and heathen writers make mention. The latter attributed the victory to the prayers or merits of the emperor, the Christians to the intercessions of the soldiers of their religion in the *Legio fulminata*, called from their success *fulminatrix*. It is curious, however, that this legion (twelfth) is not mentioned here. The commander was probably Pertinax (see *Chronicon Paschale*), not Pompeianus, the son-in-law of Marcus. The word δράκοντες (serpents, *i.e.* standards of cohorts) is also used by Lucian, *Quom. Hist.* 29. It here stands for the name of the barbarian regiments or divisions (Drungi). For the victory see Claudian *De tert. Consulatu* 93.

Κοτίνῳ[1] καταλαμβανομένου μου ὑπὸ δρακόντων ἑβδομήκοντα τεσσάρων ἀπὸ μιλίων ἐννέα. γενομένων δὲ αὐτῶν ἐγγὺς ἡμῶν ἐξπλωράτωρες ἐμήνυσαν ἡμῖν, καὶ Πομπηιανὸς ὁ ἡμέτερος πολέμαρχος ἐδήλωσεν ἡμῖν, ἅτινα εἴδομεν—καταλαμβανόμενος δὲ ἤμην ἐν μεγέθει πλήθους ἀμίκτου, καὶ στρατευμάτων λεγεῶνος πρίμας, δεκάτης γεμίνας, Φρεντησίας,[2] μῖγμα κατηριθμημένον—πλήθη παρεῖναι παμμίκτου ὄχλου χιλιάδων ἐνακοσίων ἑβδομήκοντα ἑπτά.

2. Ἐξετάσας οὖν ἐμαυτὸν καὶ τὸ πλῆθος τὸ ἐμὸν πρὸς τὸ μέγεθος τῶν βαρβάρων καὶ πολεμίων, κατέδραμον εἰς τὸ θεοῖς εὔχεσθαι πατρῴοις. ἀμελούμενος δὲ ὑπ' αὐτῶν καὶ τὴν στενοχωρίαν μου θεωρήσας τῆς δυνάμεως παρεκάλεσα τοὺς παρ' ἡμῖν λεγομένους Χριστιανούς· καὶ ἐπερωτήσας εὗρον πλῆθος καὶ μέγεθος αὐτῶν, καὶ ἐμβριμησάμενος εἰς αὐτούς, ὅπερ οὐκ ἔπρεπε διὰ τὸ ὕστερον ἐπεγνωκέναι με τὴν δύναμιν αὐτῶν.

3. Ὅθεν ἀρξάμενοι οὐ βελῶν παράρτησιν οὔτε ὅπλων οὔτε σαλπίγγων . . διὰ τὸ ἐχθρὸν εἶναι τὸ τοιοῦτο αὐτοῖς διὰ τὸν θεόν, ὃν φοροῦσι κατὰ συνείδησιν.[3] εἰκὸς οὖν ἐστιν, οὓς ὑπολαμβάνομεν ἀθέους εἶναι, ὅτι θεὸν ἔχουσιν αὐτόματον ἐν τῇ συνειδήσει τετειχισμένον. ῥίψαντες γὰρ ἑαυτοὺς ἐπὶ τὴν γῆν οὐχ ὑπερ ἐμοῦ μόνον ἐδεήθησαν ἀλλὰ καὶ ὑπὲρ τοῦ παρόντος στρατεύματος, παρήγορον γενέσθαι δίψης καὶ λιμοῦ τῆς παρούσης. πεμπταῖοι γὰρ ὕδωρ οὐκ εἰλήφειμεν διὰ τὸ μὴ παρεῖναι· ἦμεν γὰρ ἐν τῷ μεσομφάλῳ τῆς Γερμανίας καὶ τοῖς ὅροις αὐτῶν. ἅμα δὲ τῷ τούτους ῥῖψαι ἐπὶ τὴν γὴν ἑαυτοὺς καὶ

[1] Emended to Καρνούντῳ. The Cotini were south of the Vistula.

[2] MSS. have γεμινοφρεντησίας. The tenth legion consisted of two legions, *decima gemina* and *Fretensis*.

[3] *cf. Thoughts*, III. 16.

surprised in Cotinum by seventy-four regiments from nine miles away. Our scouts informed us when they had come near us, and Pompeianus, our commander, shewed us what we also saw for ourselves—for I had been suddenly surrounded by a huge and savage multitude while having with me a composite and moderate force drawn from the First legion and the Tenth (both the Twin and the Fretensian)—that there were masses of men in a miscellaneous host numbering 977,000.

2. When, therefore, I compared myself and my numbers with the immense hordes of the barbarian enemy, I took refuge in prayer to the Gods of our fathers. But being disregarded by them, and looking at the straits to which my force was reduced, I called upon those whom we name Christians—and by enquiry I found out the greatness of their numbers—going so far as to inveigh against them, which I ought not to have done, for I afterwards learnt their power.

3. They then starting with this (bethought them of) no equipment of missiles or arms or trumpets, since this is hateful to them by reason of the God that they bear in their conscience. It is likely, then, that they whom we suppose to be godless have a self-acting God entrenched in their conscience. For casting themselves on the ground they prayed, not for me alone, but also for the whole army, that He would relieve our present drought and famine. For we had taken no water for five days, as there was none to be had, for we were in the very heart of Germany and far within their frontiers. As soon as they had cast themselves on the ground, and prayed to a God

εὔχεσθαι θεῷ, ᾧ ἐγὼ ἠγνόουν, εὐθέως ὕδωρ ἠκολούθει οὐρανόθεν, ἐπὶ μὲν ἡμᾶς ψυχρότατον, ἐπὶ δὲ τοὺς Ῥωμαίων ἐπιβούλους χάλαζα πυρώδης. ἀλλὰ καὶ εὐθὺ θεοῦ παρουσίαν ἐν εὐχῇ γινομένην παραυτίκα ὡς ἀνυπερβλήτου καὶ ἀκαταλύτου . . . .[1]

4. Αὐτόθεν οὖν ἀρξάμενοι συγχωρήσωμεν τοῖς τοιούτοις εἶναι Χριστιανοῖς, ἵνα μὴ καθ' ἡμῶν τι τοιοῦτον αἰτησάμενοι ὅπλον ἐπιτύχωσι. τὸν δὲ τοιοῦτον συμβουλεύω, διὰ τὸ τοιοῦτον εἶναι, Χριστιανὸν μὴ ἐγκαλεῖσθαι. εἰ δὲ εὑρεθείη τις ἐγκαλῶν τῷ Χριστιανῷ ὅτι Χριστιανός ἐστι, τὸν μὲν προσαγόμενον Χριστιανὸν πρόδηλον εἶναι βούλομαι . .[2] γίνεσθαι ὁμολογήσαντα τοῦτο, ἀλλὰ ἕτερον μηδὲν ἐγκαλούμενον ἢ ὅτι Χριστιανός ἐστι μόνον, τὸν προσάγοντα δὲ τοῦτον ζῶντα καίεσθαι· τὸν δὲ Χριστιανὸν ὁμολογήσαντα καὶ συνασφαλισάμενον περὶ τοῦ τοιούτου τὸν πεπιστευμένον τὴν ἐπαρχίαν εἰς μετάνοιαν καὶ ἀνελευθερίαν τὸν τοιοῦτον μὴ μετάγειν.

5. Ταῦτα δὲ καὶ τῆς συγκλήτου δόγματι κυρωθῆναι βούλομαι, καὶ κελεύω τοῦτό μου τὸ διάταγμα ἐν τῷ Φόρῳ τοῦ Τραϊανοῦ προτεθῆναι πρὸς τὸ δύνασθαι ἀναγινώσκεσθαι. φροντίσει ὁ πραίφεκτος Βιτράσιος Πολλίων εἰς τὰς πέριξ ἐπαρχίας πεμφθῆναι· πάντα δὲ τὸν βουλόμενον χρῆσθαι καὶ ἔχειν μὴ κωλύεσθαι λαμβάνειν ἐκ τῶν προτεθέντων παρ' ἡμῶν.

[1] A verb is wanted such as *κατείδομεν*, which might perhaps be read for *καὶ εὐθύ*.

[2] Some participle meaning "acquitted" must have dropped out.

whom I knew not, straightway there came water from heaven, the coolest of rain upon us, but upon the enemies of Rome fiery hail. So straightway was revealed to us at once, as they prayed, the presence of their God, as of one omnipotent and everlasting.

4. From this moment, therefore, let us allow such persons to be Christians, lest by praying they obtain such weapons against us. And I propose that no such person be accused on the ground of his being a Christian. But, if anyone be found accusing the Christian for being a Christian, I wish it to be made clear that the Christian who is brought to trial should be (acquitted), if he confesses himself to be a Christian, and no other charge is brought against him except that he is a Christian, but that his accuser shall be burnt alive;[1] and the Governor who is set over the province must not force to recant or deprive of his liberty the Christian who confesses that he is one, and is credited.

5. My will is that this should be ratified by a decree of the Senate, and I direct that this my edict be published in Trajan's Forum, that it may be open to all to read it. The prefect Vitrasius Pollio[2] will see to it that it is sent throughout the provinces. Anyone who wishes to appeal to it and to have it by him must not be prevented from obtaining a copy from the official gazette of our decrees.

[1] An impossible, because illegal, enactment for Marcus.

[2] He married Annia Faustina, a cousin of Marcus, and was Consul II. in 176. If *praef. praet.* at all, he must have succeeded Macrinus Vindex, who fell in battle in 172.

Ex Vulcatii Gallicani *Vita Avidii Cassii*, v. 5.—Epistula Marci ad Praefectum Suum

Avidio Cassio legiones Syriacas dedi diffluentes luxuria et Daphnitis moribus agentes, quas totas excaldantes[1] se repperisse Caesonius Vectilianus scripsit. Et puto me non errasse, si quidem et tu notum habeas Cassium, hominem Cassianae severitatis et disciplinae. Neque enim milites regi possunt nisi vetere disciplina. Scis enim versum a bono poeta dictum et omnibus frequentatum:

Moribus antiquis res stat Romana virisque.

Tu tantum fac adsint legionibus abunde commeatus, quos, si bene Avidium novi, scio non perituros.

Ibid. v. 9.—Rescriptum Praefecti ad Marcum

Recte consuluisti, mi Domine, quod Cassium praefecisti Syriacis legionibus. Nihil enim tam expedit quam homo severior Graecanicis militibus. Ille sane omnes excaldationes,[2] omnes flores de capite collo et

[1] A later word than the time of Marcus.
[2] A late word.

---

[1] Furius Victorinus must be meant. He was *praef. praet.* 159-167.

Letter of Marcus to his *Praefectus*[1] (*praetorio*)

? 162–163 A.D.

I have put Avidius Cassius in command of the Syrian army which is dissolved in luxury and living in the moral atmosphere of Daphne.[2] Caesonius Vectilianus described them as indulging wholesale in hot baths. And I think I have done right, for you too must have noted Cassius, a man of the old Cassian severity and discipline. Nor indeed can soldiers be ruled except by the ancient discipline. For you know that line of an excellent poet, which is in the mouths of all:

Rome on her ancient ways and men unshakably standeth.[3]

You have only to see that the troops are plentifully provided with supplies. If I know anything of Cassius[4] I am certain they will not be wasted.

Answer of the Praefect

? 162–163 A.D.

You have taken a wise step, my Lord, in setting Cassius over the Syrian army. There is nothing so salutary for grecianized soldiers as a man of unusual strictness. Be sure that he will "knock off" all these hot baths for the soldiers, these flowers

[2] A suburb of Antioch, the resort of the idle and dissolute.

[3] From the *Annals* of Ennius.

[4] He was not governor of Syria before the end of 164.

sinu militi excutiet. Annona militaris omnis parata est, neque quisquam deest sub bono duce:[1] non enim multum aut quaeritur aut expenditur.

Ibid. i. 6.—Ex Epistula Veri ad Marcum

Avidius Cassius avidus est, quantum et mihi videtur et iam inde sub avo meo, patre tuo, innotuit, imperii: quem velim observari iubeas. Omnia enim nostra ei displicent, opes non mediocres parat, litteras nostras ridet, te philosopham aniculam, me luxuriosum morionem vocat. Vide quid agendum sit. Ego hominem non odi, sed vide ne tibi et liberis tuis non bene consulas, quom talem inter praecinctos habeas, qualem milites libenter audiunt, libenter vident.

Ibid. ii. 1.—Rescriptum Marci de Avidio Cassio

Epistulam tuam legi sollicitam potius quam imperatoriam et non nostri temporis. Nam si ei divinitus debetur imperium, non poterimus interficere, etiamsi velimus. Scis enim proavi tui dictum: *Successorem suum nullus occidit.* Sin minus, ipse sponte

[1] A late word for *legatus*.

from their heads and necks and breasts. The soldiers' corn-supply is all provided, and nothing is wanting with a good general in command, for his requirements and his expenses are equally moderate.

From a Letter of Verus to Marcus

? 166 A.D.

Avidius Cassius, if my judgment counts for anything, is avid for empire, as was already patent under my grandfather,[1] your father. I would have you keep a watchful eye upon him. He dislikes our whole régime; he is gathering great wealth; he ridicules our letters; he calls you a philosophizing old woman, me a profligate simpleton. See what had better be done. Personally I do not dislike the man; but you must consider whether you are acting fairly by yourself and your children in keeping ready equipped for action such a leader as the soldiers gladly listen to, gladly see.

Answer of Marcus about Avidius Cassius

? 166 A.D.

I have read your letter, which savours more of the alarmist than the Imperator, and is out of keeping with the times. For if the empire is destined by heaven for Cassius we shall not be able to put him to death, however much we may desire it. You know your great-grandfather's saying, *No one ever killed his own successor.*[2] But if the empire is not so destined,

[1] Lucius, like Marcus, was officially and by adoption son, not grandson, of Pius, though he was also son-in-law of Marcus. [2] See Suet. *Tit.* 92.

sine nostra crudelitate fatales laqueos inciderit. Adde quod non possumus reum facere quem et nullus accusat et, ut ipse dicis, milites amant. Deinde in causis maiestatis haec natura est, ut videantur vim pati etiam quibus probatur. Scis enim ipse quid avus tuus [Hadrianus] dixerit: *Misera condicio imperatorum, quibus de adfecta tyrannide nisi occisis non potest credi.* Eius autem exemplum ponere malui quam Domitiani, qui hoc primus dixisse fertur. Tyrannorum enim etiam bona dicta non habent tantum auctoritatis, quantum debent.

Sibi ergo habeat suos mores, maxime quom bonus dux sit et severus et fortis et reipublicae necessarius. Nam quod dicis liberis meis cavendum esse morte illius, plane liberi mei pereant, si magis amari merebitur Avidius quam illi, et si reipublicae expediet Cassium vivere quam liberos Marci.

Ex Iulii Capitolini *Vita Albini*, x. 6.—Marcus Aurelius Antoninus praefectis suis salutem

Albino ex familia Ceioniorum, Afro quidem homini sed non multa ex Afris habenti, Plautilli genero, duas cohortes alares regendas dedi. Est homo exer-

[1] Suet. *Dom.* 20.
[2] Marcus had two *praef. praet.* at once only between 169 and 172, viz. M. Bassaeus Rufus and Macrinius Vindex.

he will himself of his own accord, without any harsh measures on our part, be caught in the toils of Fate, let alone the fact that we cannot treat as a criminal a man whom no one impeaches and, as you say, the soldiers love. Besides, in cases of high treason, it is inevitable that even those who are proved guilty should seem to be victims of oppression. For you know yourself what your grandfather Hadrian said: *Wretched indeed is the lot of princes, who only by being slain can persuade the world that they have been conspired against!*[1] I have preferred to father the remark on him rather than Domitian, who is said to have made it first, for in the mouths of tyrants even fine sayings do not carry as much weight as they ought.

Let Cassius then go his own way, more especially as he is an excellent general, strict and brave and indispensable to the State. For as to what you say that the interests of my children should be safeguarded by his death, frankly, may my children perish, if Avidius deserves to be loved more than they, and if it be better for the State that Cassius should survive than the children of Marcus.

Marcus Aurelius Antoninus to his Praefects,[2] Greeting

169–172 A.D.

To Albinus,[3] of the family of the Ceionii, an African indeed but with not much of the African in him, the son-in-law of Plautillus, I have given the command of two cavalry cohorts. He is a man who has

[3] After the death of Commodus in 193, Albinus, then governor of Britain, became a competitor for the empire, but was defeated by Severus and slain.

citatus, vita tristis, gravis moribus. Puto eum rebus castrensibus profuturum, certe obfuturum non esse satis novi. Huic salarium duplex decrevi, vestem militarem simplicem, sed loci sui stipendium quadruplum. Hunc vos adhortamini, ut se reipublicae ostentet habiturus praemium quod merebitur.

Ibid. x. 9.—Ex Epistula qua idem Marcus Avidii Cassii temporibus de hoc eodem Scripsit

Laudanda est Albini constantia, qui graviter deficientes exercitus tenuit, quom ad Avidium Cassium confugerent. Et nisi hic fuisset, omnes fecissent. Habemus igitur virum dignum consulatu, quem sufficiam in locum Cassii Papirii, qui mihi exanimis prope iam nuntiatus est. Quod interim a te publicari nolo, ne aut ad ipsum Papirium aut ad eius adfectus perveniat, nosque videamur in locum viventis consulem subrogasse.

Ex Aelii Spartiani *Vita Pescennii*, iv. 1.—Marcus Antoninus ad Cornelium Balbum

Pescennium mihi laudas. Agnosco: nam et decessor tuus eum manu strenuum, vita gravem, et iam

seen service, is of austere life and serious character. I think that his appointment will be of advantage to the army; that it will not be disadvantageous, I am sure. I have granted him double allowances, a simple military robe, but four times the pay of his rank. Exhort him to shew himself a pattern to the State for he is assured a reward equal to his deserts.

From a Letter about Albinus written by Marcus during the Rebellion of Avidius Cassius

? 175–176 A.D.

The loyalty of Albinus is worthy of all praise in that he kept to their allegiance troops that were seriously disaffected, when they were ready to go over to Cassius. And had he not been on the spot, the defection would have been general. In him then we have a man worthy of the consulship, and I will appoint him in the room of Cassius Papirius, who, as I have just been told, is dying. But I would rather not have this appointment made public at present, that it may not get to the ears of Papirius himself or his relations, lest we seem to have elected a consul to take the place of one who is still alive.

Marcus Antoninus to Cornelius Balbus

Circa 178 (?) A.D.

You praise Pescennius[1] to me. I am not surprised, for your predecessor also spoke of him as energetic in action, serious in character, and even

[1] Pescennius Niger, like Albinus, became a claimant for empire, but was defeated and slain by Severus.

tum plus quam militem dixit. Itaque misi litteras recitandas ad signa, quibus eum trecentis Armenicis[1] et centum Sarmatis et mille nostris praeesse iussi. Tuum est ostendere hominem non ambitione, quod nostris non convenit moribus, sed virtute venisse ad eum locum, quem avus meus Hadrianus, quem Traianus non nisi exploratissimis dabat.

Ex Vulcatii Gallicani *Vita Avidii Cassii*, ix. 7.—Epistula Marci ad Faustinam

Verus mihi de Avidio verum scripserit, quod cuperet imperare. Audisse enim te arbitror, quod heri[2] statores de eo nuntiarent. Veni igitur in Albanum, ut tractemus omnia dis volentibus, nil timens.

Ibid. ix. 11.—Epistula Faustinae ad Marcum

Ipsa in Albanum cras, ut iubes, veniam. Tamen iam hortor ut, si amas liberos tuos, istos rebelliones acerrime persequaris. Male enim adsueverunt duces et milites qui, nisi opprimuntur, oppriment.

[1] A late form not recognised in the dictionary.
[2] Editors read *Veri*. For this Martius Verus see Dio, lxxi. 23, § 3.

then more than a mere soldier. And so I have sent a letter to be read to the troops, in which I have given him the command of three hundred Armenians and a hundred Sarmatians and a thousand regulars. It is your part to shew that the man has reached this rank, which my grandfather Hadrian and my great-grandfather Trajan reserved for the most tried soldiers, not by partiality, which is abhorrent to our principles, but by merit.

Marcus to Faustina

175 A.D.

Verus was verity itself when he wrote to me of Cassius that he coveted the empire. For I suppose you have heard what news messengers brought of him yesterday. So come to Albanum[1] that by the Gods' goodwill we may deal with the situation, and do not be alarmed.

Faustina to Marcus

175 A.D.

I will come myself as you suggest to Albanum to-morrow. But in the meantime I urge you, as you love your children, take the severest measures against these rebels. For the morale of generals and soldiers is thoroughly bad, and unless you crush them they will crush us.

[1] The villa of Domitian on the Alban hills. This afterwards became the town of Albanum.

Ibid. x. 1.—Epistula Faustinae ad Marcum

Mater mea Faustina patrem tuum Pium [eiusdem] in defectione Celsi cohortata est ut pietatem primum circa suos servaret, sic circa alienos. Non enim pius est imperator, qui non cogitat uxorem et filios. Commodus noster vides in qua aetate sit; Pompeianus gener et senior est et peregrinus. Vide quid agas de Avidio Cassio et de eius consciis. Noli parcere hominibus qui tibi non pepercerunt, et nec mihi nec filiis nostris parcerent, si vicissent. Ipsa iter tuum mox consequar. Quia Fadilla nostra aegrotabat, in Formianum venire non potui. Sed si te Formiis invenire non potuero, adsequar Capuam, quae civitas et meam et filiorum nostrorum aegritudinem poterit adiuvare. Soteridam medicum in Formianum ut dimittas rogo. Ego autem Pisitheo nihil credo, qui puellae virgini curationem nescit adhibere. Signatas mihi litteras Calpurnius dedit, ad quas rescribam, si tardavero, per Caecilium senem spadonem, hominem ut scis fidelem. Cui verbo mandabo quid uxor Avidii Cassii et filii et gener de te iactare dicantur.

Ibid. xi. 2.—Rescriptum Marci ad Faustinam

Tu quidem, mea Faustina, religiose pro marito et pro nostris liberis agis. Nam relegi epistulam tuam

[1] He married Lucilla, the daughter of Marcus and widow of Lucius Verus. He was Consul II. in 173.

[2] Born about 150. She married Claud. Severus.

Faustina to Marcus

175 A.D.

My mother Faustina exhorted your father Pius, on the revolt of [the same] Celsus, that he should shew loyalty in the first place to his own family and then to others. For an Emperor cannot be called *Pius* who does not think of wife and children. You see how young our Commodus is: Pompeianus, our son-in-law,[1] is both aged and a provincial. See how you deal with Avidius Cassius and his accomplices. Spare not men who have not spared you, and would have spared neither me nor your children, had they succeeded. I will myself soon follow you on your journey. As our Fadilla[2] was ill, I could not come to the Formian Villa.[3] But if I cannot find you at Formiae, I will go on to Capua, a place which is likely to benefit my health and our childrens'. I beseech you send Soteridas the physician to the Formian Villa. I have no faith in Pisitheus, who does not know how to cure our little maid.[4] Calpurnius gave me the sealed letter to which I will send an answer. If I fail to get it off at once, by Caecilius the old eunuch, a man, as you know, to be relied on, I will entrust him with an oral message of what the wife of Avidius Cassius and his children and son-in-law are reported to say about you.

Answer of Marcus to Faustina

175 A.D.

The anxiety which you shew for your husband and our children, my Faustina, is natural. For I have

[3] We know of no imperial villa here.

[4] An inscription (*Corp. Inscr. Graec.* 1124 b) found at Tibur was dedicated to Artemis ὑπὲρ σωτηρίας Μάρκου καὶ Φαδίλλας.

in Formiano, qua me hortaris ut in Avidii conscios vindicem. Ego vero et eius liberis parcam et genero et uxori, et ad senatum scribam, ne aut proscriptio gravior sit aut poena crudelior. Non enim quicquam est quod imperatorem melius commendet gentibus quam clementia. Haec Caesarem deum fecit, haec Augustum consecravit, haec patrem tuum specialiter Pii nomine ornavit. Denique, si ex mea sententia de bello iudicatum esset, nec Avidius esset occisus. Esto igitur secura :

Di me tuentur, dis pietas mea cordi est.

Pompeianum nostrum in annum sequentem consulem dixi.

---

[1] See *Vit. Avid. Cass.* 12.

[2] The name *Pius* was given him either because of his benevolent and gracious disposition (as here and Capit. *Vit. Hadr.* ii. 7) or because of his dutiful loyalty to Hadrian. *Pietas*

read your letter again in the Formian Villa, in which you urge me to take vengeance on the accomplices of Cassius. But I intend to spare his children and son-in-law and wife,[1] and I shall write to the Senate not to permit any severer persecution or harsher penalty being inflicted on them. For there is nothing that can commend an emperor to the world more than clemency. It was clemency that made Caesar into a God, that deified Augustus, that honoured your father with the distinctive title of Pius.[2] Finally, if my wishes had been followed in respect to the war, not even Cassius would have been slain. So do not be troubled:

The Gods protect me, to the Gods my loyalty is dear.[3]

I have named our Pompeianus[4] consul for the ensuing year.

meant a conscientious sense of duty or loyalty to the Gods or country or relations or mankind in general.

[3] Hor. *Od.* i. 17, 13.

[4] Claud. Pompeianus Quintianus, not the son-in-law of Marcus, was *consul suffectus* in 176.

ADDENDUM

A rescript of some length and not without interest, though much mutilated in the last half, has been omitted as not being strictly a letter. It was sent in 162 or 163 from Marcus and Verus conjointly to the logister or "curator" of the Senate of Ephesus in answer to three questions which he had put. After being reproved for applying direct to the Emperor instead of through the proper channels, he was told about the obsolete statues of the emperors in the Senate house of Ephesus, as to which he had asked, whether they, if unidentified, should be altered to represent the reigning Emperor and re-dedicated, that this should of course on no account be done, since the Emperors had not in other cases shown any hankering for honours, much less a wish to take honours from others.

The other matter referred to by Eurycles concerned a certain Saturninus, a slave or servant of the Senate, and the management of the public money.

INDEXES

I.—INDEX OF NAMES

A

Abercius, bishop of Hieropolis, an apocryphal letter of M., II. 299

Accius (Attius) L., born 170 B.C., a Roman tragic poet: chooses out his words, I. 5; Marcus to fill himself with, II. 5; bracketed with Plautus and Sallust as using a certain kind of word (passage mutilated), II. 115; Niebuhr, *Accio* for *Titio*, I. 167; called *inaequalis*, II. 49

Acheruns, the Lower World, "walled in" with rivers, etc., II. 14; herb of death sought in its meadows, II. 17

Achilles, his armour-bearer Patroclus (Patricoles, Cod), I. 167, II. 175; fleetness of, II. 61; exploits of, II. 199; shield of, II. 109

Acilius, censor, "marks" M. Lucilius a tribune for illegal conduct, I. 215

Acilius Glabrio slays a lion in the amphitheatre at Albanum, I. 211

Adherbal, King of Numidia, his character (from Sallust), II. 163; his letter to the Senate while besieged in Cirta, II. 143

Adurselius (?), m[1] Cod. Ambr. 62, I. 168*n*.

Aedon, a vowel in, dwelt on by harpers, II. 107

Aegrilius Plarianus, *see* Plarianus

Aelius Stilo, copyist of the works of Cicero and other writers, I. 167

Aemilius Pius, apparently a pupil of Fronto, recommended to Passienus Rufus, II. 191

Aenaria, an island off Naples with inland lake, I. 85, 39

Aeschines, the philosopher and disciple of Socrates, mentioned in mutilated passage, II. 50

Aesculapius, specially worshipped by Pius and Marcus, I. 50*n*.; God of Pergamum, I. 51

Aesopus, a great tragic actor of Cicero's time, I. 165; how he practised acting with a mask, II. 69

Africa, taxes of, farmed by Saenius Pompeianus, I. 233; Africans taken captive by Scipio, II. 29; *tres triumphi de Africanis . . .*, II. 151

Africanus, *see* Scipio

Agamemnon, Homer's description of, I. 94, 99

Agrigentines, inventors (?) of ploughs (Cato), II. 201

Ajax, the bull's-hide shield of, II. 107

Albanum, Domitian's villa in the Alban Hills, I. 211; Marcus at (?), II. 315

Albinus, Aulus Postumius, defeated at Cirta (? Suthul), II. 21; Sallust's description of Spurius Albinus' army, II. 163

Albinus, Clodius, proclaimed emperor in Britain and slain by Severus, promoted by Marcus, 311, 13; loyal to M. *ibid.*

Albucius, an old Roman poet called by Fr. *aridus*, II. 49; where Minton Warren suggests *Abuccius* from Varro, *R. R.* III. 6, 6

Alcibiades, as pupil of Socrates, I. 103; II. 11, 61

Alexander, council at his death, from a Gallic rhetorician, II. 111; his empire divided into satrapies (*praefecturae*), II. 203; and Apelles, II. 59

INDEX OF NAMES

INDEX OF NAMES

INDEX OF NAMES

D

INDEX OF NAMES

I

J

INDEX OF NAMES

INDEX OF NAMES

INDEX OF NAMES

INDEX OF NAMES

Q

T

U

II.—LATIN AND GREEK INDEX

Words apparently not found elsewhere are given in Italics; doubtful words are obelized. For complete lists of words in Fronto drawn from ancient writers or of a poetical cast, or used in a different sense, see Priebe, de Frontone etc., *pp.* 10–18.

A

a cubito infirmus, F. I. 218
abludo† for MS. abluo, II. 100
abs te (absque), F. I. 232; II. 130; II. 264 (Gellius); absque te, I. 232
accusative of respect, quae conscius sim, F. II. 228
accipio = treat well, M. I. 216
acclamatio (ἐπιφωνήματα M.), I. 208*n*.
acentetus (Greek), II. 6
acta cognitionum, II. 92
actus, a holding of land, F. II. 112
ad = apud (Cod.), I. 180
adaeque (Plaut.) F. II. 217
ad aliquem modum (iuvare), M. I. 140
adcensus† (MS.), F. I. 8
addubito with dat., F. I. 56, with acc., F. I. 64
adflixint (sacerdotal), I. 64
admurmuror, dep., F. I. 118
adorea, F. II. 20
adparatus verborum, F. I. 288
adpiciscor, F. I. 226
adpropinquatio (Cicero), M. I. 246
adquiesco, M. II. 18; M. 128, F. 228; *see also Exempla Elocutionum*, Mai, p. 336
ἁδρός, F. of style, I. 104
adseveratio, F. I. 40
adsiduus, F., a man of substance, II. 260; adsidue diei, I. 90, cp. I. 122
aerumna, F. II. 20, 40; of Hercules' labours, F. II. 100, 200
agere satis pro, M. I. 202
alcedonia, F. II. 6
alienus mihi, F. I. 122
alipta, M. I. 151
aliquo = aliquanto, M. II. 32
altercator (Quintilian only), F. II. 132
altipendulus (? Novius), I. 182
amici = consilium, M. II. 96
amplificus, F. I. 74
animans opicus, M. I. 142
animadverto with acc., F. II. 210
annona = corn-supply, F. II. 216
ἀντίδοσις, of property, F. I. 276
antiqui veteres, F. II. 92
antiquius (*cp.* πρεσβύτερον), F. II. 114
antiquitas (Sallust), II. 114
anucella†, F. II. 90
anxius = laboured, F. I. 100
apopsis, F. II. 6
ἀποτίμησις, F. I. 276
arcana amicitiae, I. 258
arena (harena) = amphitheatre, F. II. 216; arena or arenae, II. 253; *cp*. I. 160
arma, plural only, 255, 257, 261
ἁρμόζειν, F. II. 108
ἀρθριτικός, II. 252
ἀρτηρία, M. I. 184
asa, Umbrian for ara, in law of Numa, *see* Gellius, iv. 3. 3, F. I. 44; Assa nutrix—dry nurse, 124
aspergor paululum pluviae (Cod), M. I. 174
astus, I. 46; II. 143
Atellaniola, F. I. 138
atque as used by Cato, M. I. 152; M. I. 76; F. I. 6
attat (Cato), II. 44

LATIN AND GREEK INDEX

plural in *um* not *ium*, mensum (MS.), I. 158; Atheniensum (Cod. Vat. 137), I. 216; pare tum in speech Pro Ptolemaeensibus, *see* Charisius *Ars Gram.* I. 138
Greek, Achilli, Alcibiadi, Euphrati, Herculi, Polycrati, Alixi, Socrati, but Achillis, II. 109 *cp.* Parthamasiri, II. 215
gerundive use: res laetundae, F. I. 130, usus communicandi artium, F. II. 244; fovendi infantum faucibus (?), F. II. 42
genum, neut. F. I. 246
gibberosos, only here figuratively, F. II. 70
glaucus in Vergil, II. 264, 266
γλαυκῶπις, II. 267
glisco, M. I. 142
γλωσσόκομον, (rejected by Phrynichus), M. II. 291
gnome (or *gnoma*), I. 12, 14
γνώμη, I. 16, 54
Graecia terra, M. I. 142
Graeciensis (Gellius), II. 272
gratia sententiae fiat, I. 304
gravatius, F. I. 208
gravedo, a cold, F. I. 194
gravius magno pondere amo (*cp.* Cic. *De Officiis*, iii. 8), F. I. 172
gustum, neut., F. II. 198

H

hamatalis (Plautus), I. 6
hastatus miles, added to extract from Sallust, II. 164*n*.
hastula, II. 107
hora decimam tangit (decimum in text is a misprint), F. I. 90
horae quid for qua hora, II. 96
hordeum, no plur., II. 254*n*.
horribiliter, "awfully," M. I. 130
Horti Maecenatiani, F. I. 122
humanitas (Ennius and Cicero), II. 189*n*.; I. 298; II. 188; humanissime, I. 296
humanitus, F. II. 152
hyaenae (m² for leones Cod. Ambr. 349), II. 110; I. 133

I

ἱερὸν ὀστοῦν (Suetonius), II. 175
imago = simile, I. 36
illatenus (Apuleius), M. II. 18
imperandum, ad, for ordering, *i.e.*, being ordered, II. 54
ignominia, II. 181, 187
implicisco (noted in marg.), F. I. 222
impoene (Cato), II. 46
imposivi (Cato), II. 44
impotentia, *also plur.*, II. 255
impraesentiarum (colloquial), M. I. 184
impressio, only here in this sense, F. I. 230
incido with acc. (late), II. 310
incitator (first used), F. II. 67
incubare, "to sit tight upon," I. 158; with acc., F. II. 210
incuria, also in plur., II. 255
inconstantius, M. I. 60
indecorius, F. II. 38
induciae, sometimes sing., II. 259
industriosius, F. I. 4
infamia, F. II. 180 f.
infercire verba (Cicero), I. 40
inferiae, never sing., II. 259
infinitive with adj., obscurus involvere, etc., F. II. 48; dignus laudari, I. 108; historic, F. I 56
infrequens a, F. I. 44; infrequens amicus, F. II. 230
inguem, marg. Cod. Vat. 65, for inguen (perh. from Lucilius, *see* Klussmann, p. 78), I. 246
inlibatus, M. I. 82, 196; II. 112
inluculasco, F. II. 126
inornatius, F. II. 144
inridentius, false reading (Mai), Nab. p. 142 *see* II. 58, §6
insupra (?), Nepos ? II. 174
insuper habere (Fronto first), F. I. 10; II. 210
intenditus, error for intenditur, F. II. 8
intensius, F. II. 10
interim, II. 184
internatium, F. II. 174 (emendation)
intro, legal expression, M. I. 154
introferre pedem (Marcus only), I. 130
invio, adv., F. II. 54
invocatus, subst. F. II. 50
ipsus, Cod. according to Brakman, F. I. 214
irascor† used passively with subj. in nom., M. I. 210

LATIN AND GREEK INDEX

LATIN AND GREEK INDEX

LATIN AND GREEK INDEX

III.—TABLE OF MATTERS

TABLE OF MATTERS

TABLE OF MATTERS

TABLE OF MATTERS

TABLE OF MATTERS

CONSPECTUS OF PAGES IN NABER'S EDITION AND THE LOEB

	Naber. Page	Loeb. vol.	p.	No. of Letter
Ad M. Caes. i. 1, F.	3	I.	80	(24)
Ad M. Caes. i. 2, M.	3	„	80	(25)
Ad M. Caes. i. 3, F.	5	„	82	(26)
Ad M. Caes. i. 4, M.	9	„	90	(27)
Ad M. Caes. i. 5, F.	11	„	96	(28)
Ad M. Caes. i. 6, M.	13	„	154	(53)
Ad M. Caes. i. 7 F.	17	„	162	(54)
Ad M. Caes. i. 8, F.	20	„	118	(37)
Ad M. Caes. ii. 1, F.	25	„	108	(33)
Ad M. Caes. ii. 2, M.	26	„	112	(34)
Ad M. Caes. ii. 3, M.	28	„	128	(40)
Ad M. Caes. ii. 4, M.	29	„	116	(35)
Ad M. Caes. ii. 5, M.	29	„	116	(36)
Ad M. Caes. ii. 6, M.	30	„	140	(44)
Ad M. Caes. ii. 7, F.	32	„	144	(45)
Ad M. Caes. ii. 8, F.	32	„	144	(46)
Ad M. Caes. ii. 9, M.	33	„	146	(47)
Ad M. Caes ii. 10, M.	33	„	136	(42)
Ad M. Caes. ii. 11, M.	35	„	140	(43)
Ad M. Caes. ii. 12, M.	35	„	150	(49)
Ad M. Caes. ii. 13, M.	36	„	152	(50)
Ad. M. Caes. ii. 14, M.	36	„	152	(51)
Ad M. Caes. ii. 15, M.	37	„	154	(52)
Ad M. Caes. ii. 16, F.	37	II.	94	(186)
Ad M. Caes. ii. 17, M	38	„	96	(187)
Ad M. Caes. iii. 1, F.	40	I.	52	(13)
Ad M. Caes. iii. 2, M.	40	„	58	(16)
Ad M. Caes. iii. 3, F.	41	„	62	(17)
Ad M. Caes. iii. 4, F.	43	„	66	(18)
Ad M. Caes. iii. 5, M.	43	„	66	(19)
Ad M. Caes. iii. 6, F.	44	„	68	(20)
Ad M. Caes. iii. 7, M.	44	„	32	(7)
Ad. M. Caes. iii. 8, F.	45	„	34	(8)
Ad M. Caes. iii. 9, M.	47	„	50	(11)
Ad M. Caes, iii. 10, F.	48	„	52	(12)
Ad. M. Caes. iii. 11, F.	48	„	12	(2)
Ad M. Caes. iii. 12, M.	49	„	14	(3)
Ad M. Caes. iii. 13, F.	50	„	218	(110)
Ad M. Caes. iii. 14, M.	52	„	100	(29)
Ad M. Caes. iii. 15, F.	52	„	100	(30)

CONSPECTUS OF PAGES

	Naber. Page	*Loeb. vol. p.*	*No. of Letter*
Ad M. Caes. iii. 16, F.	53	I. 104	(31)
Ad M. Caes. iii. 17, M.	55	,, 106	(32)
Ad. M. Caes. iii. 18, M.	56	,, 78	(23)
Ad M. Caes. iii. 19, M.	56	,, 170	(56)
Ad M. Caes. iii. 20, F.	56	,, 172	(57)
Ad M. Caes. iii. 21. M.	57	,, 172	(58)
Ad M. Caes. iv. 1, F.	58	,, 70	(21)
Ad M. Caes. iv. 2, M.	60	,, 74	(22)
Ad M. Caes. iv. 3, F.	61	,, 2	(1)
Ad M. Caes. iv. 4, M.	66	,, 174	(59)
Ad M. Caes. iv. 5, M.	68	,, 178	(60)
Ad M. Caes. iv. 6 ,M.	69	,, 180	(61)
Ad M. Caes. iv. 7, M.	70	,, 184	(62)
Ad M. Caes. iv. 8, M.	71	,, 184	(63)
Ad M. Caes. iv. 9, F.	71	,, 186	(65)
Ad M. Caes. iv. 10, M.	72	,, 188	(66)
Ad M. Caes. iv. 11, M.	72	,, 202	(99)
Ad M. Caes. iv. 12, F.	72	,, 202	(100)
Ad M. Caes. iv. 13, M.	75	,, 214	(108)
Ad M. Caes. v. Index (8 letters F.; 7 letters, M.)	76, 77	I. 190	(71-85)
Ad M. Caes. v. 1, F.	77	I. 188	(67)
Ad M. Caes, v. 2, M.	78	,, 188	(68)
Ad M. Caes. v. 3, F.	78	,, 188	(69)
Ad M. Caes. v. 4, M.	78	,, 190	(70)
Ad M. Caes. v. 5, (20), M.	78	,, 192	(86)
Ad M. Caes. v. 6 (21), F.	78	,, 192	(87)
Ad M. Caes. v. 7 (22), M.	79	,, 194	(90)
Ad M. Caes. v. 8 (23), M.	79	,, 196	(91)
Ad M. Caes. v. 9 (24), F.	79	,, 196	(92)
Ad M. Caes. v. 10 (25), F.	80	,, 194	(88)
Ad M. Caes. v. 11, (26), M.	80	,, 194	(89)
Ad M. Caes. v. 12 (27), F.	80	,, 198	(43)
Ad M. Caes. v. 13 (28), M.	80	,, 198	(94)
Ad M. Caes. v. 14 (29), F.	81	,, 198	(95)
Ad M. Caes. v. 15 (30) M.	81	,, 200	(96)
Ad M. Caes. v. 16 (31), M.	81	,, 200	(97)
Ad M. Caes. v. 17 (32), F.	81	,, 200	(98)
Ad M. Caes. v. 18 (33), F.	81	,, 224	(111)
Ad M. Caes. v. 19 (34), M.	81	,, 224	(112)
Ad M. Caes. v. 20 (35), F.	82	,, 226	(115)
Ad M. Caes. v. 21 (36), M.	82	,, 226	(116)
Ad M. Caes. v. 22 (37), F.	82	,, 210	(102)
Ad M. Caes. v. 23 (38), M.	82	,, 210	(103)
Ad M. Caes. v. 24 (39), M.	83	,, 212	(104)
Ad M. Caes. v. 25 (40), F.	83	,, 212	(105)
Ad M. Caes. v. 26 (41), M.	83	,, 212	(106)
Ad M. Caes. v. 27 (42), F.	83	,, 214	(107)
Ad M. Caes. v. 28 (43), M.	84	,, 208	(101)
Ad M. Caes. v. 29 (44), F.	84	,, 218	(109)
Ad M. Caes. v. 30 (45), F.	84	,, 228	(119)
Ad M. Caes. v. 31 (46), M.	85	,, 230	(120)

CONSPECTUS OF PAGES

	Naber. Page	*Loeb. vol. p.*	*No. of Letter*
Ad M. Caes. v. 32 (47), M.	85	I. 230	(126)
Ad M. Caes v. 33 (48), F.	85	„ 232	(122)
Ad M. Caes. v. 34 (49), F.	86	„ 232	(123)
Ad M. Caes. v. 35 (50) M.	86	„ 234	(124)
Ad M. Caes. v. 36 (51), M.	86	„ 234	(125)
Ad M. Caes. v. 37 (52), F.	87	„ 238	(127)
Ad M. Caes. v. 38 (53), F.	87	„ 240	(128)
Ad. M. Caes v. 39 (54) M.	87	„ 240	(129)
Ad M. Caes. v. 40 (55), F.	87	„ 240	(130)
Ad. M. Caes. v. 41 (56), M.	88	„ 242	(131)
Ad. M. Caes. v. 42 (57), F.	88	„ 244	(132)
Ad. M. Caes. v. 43 (58), M.	89	„ 244	(133)
Ad M. Caes. v. 44 (59), F.	89	„ 246	(134)
Ad M. Caes. v. 45 (60), M.	90	„ 246	(135)
Ad M. Caes. v. 46 (61), F.	90	„ 248	(136)
Ad M. Caes. v. 47 (62), M.	90	„ 248	(137)
Ad M. Caes. v. 48 (63), F.	90	„ 248	(138)
Ad M. Caes. v. 49 (64), M.	90	„ 248	(139)
Ad M. Caes. v. 50 (65), F.	90	„ 224	(113)
Ad M. Caes. v. 51 (66), M.	90	„ 226	(114)
Ad M. Caes. v. 52 (67), F.	91	„ 250	(140)
Ad M. Caes. v. 53 (68), M.	91	„ 250	(141)
Ad M. Caes. v. 54 (69), F.	91	„ 252	(142)
Ad M. Caes. v. 55 (70), M.	91	„ 252	(143)
Ad M. Caes. v. 56 (71), F.	92	„ 252	(144)
Ad. M. Caes. v. 57 (72) M.	92	„ 252	(145)
Ad M. Caes. v. 58 (73), F.	92	„ 186	(64)
Ad M. Caes. v. 59 (74), M.	92	„ 52	(14)
Ad Antoninum Imp. i. 1, M.	94	II. 30	(173)
Ad Antoninum Imp. i. 2, F.	94	„ 32	(174)
Ad Antoninum Imp. i. 3, F.	101	„ 118	(191)
Ad Antoninum Imp. i. 4, M.	101	„ 120	(192)
Ad Antoninum Imp. i. 5, F.	102	„ 122	(193)
Ad Antoninum Imp. i. 6, M.	93 (Index) only.	126	(194)
Ad Antoninum Imp. i. 7 F.		128	(195)
Ad Antoninum Imp. i. 8, M.			(196)
Ad Antoninum Imp. i. 9, F.			(197)
Ad Antoninum Imp. i. 10, M.			(198)
Ad Antoninum Imp. ii. 1, M.	104	I. 300	(161)
Ad Antoninum Imp. ii. 2, F.	105	„ 302	(162)
Ad Antoninum Imp. ii. 3, F.	106	II. 128	(199)
Ad Antoninum Imp. ii. 4, M.	106	„ 156	(202)
Ad Antoninum Imp. ii. 5, F.	107	„ 156	(203)
Ad Antoninum Imp. ii. 6, F.	107	II. 158	(204) (219*n*)
Ad Antoninum Imp. ii. 7, M.	111	II. 218	(217)
Ad Antoninum Imp. ii. 8, F.	111	„ 220	(219)
Ad Antoninum Imp. ii. 9, F.	112	„ 218	(218)
Ad Antoninum Imp. ii. 10, F.	112	II. 219*n*	(218)
Ad Antoninum Imp. ii. 11, M.	112	„ 219*n*	(218)
Ad Verum (?) Imp. i. 1, F.	113	II. 46	(175)
Ad Verum Imp. i. 2, V.	115	I. 304	(163)

CONSPECTUS OF PAGES

	Naber. Page	*Loeb. vol. p.*	*No. of Letter*
Ad Verum Imp. i. 3, V.	116	I. 294	(159)
Ad Verum Imp. i. 4, F.	117	,, 296	(160)
Ad Verum Imp. i. 5, ?	118	,, 306	(164)
Ad Verum Imp. ii. 1, F.	119	II. 128	(200)
Ad Verum Imp. ii. 2, V.	129	,, 116	(190)
Ad Verum Imp. ii. 3, V.	131	,, 194	(214)
Ad Verum Imp. ii. 4, F.	132	,, 236	(224)
Ad Verum Imp. ii. 5, V.	132	,, 236	(225)
Ad Verum Imp. ii. 6, F.	133	,, 84	(180)
Ad Verum Imp. ii. 7, F.	133	,, 150	(201)
Ad Verum Imp. ii. 8, F.	136	,, 238	(226)
Ad Verum Imp. ii. 9, F.	137	,, 232	(222)
Ad Verum Imp. ii. 10, V.	138	,, 234	(223)
Ad Anton. De Eloquentia, 1, F.	139	,, 52	(176)
Ad Anton. De. Eloqu. 2, F.	148	,, 70	(177)
Ad Anton. De Eloqu. 3, F.	149	,, 72	(178)
Ad Anton. De Eloqu. 4, F.	153	,, 80	(179)
Ad Anton. De Orationibus, F.	155	,, 100	(189)
Ad Pium, 1, F.	163	I. 126	(38)
Ad Pium, 2, P.	163	,, 126	(39)
Ad Pium, 3, F.	164	,, 254	(146)
Ad Pium, 4 (really *ad Marcum*)	167	,, 260	(148)
Ad Pium, 5, F.	167	,, 226	(117)
Ad Pium, 6, P.	167	,, 228	(118)
Ad Pium, 7 (really *ad Gavium Maximum*) F.	168	,, 258	(147)
Ad Pium, 8, F.	169	,, 236	(126)
Ad Pium, 9, F.	170	,, 262	(149)
Ad Amicos, i. 1, F.	172	,, 282	(154)
Ad Amicos, i. 2, F. (Greek)	173	,, 286	(155)
Ad Amicos, i. 3, F.	175	,, 278	(152)
Ad Amicos, i. 4, F.	176	,, 288	(156)
Ad Amicos, i. 5, F.	177	,, 290	(157)
Ad Amicos, i. 6, F.	178	II. 190	(212)
Ad Amicos, i. 7, F.	179	,, 168	(205)
Ad Amicos, i. 8, F.	179	,, 190	(211)
Ad Amicos, i. 9, F.	180	,, 240	(227)
Ad Amicos, i. 10, F.	180	,, 242	(228)
Ad Amicos, i. 11, F.	181	,, 86	(181)
Ad Amicos, i. 12, F.	181	,, 170	(205)
Ad Amicos, i. 13, F.	182	,, 174	(207)
Ad Amicos, i. 14, F.	183	,, 98	(188)
Ad Amicos, i. 15, F.	184	,, 88	(182)
Ad Amicos, i. 16, F.	185	,, 90	(183)
Ad Amicos, i. 17, F.	185	,, 90	(184)
Ad Amicos, i. 18, F.	185	,, 92	(185)
Ad Amicos, i. 19, F.	187	,, 192	(213)
Ad Amicos, i. 20, F.	187	,, 242	(229)
Ad Amicos, i. 21, 22, 23, F. (Index)	172	II. 244*n*	(232–4)
Ad Amicos, i. 24, F.	188	II. 244	(230)
Ad Amicos, i. 25, F.	188	,, 244	(231)
Ad Amicos ii. 1, F.	190	I. 306	(165)
Ad Amicos ii. 2, F.	190	,, 308	(166)

CONSPECTUS OF PAGES

	Naber. Page	*Loeb. vol. p.*	*No. of Letter*
Ad Amicos ii. 3, F.	191	I. 308	(167)
Ad Amicos ii. 4, F.	191	,, 282	(153)
Ad Amicos ii. 5, F.=ad Pium 7	168	,, 258	(147)
Ad Amicos, ii. 6, F.	191	II. 174	(208)
Ad Amicos, ii. 7, F.	192	,, 176	(209)
Ad Amicos, ii. 8, F.	199	,, 188	(210)
Ad Amicos, ii. 9, F. (Index only)	189	II. 190*n*	(210†)
Ad Amicos, ii. 10, F. (Index only)	189	I. 292*n*	(158†)
Ad Amicos, ii. 11, F.	200	I. 292	(158)
Principia Historiæ (letter ad Marcum) F.	202	II. 196	(215)
Principia Historiæ (letter ad Marcum) F.	202	,, (198)	(216)
Laudes Fumi et Pulve s, F.	211	I. 38	(9)
Laudes Neglegentiae, F	214	,, 44	(10)
De Bello Parthico, F.	217	,, 20	(172)
De Feriis Alsiensibus, 1, M.	223	II. 2	(168)
De Feriis Alsiensibus, 2, F.	223	,, 2	(169)
De Feriis Alsiensibus, 3, F.	224	,, 4	(170)
De Feriis Alsiensibus, 4, M.	230	,, 18	(171)
De Nepote Amiss, 1, M.	231	,, 220	(220)
De Nepote Amiss, 2, F.	232	,, 222	(221)
Arion, F.	237	I. 54	(15)
Epistulae Graecae, 1, F.	239	,, 130	(41)
Epistulae Graecae, 2, F.	242	,, 146	(47)
Epistulae Graecae, 3, F.	243	,, 168	(55)
Epistulae Graecae, 4, Appian	244	,, 264	(150)
Epistulae Graecae, 5, F.	246	,, 268	(151)
Epist. Graecae (Latin), 6, M.	252	,, 18	(4)
Epist. Graecae (Latin), 7, M.	253	,, 30	(6)
Epist. Graecae, 8, F.	255	,, 20	(5)
Pro Carthaginiensibus, F.	260	II. 280	—